The
Choice

AMERICA
AT THE
CROSSROADS
OF RUIN
AND REVIVAL

Sammy Tippit

MOODY PRESS
CHICAGO

ISBN: 0-8024-5247-7

1 3 5 7 9 10 8 6 4 2

Printed in the United States of America

To my dear Aunt Eunice,
who was like an ark of safety for me
during the turbulent '60s.
Her listening ear and compassionate heart
helped me to stay afloat
during a stormy time of life.

CONTENTS

FOREWORD

---★---

With the publication of this, Sammy Tippit's latest book, a secret will be revealed that I once feared was known only to me.

Anyone who knows Sammy, and I have known him twenty-five years, recognizes him as a consummate evangelist. He's one preacher as evangelistically minded in private as in public. It is not the big crowds that draw him; it is the individual heart. The tens of thousands at a time who listen to him at crusades on every continent each year are merely one way he reaches individuals.

He was an accomplished orator even in high school in the '60s, before he became a Christian. He had an international view even then, winning speaking competitions in the United States.

So what secret about Sammy is now revealed? I sensed from the day I met him and interviewed him for a magazine article in 1972—and this was confirmed when I was privileged to serve as his writer on his first several books—that he was more than a preacher, more than a Bible student. He is also an astute observer of geopolitical developments.

Early in his ministry, when still in his twenties, Sammy was invited to conduct a question-and-answer session on modern youth with the large editorial team at Scripture Press Publications. Someone had the foresight to tape the entire session. I was as surprised as anyone that my new friend, young as he was, was so articulate on social and political trends as well as spiritual issues.

Because Sammy primarily preaches internationally, he is less known in North America for his singular preaching gift. Anyone aware of his schedule knows he must be a good preacher. But unless they have heard him expound, based on hundreds of international journeys through the decades, they will not know of his incisive analysis.

Until now.

In these pages you will be exposed to a surgical thinker. Though like his model, Billy Graham, he preaches a clear, simple, unchanging message, he's also on the cutting edge of international thought. Here he turns his gaze toward his homeland.

Sammy doesn't apologize for his good ol' boy Louisiana roots, and the accent is still evident. But he's come a long way from Baton Rouge, and I'm pleased to see the release of his deepest, most ambitious, and most important book.

My only regret is that this makes clear he's way past needing the help of a writer. I envy you your first exposure to the deep thinking behind the evangelist's heart.

> Jerry B. Jenkins
> Writer-in-Residence
> Moody Bible Institute

PREFACE

After Bill Clinton was elected president of the United States, I was speaking with one of my friends about the election. I told him, "Whatever you think of Bill Clinton, good or bad, there's something that the people of America must come to grips with. The post World War II baby boomers have come of age." President Clinton was born the first year after the close of the war. He was a part of the first wave of what has become known as the "boomer generation." Not only has a boomer become the leader of the world's greatest superpower, but boomers have moved into positions of leadership in every sphere of American society. And we (I'm a boomer) have brought our philosophies and values with us into those arenas.

I've discovered through much of my research that the values of the boomers are different from those of any previous group in American history. After I began work on this book, I found myself with my head in my hands, weeping and saying, "I just didn't know it was this bad." God had awakened my heart to the needs of America. I've concluded that there will never be a spiritual awakening in the land until someone's heart breaks and weeps for the soul of the nation. The first section of this book is filled with research and data that will awaken you to the great spiritual, social, and moral needs of America.

But as great as the problems seem to be, there is also hope in the land that is equal to or greater than the needs. God has promised that He will hear those who repent and call upon Him, and many of His people are doing just that. After interviewing some of America's most respected Christian leaders, I have reason for hope. God has raised up men such as Mike Huckabee, governor of Arkansas; James Dobson, president of Focus on the Family; Tom Elliff, a pastor and the president of the Southern Baptist Convention; and Bill Bright, president and founder of Campus

Crusade for Christ, for "such a time as this." I think that you'll find my interviews with them not only interesting, but deeply convicting. They offer hope to the nation.

This book deals with issues that involve people from positions as high as the chief political adviser to the president of the United States and as low as one of America's wealthiest publishers of pornography. In order to deal with those issues, strong stands against what I believe to be wrong are necessary. I make no apologies for those stands. The time has come for men and women of God to stand up and say, "Right is right and wrong is wrong." But it's also important to note that love and grace are offered to anyone entangled in the matters about which this book speaks. My desire is that all involved in these issues would come to genuine repentance and sincere faith in Jesus Christ.

Ultimately, common, ordinary Americans have a choice to make. We can continue down the road that leads to ruin, or we can by faith take the high road that leads to spiritual revival and moral renewal. The choice is ours. The only question that remains is simply, "Do we have the character and moral courage to change directions?" The answer to that question lies in the hearts of ordinary American citizens. The choice is ours.

ACKNOWLEDGMENTS

———————★———————

Several people have been an encouragement to me in this project. The person who gave me the most help was my daughter, Renee. She helped immensely with the research part of the book. She spent many hours in libraries and on-line finding needed information. Also, my wife, Tex, has been an encouragement to me. She has continued to give me helpful suggestions.

Washington D.C. journalist Matt Labash gave me helpful suggestions about how and where to find certain pieces of information that I needed. Mike Wirth has been a prayer warrior for me as I have written. His encouragement has been especially appreciated. Finally, a special word of thanks is given to Moody Press for their continued support and encouragement of my writing.

SECTION ONE

★

The Road to Ruin

1
THE SIGNS OF
CULTURAL DECAY

*Of all the dispositions and habits which lead to political pros-
perity, religion and morality are indispensable supports. . . .
And let us with caution indulge the supposition, that morality
can be maintained without religion. Whatever may be conceded
to the influence of refined education on minds of peculiar structure, reason and experience both forbid us to expect that national morality can prevail in exclusion of religious principle.*[1]

GEORGE WASHINGTON
September 19, 1796
(excerpt from Farewell Address)

THE SEEDS OF CULTURAL CHANGE

1960s: THE SEED IS SOWN—Post World War II baby boomers
reject the biblical values of their forefathers.

1970s: THE SEED TAKES ROOT—Boomers begin to slip into
America's institutions, bringing with them a new set of values.

1980s: A TREE COMES FORTH—Society begins to embrace a
new set of standards and values espoused by the boomers.

1990s: THE FRUIT IS PRODUCED—A cultural revolution is in
full swing. The new morality brings with it social catastrophe.

JUDGMENT IS PENDING

THE SIGNS OF CULTURAL DECAY

Belief in the God of the Bible was the rock upon which this democratic society was built. It has been the foundation that enabled its people to withstand the storms that have blown across the pages of its history. This faith has never been forced upon America's inhabitants. But the nation has, until recently, recognized the importance of God, Christ, and the morality of the Bible in building and sustaining a civilized society.

From the time that George Washington warned the nation in his farewell address that "reason and experience both forbid us to expect that national morality can prevail in exclusion of religious principle" until the turbulent '60s, faith in God was respected and viewed as necessary to the health of the nation. But something has changed over the last thirty years. Good is touted as evil, and that which was seen as evil to previous generations has become the new standard of morality. The consequences have been devastating. Social ills are spreading like wildfire, leaving behind a trail of broken lives. Crime has soared. Families have been destroyed. Millions of babies have been killed in their mothers' wombs. Suicide and violent crime are both at the top of the list of the leading killers of America's youth, who are the children of the baby boomers. In the last ten years sexually transmitted diseases have killed nine times more people than died in the ten worst years of the Vietnam War. Signs of a society gone haywire show up everywhere.

A tree of immorality and selfishness has been cultivated in our midst for decades, and its roots are firmly entwined in our nation. And now America must make a choice: Are we willing to do the hard work to uproot it, or will we ignore it or even continue to nurture it? The United States is above all things a nation "of the people, by the people, for the people." The people ultimately have responsibility for the direction of the nation. We cannot blame a political dictator, for we have never existed under a dictatorial regime. The manner in which the Founding Fathers structured the nation left full responsibility in the hands of the people. The greatness of America is directly related to the moral character of her citizens. The nation will rise or fall on the moral constitution of its inhabitants.

Even though America continues to prosper economically and militarily, a case could easily be made that she has lost her moral and spiritual greatness. America faces a choice: to continue down the road leading to God's judgment or to rush toward the road that ushers us to moral renewal and spiritual revival.

INVERTED MORALITY, HOLLYWOOD STYLE

Already the paradigm of what is right or wrong has changed. The Founding Fathers would have been shocked at much of what is being extolled as heroic, as well as appalled by what is propounded as anti-American today. Perhaps there's not a more vivid illustration of this inversion of moral values being thrust upon the general American population than Oliver Stone's movie *The People vs. Larry Flynt.* The movie was released in theaters throughout America at the beginning of 1997, and it received five Golden Globe nominations. Stone, an award-winning Hollywood producer, depicts Flynt as the champion of the First Amendment of the Constitution. The movie's villain is Baptist pastor Jerry Falwell. In Stone's version of history, Falwell would like to take away the basic freedoms of Americans, including the freedom of speech and the press. But courageous Larry Flynt, even though he might be a little eccentric, fights for the freedoms of every American.

The movie is based on Flynt's autobiography. The story centers around Flynt's pornography empire and a parody that *Hustler* magazine did on Jerry Falwell and his deceased mother. In the parody, Flynt suggests that Falwell's first experience with sex was with his mother in an outhouse. Flynt was parodying advertisements of Campari, an Italian liquor company, that asked the question, "What was it like the first time you tried it?"

Falwell sued Flynt, claiming malice, and won a $200,000 settlement. Flynt appealed the decision, and the case went to an appeals court. Falwell won again. But Flynt appealed all the way to the Supreme Court. Oral arguments were given on December 2, 1987. On February 24, 1988, the Court published its 8 to 0 judg-

ment to reverse the appeals court decision. Flynt was no longer
held liable for his obscene and demeaning parody of Pastor Falwell.

Hollywood's depiction of Flynt as the Constitutional hero and
Falwell as the villain raises numerous questions about what has
happened to the moral fiber of America. Of course, it isn't the
first time that Hollywood has portrayed the religious establish-
ment in America as the bad guys. Media critic Michael Medved
documents numerous incidents of "God bashing" by Hollywood
in his video *Hollywood vs. Religion*. Medved stated that recently
Hollywood has produced twenty-five movies with total cumula-
tive costs of one billion dollars in which they portray believers as
psychopaths, killers, and child molesters.[2] In one movie, a black
minister shoots his cocaine-addicted son in the groin and then
lays his gun on an open Bible. In another movie, a woman looking
for the rapture of the church shoots her daughter in the middle of
a desert. In yet another movie, "born again" Christians take over
America and begin to have people who had committed adultery
hanged to death.[3]

Many of today's movies show believers in such a perverted
manner, but that hasn't always been the case. There was a time in
American life in which most movies portrayed religion and belief
in God as something good and healthy for Americans. For instance, in 1959 *Ben Hur*, a movie about the time of Christ, won
more Oscars than any other movie. Medved documents in his
video numerous other movies before the '60s where religion and
religious leaders were portrayed as heroes. Members of the clergy
were depicted as good guys rather than villains. *The Sound of
Music*, the beloved Oscar-winning musical released in 1968, depicted religious people as wholesome and respectable. But today
is a different day.

Pop Culture and the Media

Something has happened to change the climate of popular
culture. Religious stereotyping has become the norm. I saw firsthand the consequences of such stereotyping by the mass media
when I visited Rwanda in 1995. More than 500,000 Tutsis had
been slaughtered in one month during the previous year. The horror stories of the attempted genocide were like nothing I had ever
heard. The Tutsis were killed for one reason—their ethnic origin.

I kept asking how such a horrible thing could occur at the close of the twentieth century. The only answer that I received was that months prior to the mass killings, a constant barrage of media told the people how terrible the Tutsis were. People were brainwashed to believe that the Tutsis were the lowest form of humanity. When an order was given to exterminate the Tutsis, people thought they were doing the nation a service. They had to first believe the worst about another ethnic group before they could rationalize their murderous actions.

Michael Medved, a leader in his local synagogue and media critic for the *New York Post,* succinctly stated the danger of American mass media's stereotyping of religious groups: "The real power of mass media is to define our idea of what constitutes normal behavior. If you show some kind of weird extreme often enough, then it's not only accepted, eventually it's expected. . . . If movie after movie features killer Christians, won't people become more cynical about religious faith, and more fearful of its influence?"[4] If believers are characterized long enough as evil, radical extremists, then certain portions of the population will begin to believe that description. That could ultimately be extremely dangerous.

That's why Stone's portrayal of Flynt as a Constitutional hero should raise some serious questions about where we're headed as a nation. Also, such a public characterization of Flynt and Falwell shouldn't go unchallenged for two reasons. First, many recent movies have prejudicially portrayed believers as the bad guys. Second, this movie is not presented as something fictional, but rather biographical. It would be easy for the American public to accept the movie as history when, in reality, much of it is pure fiction.

Unanswered Questions

Therefore, several critical questions need to be answered about what has been presented to the American public as factual. First, if Flynt is a new kind of American hero, then we should know who he is, how he has conducted himself, and what he believes. Who is Larry Flynt? Second, how accurate is the movie? Third, why was the scapegoat chosen from the religious community? And, finally, have the courts always viewed obscenity in the same manner as the Supreme Court's decision in the Flynt/Falwell case? The answers to all these questions are warning signs pointing to the direction America is headed.

The Flynt movie is but one example of a national trend to invert moral values. Hollywood seemed to be running full speed in upending biblical values during 1997. Not only did the entertainment elite begin the year with the Flynt movie, but they also introduced the first lead character in a major sitcom to openly announce her homosexuality. Ellen Morgan, the lead character in *Ellen* (played by Ellen DeGeneres), revealed in a spring edition of the sitcom that she was a lesbian. The real life Ellen DeGeneres also "came out" and told the world that she was a lesbian. According to *Newsweek* magazine, Ellen would be the "first show built around a lesbian—and starring one."[5] The moral direction of a core of Hollywood decision makers has been headed toward an all-out assault on the biblical standard of morality for some time. There were two dozen minor roles of homosexuals being broadcast on prime-time television and a "lesbian wedding practically every other week."[6] Hollywood seems to be unwavering in its attempt to reindoctrinate Americans with this new set of values.

Just the Facts

Where is Hollywood's new morality headed? The Larry Flynt movie gives us an idea of the kind of depravity that Hollywood would like to thrust upon America. Flynt describes himself in his book as someone who is candid and frank in discussing his sexual appetites. Oliver Stone attempts to answer the question, "Who is Larry Flynt?" in the foreword to Flynt's autobiography. He says, "I find him personally to be more in the rapscallion tradition of Mark Twain's Huckleberry Finn—the country boy, misunderstood by so many trying to figure it all out, rafting down the American psyche gone wacko. . . . Larry, by some standards, is a First Amendment hero and defender of the Constitution."[7]

Is Flynt just another Huckleberry Finn? He boasts in his biography of having sex with a chicken as a young boy and claims that bestiality was quite common in eastern Kentucky.[8] I don't think that Stone's portrayal and Flynt's straightforward description of his own actions would have been seen so positively by previous generations. They would more likely have been understood to be confessions of utter filth and perversion.

Not only are Flynt's claims offensive to the sensibilities and morality of most Americans, but millions of ordinary citizens would shudder in horror at his portrayal of women. Michael Levin wrote in the *Los Angeles Times,* "I miss the time in our culture when movies were about heroes. In a bygone era Flynt wouldn't be the hero of a movie. He'd be a villain. . . . The same Larry Flynt who ran the notorious depictions of a woman run through a meat grinder and turned into hamburger, and of a woman strapped to the hood of a Jeep after a hunting trip, now comes before us as a symbol of what is right with America."[9]

Not only does Mr. Flynt believe that his manner of life and portrayal of women is acceptable morality, but he also believes that religion is a terrible idea. He concluded his book stating, "I have come to think religion has caused more harm than any other idea since the beginning of time."[10] He reiterated that claim in an interview with Larry King. That's a huge accusation that cannot go unchallenged.

Because Mr. Flynt has brought this issue into the public arena, and because he is pictured as a hero to the American public, then we must investigate his claims. Has faith in God been harmful to American society? Or does America stand in need of a great spiritual revival? Which direction should America go? Actually, a great deal of research has already been done in the scientific community about the benefit of religion upon Americans and society in general.

RELIGION AND SOCIETY: THE RESEARCH

Researchers David and Susan Larson wanted to discover if what is told to the American public about religion is based in fact. In their study *The Forgotten Factor,* they stated, "If academic science is to remain true to its claim of objectivity and of openness to new discoveries, we felt this unquestioned tenet—that religion is primarily harmful—deserved some investigation. We wanted to know, based on research findings, if indeed religious commitment was harmful, neutral or even beneficial."[11]

Their research brought together studies from numerous physical and mental health caregivers. It produced some very interesting results in light of what is being sold to the American public about religion. For instance, one study showed that "a national decline in church attendance has been found to predict heightened suicide rates." And a large-scale study found that "persons who did not attend church were four times more likely to kill themselves than were frequent church attenders."[12] Another study found that the "most important predictor of marital stability is church attendance."[13]

Not only have many studies proven that faith in God produces personal and family security, but also it is a great prevention for many of the social ills facing America. A number of researchers report that "drug abuse is related to the lack of religion in a person's life."[14] A parallel finding was discovered about alcohol abuse. Researchers found that "alcohol abusers rarely had a strong religious commitment . . . and those with a higher level of commitment are less likely to use or abuse drugs."[15] A study on juvenile delinquency showed that "religious participation has consistently been shown to be a deterrent to delinquency."[16] One of the most interesting findings by researchers relates to prejudice. They discovered that "the least prejudiced people are those who attend church often and those who never attend. The most prejudiced are those who attend church occasionally."[17]

But researchers have discovered that a deep belief in God not only is good for personal, familial, and societal stability, but actually is good for one's physical health. Committed believers have lower risks of such sicknesses as heart disease, pulmonary emphysema, hypertension, and cirrhosis of the liver.[18] A study by Drs. Levin and Vanderpool determined, "The comprehensive review of nearly 250 epidemiological studies found positive associations between religious commitment and health. . . . In general, these studies suggest that infrequent religious attendance should be regarded as a consistent risk factor for morbidity and mortality of various types."[19]

In spite of the evidence, there seems to be an antireligious bias in many Hollywood circles. This bias is often presented to the American public as fact. Truth isn't necessarily the most important issue to some of Hollywood's executives. In fact, the movie *The People vs. Larry Flynt* has plenty of historical inaccuracies.

MOVIE INACCURACIES

Matt Labash, a journalist for a Washington conservative political magazine, *The Weekly Standard*, investigated the truthfulness of the Flynt movie. He documented numerous inaccuracies in the movie in his cover story, "The Truth vs. Larry Flynt." Labash, commenting on the many untruths in the film, stated, "Nor can its inaccuracies be excused as the result of the filmmakers' desire to entertain, rather than deliver a rigorously factual documentary. The truth is that, scene by scene and line by line, the distortions, omissions, and outright fabrications in 'The People vs. Larry Flynt' make it a dishonest piece of work in almost every particular."[20]

In one instance, the movie's creators apparently felt a need to beef up their portrayal of Falwell as a villain. The only way they could make a case for turning good into evil was to bring another character into the story. The producers connected Wall Street's Charles Keating, who had been convicted of insider trading, with Falwell and his lawyers. The movie depicts Keating advising Jerry Falwell's lawyers. In one of the final scenes of the movie, Falwell, Keating, and Flynt stand outside the Supreme Court building. The press gathers around them and asks Keating why he was at the hearing. Keating says, "To show support for those people who believe that pornography should be outlawed." The published screen script had him also saying, "This smut is the most dangerous menace to our country today! All decent citizens demand *action!* They want pornography where it belongs—*in jail!*"[21] The movie ends shortly thereafter and the credits roll. The final credit reads, "Charles Keating is the central figure in the Lincoln Savings and Loan scandal, which cost taxpayers over 2 billion dollars." Only one conclusion is left for the viewer—"These religious guys are a bunch of phonies costing common ordinary Americans billions of dollars."

The only problem is that in real life Falwell and Keating say that they don't know each other. *On Larry King Live,* Falwell denied having met Keating except for a brief encounter in a hotel lobby in Phoenix years after the trial. Keating told journalist Labash that "he has never had a conversation with Falwell."[22] If they were lying, the press could have proven them wrong immediately, since the movie depicts them at a press conference together. It's at this point that there seems to be great danger. Hollywood bolsters its argument against Falwell by bringing another "villain" into the story and then connecting the two "villains." This is making a case for prejudices rather than presenting genuine biography.

GRAVER DANGERS

But the lack of truthfulness in Stone's movie isn't the only concern. The most serious consideration is not just that popular culture stands in opposition to the foundation of Western civilization, but that the institutions of the nation have changed their views of right and wrong. I've read what critics of the Stone movie have written and also discussed the movie with several people. There's a greater issue than a movie's portrayal of a pastor and a pornographer. It's easy to find those who are critical of the movie because of the sleaze of Larry Flynt. But I've yet to find anyone who believes the Supreme Court's decision in the case should be questioned.

That's quite disturbing because during most of the history of this nation the Supreme Court would have likely ruled differently in the case. Flynt's argument was simply that the statements about Falwell were a parody and clearly stated as such. Therefore, Flynt should not be held liable. Falwell's argument was that there are boundaries of decency, and when a person steps across those, he isn't protected by the First Amendment.

The courts have historically recognized the importance of faith in God and the limitations of obscenity in public speech. President Clinton quoted from Alexis de Tocqueville in one of his 1997 inaugural celebration speeches. Tocqueville was a French leader who visited America during the mid-1800s. He observed American life for nine months and wrote a classic book entitled *Democracy in America.* The book is studied by students of political science and is considered to have some of the keenest insights about American democracy ever written. When one reads this classic, he cannot escape the fact of how important Tocqueville viewed the religious nature of the American people to be. He understood that the religious character of the American people was foundational to American democracy.

Tocqueville wrote in his observances, "For the Americans the ideas of Christianity and liberty are so completely mingled that it is almost impossible to get them to conceive of one without the other."[23] Tocqueville cited an interesting article from the *New York Spectator* on August 23, 1831. The newspaper carried a story of a case in which an atheist was a witness in a court of law. The article stated the following:

The court of common pleas of Chester county (New York) a few days since, rejected a witness who declared his disbelief in the existence of God. The presiding judge remarked that he was not before aware that there was a man living who did not believe in the existence of God; that this belief constituted the sanction of all testimony in a court of justice; and that he knew of no case in a Christian country, where a witness had been permitted to testify without such belief.[24]

I wouldn't attempt to say that American courts should do the same today. But it should be clear that the courts have historically recognized the importance of belief in God in American life. Not only has such acknowledgment been important to American society, but the courts have also in past times accepted limitations on freedom of speech. Francis Canavan, professor emeritus of political science at Fordham University, in discussing a 1973 California court decision says, "The First Amendment doesn't protect all speech simply because it is speech, any more than freedom protects all action simply because it is action. We must always ask, what kind of action? Who is doing what? And—as they say—to whom?" He went on to say, "Consider the history of our own country. A regime of unlimited freedom of expression came in only in the 1960s."[25]

Professor Canavan cites a 1942 Supreme Court decision in *Chaplinsky v. New Hampshire* that says:

There are certain well-defined and narrowly limited classes of speech, the prevention and punishment of which have never been thought to raise any constitutional problems. These include the lewd and obscene, the profane, the libelous, and the insulting or "fighting" words—those which by their very utterance inflict injury or tend to incite an immediate breach of the peace. It has been well observed that such utterances are no essential part of any exposition of ideas and are of such slight social value as a step to truth that any benefit that may be derived from them is clearly outweighed by the social interest in order and morality.[26]

That 1942 Supreme Court would have likely viewed the Flynt/Falwell case much differently than it's perceived today. The "social interest in order and morality" was the defining line that could not be crossed in 1942. How did we arrive at this place in history where good is viewed as evil and wrong is now considered right? How is it that faith has now become the scourge of the mass media, and why isn't the story that doctors and scientists have discovered the benefits of faith in God getting out to the general public? What has happened in our basic institutions that has caused them to side with perversion rather than "order and morality"? Why has the general public accepted and embraced such depictions? But the greatest question is "Where are we now headed?"

THE CHALLENGE

Perhaps the most accurate thing about Stone's movie is its ti-tle—*The People vs. Larry Flynt.* The people lost. Larry Flynt won. That sums up the past thirty years of the social and moral decline of America. And things could get much worse if they don't change soon. William Bennett, former U.S. secretary of education, cited statistics that "the average child watches up to 8,000 made-for-TV murders and 100,000 acts of violence by the end of grade school."[27] This generation is the most visually oriented one in history. It is being fed a steady diet of "Religion is bad. Sexual perversion is good. Violence is normal." That's a sure formula for disaster. The seed planted in the '60s has begun to bear fruit. Judgment is pending. Will the church have the spiritual and moral courage to declare the gospel boldly and live out Scripture's truths? Will the American people recognize the current cultural direction as a failure before it's too late?

2
SHIFTING VALUES:
THE FRUIT OF THE SIXTIES

We have grown in numbers, wealth and power, as no other nation has ever grown. But we have forgotten God. We have forgotten the gracious hand which preserved us in peace, and multiplied and enriched and strengthened us; and we have vainly imagined, in the deceitfulness of our hearts, that all these blessings were produced by some superior wisdom and virtue of our own. Intoxicated with unbroken success, we have become too self-sufficient to feel the necessity of redeeming and preserving grace, too proud to pray to the God that made us!

It behooves us then, to humble ourselves before the offended Power, to confess our national sins, and to pray for clemency and forgiveness.[1]

> ABRAHAM LINCOLN
> March 30, 1863
> Proclamation—National Day to Fast

THE TREE OF IMMORALITY GROWS

1960: THE SEED IS SOWN—439,000 couples in the U.S. live together outside the bonds of marriage.

1970: THE SEED TAKES ROOT—523,000 couples in the U.S. live outside the bonds of marriage.

1980: A TREE COMES FORTH—1,589,000 couples in the U.S. live together outside the bonds of marriage.

1994: THE FRUIT IS PRODUCED—3,661,000 couples in the U.S. live outside the bonds of marriage.[2]

JUDGMENT IS PENDING

SHIFTING VALUES:
THE FRUIT OF THE SIXTIES

It was a beautiful, sunny Sunday afternoon as I drove into Washington, D.C. I had been speaking in nearby Annapolis, Maryland, and I jumped at the chance for a short visit into the city. It wasn't often that I was able to go into the city by myself and spend time thinking about and praying for our nation. Twenty-six years earlier I had spent several days in D.C. praying and fasting for spiritual and moral renewal within the country. Much had changed since then; I didn't realize how much. But what I experienced on my short visit affected me in a profound manner.

When I've had the opportunity to visit the nation's Capitol during the last several years, I've gone to the Vietnam War Memorial. The Vietnam War seems to be the reference point from which my generation views history. Certainly our lives were deeply affected by it. Many social historians have tried to analyze what happened during those turbulent years. But investigation and study can't describe the human emotions that many of us felt.

Those emotions first gripped my heart during the late '60s when I was a new Christian attending a conference at a church in my hometown, Baton Rouge. An old high school friend, David, came limping into the church, wearing a leg brace. He had been a national competitor in gymnastics during high school. David had so much athletic ability, but that potential was now gone.

While in Nam, David was engaged in a firefight in the rice patties. He took a hit and a hole was blown in his leg. He lay there thinking he would die. An African-American soldier rushed to pull him to safety. David's life was saved, but the black soldier was killed rescuing him. That was pretty heavy stuff for a white Southern boy. The culture in which we grew up taught us that blacks weren't our equals. We went through forced integration during high school. Many of us were taught to oppose any attempt of

African Americans to enter our schools, and we were taught not to have friendships with black young people.

David's entire outlook on life was shattered through the death of that soldier. He began to question everything he had been taught. At first, he began drinking heavily, thinking that he could drown the memories. But he couldn't. They haunted him day and night until one day he turned to Christ and made peace with God. When David walked into that church, I saw myself, my colleagues, and an entire generation struggling to find out what was right or wrong, a truth or a lie. David discovered the truth of the gospel. But not everyone had that opportunity.

Many became disillusioned. I saw a number of my contemporaries destroy their mental and physical health with mind-expanding drugs. Others were killed before they had an opportunity to figure out why everything was changing so rapidly. Tommy was one of those. Tommy was a really nice guy. When I heard that he was killed in Vietnam, I remember asking myself, *Why? Why Tommy? He had more to offer society than a lot of others* (including myself). Those were difficult days—confusing times. There were no easy answers.

When I visit the Vietnam War Memorial, I always spend time at the place where Tommy's name is inscribed. The memorial pulls tender emotions out of me, and the mental fog seems to lift. I find myself able to see a little more clearly where we are as a nation and where we've come from. It helps me to clarify in my mind what can be done to bring healing to a nation that so desperately needs it.

THE CONSEQUENCES OF UNFETTERED FREEDOM

While at the memorial that afternoon, I saw something that affected me deeply. Tens of thousands of marchers walked peacefully down the streets. They didn't look like the radical types of the '60s. They were clean-cut and well dressed, and they behaved appropriately. They were the boomers come of age. Many were carrying signs—but these were quite different from the '60s demonstrations. The march was an attempt to raise money for AIDS research. Instead of "Make Love—Not War" signs, theirs advertised some of the major American businesses and their fight against AIDS. For the first time, I saw a linkage between what happened in Vietnam and the AIDS virus. I understood that they

were tied by a spiritual and moral outlook on life that was planted
in the heart of an entire generation in the '60s and has produced
its full fruit in the '90s. In our youthful confusion while attempting to find a "bridge over troubled waters," we decided to forsake
that age-old bridge, the Bible, upon which our forefathers had
traveled for nearly two hundred years.

We began a process of sowing a seed of selfishness, and today
we're reaping its full harvest. It has been my experience that a
seed (whether good or bad) sown in an individual's life takes
about ten years before it begins to bear its full crop of fruit. But in
a nation, it takes longer. The seed sown by individuals takes time
to be grown in society. It has taken twenty-five to thirty years to
bear the fruit of what transpired in the '60s. We sowed immorality
in the '60s, and we're reaping a culture of death in the '90s. We rejected God's law in the '60s, and violent crime and suicide are two
of the leading killers of our children in the '90s. Only 439,000 couples lived together outside of marriage in 1960, but there are
more than 3,600,000 couples living outside of marriage in the
1990s—approximately a 900 percent increase.[3] The immorality of
the '60s has become the social catastrophe of the '90s. The solution of the '60s was to rid ourselves of the puritanical values of our
forefathers. The solution of the '90s is "uh oh, pass out the condoms."

SIXTIES CULTURAL SHIFTS

The boomers were larger in number than any previous generation. Our fathers returned from World War II, got married, and
began having children. But more important perhaps than our
numbers is the influence we have had on the thoughts and actions of Americans. There's no doubt that the moral climate in
America began to change in the latter part of the 1960s. Most social scientists and observers agree that a dramatic shift in values
took place. James Lincoln Collier documents this shift in moral
behavior in his book *The Rise of Selfishness in America*. He cites
a change of attitude and behavior in two distinct areas of life in
the 1960s—drug use and sexual promiscuity. Speaking of drug
use in the '60s he writes, "This sudden acceptance of drugs,
which took place in a span of about ten years, is one of the most
dramatic cultural shifts to occur during the American twentieth
century. A behavior pattern that had been universally anathema-

tized throughout the entire society, except in a tiny fringe underclass, overnight became accepted and widely practiced in a new generation, and was even beginning to spread into older cohorts."[4] A Bureau of Narcotics and Dangerous Drugs report showed that from 1960 to 1969 there was a "51 percent increase in the number of active addicts and the number of addicts under 21 years of age increased by 173 percent."[5]

But a rise in drug abuse wasn't the only dramatic shift in culture. Sexual attitudes changed. The boomers even affected their parents' outlook. Collier pointed to a study of the changing attitudes toward sex in the '60s and '70s. A 1976 survey showed that "32 percent of American middle class women in the thirty-five to forty year age bracket had had extramarital sex at least once. . . . Further evidence that the change in attitude was moving through the society comes from a study of 1954 college graduates and their daughters. These mothers belonged to the same cohort of women in the adultery (1976 survey) study and showed the conservatism toward sex prevalent at the time: 94 percent of them were virgins at their high school graduations. . . . But 55 percent of them said that their daughters had helped to liberalize their attitudes toward sex."[6]

Former Supreme Court nominee Judge Robert Bork summed up the moral state of the '60s, "Unlike any previous decade in American experience, the Sixties combined domestic disruption and violence with an explosion of drug use and sexual promiscuity; it was a decade of hedonism and narcissism; it was a decade in which popular culture reached new lows of vulgarity."[7] I'm convinced that what happened in the '60s was much more than America's slide into moral poverty. Something deeper than moral degradation was taking place in culture. Something deeply spiritual transpired that became the foundation for a generation that rejected God's law.

A Pivotal Supreme Court Decision

Many factors caused the '60s to be unique in American history. But one fundamental decision made in 1962 reconstructed the spiritual landscape of America. Until 1962, belief in God and Judeo-Christian values was deeply rooted and intertwined in the fabric of American society. But during that year, the Supreme Court of the United States banned prayer in public schools. Before the ruling, there was an acknowledgment in American life and our institutions that we needed God. That began to be dismantled in 1962. Since we started to throw God out of our public institutions in the '60s, a flood of other religions has rapidly spread across America. That would make a return to the kind of praying in our schools that we experienced in the '60s very difficult because of the multiculturalism that has been ingrained in American culture.

The lone dissenting voice in that 1962 Supreme Court decision was the Honorable Justice Potter Stewart. In his dissenting statements he said, "With all respect, I think the Court has misapplied a great constitutional principle. I cannot see how an 'official religion' is established by letting those who want to say a prayer say it. On the contrary, I think to deny the wish of these school children to join in reciting this prayer is to deny them the opportunity of sharing in the spiritual heritage of our Nation. . . . It was all summed up by the Court just ten years ago in a single sentence: 'We are a religious people whose institutions presuppose a Supreme Being.' Zorach v. Clauson, 343 U.S. 306, 313."[8]

In this institutional disregard for God, we did what Abraham Lincoln described ninety-nine years earlier. In one of the darkest moments of American history, the Civil War, Lincoln stated, "We have grown in numbers, in wealth and power, as no other nation has ever grown. But we have forgotten God. . . . Intoxicated with unbroken success, we have become too self-sufficient to feel the necessity of redeeming and preserving grace, too proud to pray to the God that made us!"[9]

Economics and Selfishness

The boomers were vulnerable to spiritual forces that would change life in America for many generations to come and possibly forever. Several elements produced this kind of vulnerability. First, many of the parents of the boomers had grown up during times of great economic hardships as well as having gone through World War II. But following the war came a time of unprecedented prosperity. The parents of the boomers wanted a better life for their children than they had experienced, so those parents indulged their children. The boomers grew up with the televisions and cars that their parents didn't have at their age. Collier says of the boomers, "They had been raised in a prosperity no society anywhere in the history of the world had ever provided for its general populace."[10]

The bottom line was that we were spoiled. I recall my father talking about how many miles he walked to school every day. But not me. Even though I grew up in a blue-collar family, when I was a teenager I drove to school every day. Our parents wanted to help us, but a rise of selfishness began to envelop the culture. We became creatures of comfort, and a spirit of selfishness engulfed a new generation of young people.

Rebellion

Many boomers began to challenge the standards of their parents. The older generation was seen as hypocritical. Christian churches preached love, but wouldn't allow people of other races access to their facilities. Parents were angry with their children about the use of marijuana and other drugs, but many of the parents drank alcohol. In our youthful rebellion, my generation was predisposed to throw the baby out with the bath water. We figured that if our parents weren't living up to biblical standards, then they had no right to impose them upon us.

There were also plenty of professors in the universities to feed our rebellion. Professors in many of the leading universities taught students that there were no absolutes. Everything was relative. Of course, if there were no absolutes, then we couldn't believe in a God who is absolute. And even if we did believe in God, then there were still no absolute standards by which we could live. The Bible was irrelevant. I recall one professor in a sociology class who felt it was his responsibility to debunk the "myth" of the Bible. As a new Christian, I spent much time researching and challenging his premises. I discovered that he was good at making his arguments sound intellectual, but, in fact, they had very little intellectual basis to them. But that professor gave many of my friends an excuse to indulge in behavior that was contrary to their moral upbringing. Without God, the law of God was meaningless.

Sexual Research

Another seed of deceit and destruction was sown in America's intellectual community in 1948 and 1953 that ultimately found its way into the hearts of post World War II baby boomers.

During 1948 Alfred C. Kinsey published *Sexual Behavior in the Human Male*. It was dubbed as the most comprehensive sex survey ever taken of American men. Then, in 1953, he published *Sexual Behavior in the Human Female*. Both publications challenged the moral foundation of America. Robert Knight of the Family Research Council wrote, "Kinsey's overall thesis of 'outlet sex' placed all sexual acts on the same moral, social and biological level whether in or out of wedlock, between two people of the same sex or opposite sex, or even when sex involved children or animals. By declaring that 'science' had found no value in traditional sexual morality, the Kinsey Reports, as they came to be known, provided the 'scientific' foundation for America's sexual revolution."[11]

In recent years, the Kinsey reports have been challenged by numerous scientific researchers. The Family Research Council reported that questions have been raised about "allegations of fraudulent data and child sexual abuse" (one table in the study contains "detailed data about molestations of young boys") and "allegations of improper sampling" (the heavy use of prison inmates, including sex offenders, in the study).[12] Walter Stewart of the National Institutes of Health, a scientific detective who hunts out fraud, said, "Serious questions have been raised about the validity and ethical basis [Kinsey used] and these questions are not going to go away without investigation. This is a golden opportunity for scientists to exercise their professional role in policing their own ranks."[13] Researchers are challenging the use of statistics, ethics, legality, and scientific objectivity of Kinsey's research.

It didn't matter to the kids of the '60s what would be found in the '90s about the Kinsey reports. The sexual revolution would be in full swing by then. Professors in the '60s believed a lie. They thrust that lie on a vulnerable generation. A generation that had been left without a spiritual covering believed the lie.

The Vietnam War

During the same time that we prospered, the Vietnam War was raging. Unlike our fathers' experience in World War II, it was a difficult war for us to understand. We weren't clear about Vietnam's threat to America, and we couldn't see an end in sight. We were confused. We were used to the comforts of life, but we were told we had to go to war.

Millions of boomers looked for a way to escape the war. Young men who were university students received a 2S classification with the draft board. That meant they at least had bought some time. These young students just hoped the war would end soon and they wouldn't have to go.

The Boomer Subculture

University campuses experienced phenomenal growth. Seymour Martin Lipset noted that by the end of World War II there were 1,675,000 university students and 165,000 faculty. "But in 1970, there were 7,000,000 students and over 500,000 full-time faculty. Thus, in twenty five years, the number of faculty tripled and the number of students quadrupled."[14] The intellectual challenge to students predisposed to youthful rebellion began to produce a subculture. Liberal professors gave young people a reason for their rebellion. It was like pouring fuel on dry wood and lighting a match. Sexual passions burned out of control. Mind-expanding drugs eased the pain. "If it feels good, do it" became the philosophy of many of my contemporaries. Marriage was no longer sacred. Many couples began living together outside of marriage. The illegitimacy rate began to soar. The seed of destruction was sown. A counterculture with extremely large numbers was born. The course of American life took a historically different turn.

That course of promiscuity ultimately opened the way for many sexually transmitted diseases to spread throughout America. Hundreds of thousands of boomers and their children have died or will eventually die from AIDS. The disease was unknown in America until the late '70s, but between 1980 and 1995 more than 315,000 Americans died of AIDS.[15] Robert Swenson, professor of medicine and microbiology at Temple University Health Science Center, said, "The first AIDS cases are believed to have occurred in the late 1960s. By the mid-1970s, changes in modern air travel brought HIV to the rest of the world. . . . The link to the United States appears to be homosexual males vacationing in the area of Port-au-Prince, Haiti. From there, HIV infection was carried to those areas with the largest concentrations of homosexual males, New York and San Francisco. . . . The next group infected with HIV were intravenous drug users."[16]

But what happened to the boomers? The war ended in the

early 1970s, and the "radicals" left the streets. Although the boomers generally assimilated into society, they brought with them the attitudes of the '60s. The more radical boomers moved into places of influence. Judge Robert Bork observes, "They didn't just go into the universities. The radicals were not likely to go into business or the conventional practice of the professions. They were part of the chattering class, talkers interested in policy, politics, and culture. They went into politics, print and electronic journalism, church bureaucracies, foundation staffs, Hollywood careers, public interest organizations, anywhere attitudes and opinions could be influenced."[17]

The Boomers Today: Fruit of the Sixties

The former radicals became the shapers of American philosophy. The process of changing America's fundamental institutions began in the '60s, but those changes were firmly rooted in the hearts and attitudes of the American people by the end of the '70s. The first and greatest change was found in America's most basic institution, the family. For instance, in 1960, 393,000 marriages ended in divorce in the nation. By 1962, that number had grown to 413,000. It continued to increase every year thereafter through 1970. During 1970, 708,000 divorces were granted in the United States.[18] By the time 1980 arrived, 1,189,000 families were torn apart by divorce in one year.[19] The seeds of destruction had taken root.

One of the most alarming aspects of the 1970s was the "heart trends" of the American people. As boomers were assimilated into mainstream society, they brought a lot of the '60s baggage with them. A "Study of American Families" showed that trends in attitude about divorce had taken root in the heart of the American people by the mid 1970s. The study "documented a dramatic increase in acceptance of divorce between 1962 and 1977. Whereas 51 percent of women disagreed in 1962 with the statement that 'when there are children in the family, parents should stay together even if they don't get along,' a much larger 80 percent disagreed with this statement fifteen years later in 1977."[20]

Divorce was no longer viewed as a tragedy taking place in American homes. During the 1970s divorce became more common and ultimately a part of the American cultural landscape. By the '90s, Americans had discovered that a great tragedy had taken place during the '60s and '70s. Everything from disease, depression, social maladjustment, economic hardship, crime, and suicide would be linked in the '90s to the breakdown of the nuclear family.

That spiritual and moral fruit could be seen most easily in the dramatic increase in illegitimate births. From 1960 to 1994, illegitimate births increased more than 400 percent.[21] Charles Krauthammer wrote, "Since 1960 the incidence of single parenthood has more than tripled. Almost 30 percent of all American children are now born to unmarried mothers."[22] Many scholars believe that this cultural trend could produce utter havoc within the nation by the turn of the century. Author Charles Murray has stated, "Illegitimacy is the single most important social problem of our time—more important than crime, drugs, poverty, illiteracy, welfare, or homelessness because it drives everything else."[23] When the boomers threw out traditional biblical values in the '60s, they not only lost their souls, but they abandoned the very foundation upon which any society can be sustained.

The first institution that God established was the family. When Americans abandoned that institution, we left ourselves vulnerable for spiritual and moral devastation within society as we and our forefathers have never previously known. Patrick F. Fagan, senior policy analyst for the Heritage Foundation in Washington, D.C., concluded a cultural policies study stating, "America is headed toward a 50 percent out-of-wedlock birthrate sometime in the next twelve to twenty years, inching more and more of the country closer to today's inner-city illegitimacy rate. If this trend is not reversed, Americans must prepare for extensive and serious erosion of public safety and practical freedoms."[24]

Pornography

Another trend rooted in the '60s should also cause alarm within society—the rise of pornography. *U.S. News & World Report* stated, "During the 1980s, the advent of adult movies on videocassette and on cable television, as well as the huge growth in telephone sex services, shifted the consumption of porn from seedy movie theaters and bookstores into the home. As a result, most of the profits being generated by porn today are being earned by businesses not traditionally associated with the sex industry—by mom and pop video stores; by long distance carriers like AT&T; by cable companies like Time Warner and Tele-Communications, Inc.; and by hotel chains like Marriott, Hyatt, and Holiday Inn that now reportedly earn millions of dollars each year supplying adult films to their guests."[25]

God was legislated out of the American school systems in the '60s. Immorality took root in the '70s. Then pornography was dressed up and ushered into homes throughout the nation in the '80s. According to *Adult Video News,* "The number of hard-core-video rentals rose from 75 million in 1985 to 490 million in 1992. The number climbed to 665 million, an all-time high, in 1996."[26]

But it's not just hard-core pornography that has gripped America. In a conference paper presented to the American Enterprise Institute, Jane D. Brown and Jeanne R. Steele cited studies about the major broadcast networks (ABC, CBS, NBC, and FOX). The study found that during prime time there were "an average of 10 instances of sexual behavior per hour."[27] Furthermore, the study stated, "More alarming, given current rates of STDs (sexually transmitted diseases) and unplanned pregnancy, analysis showed that few programs ever mentioned the adverse consequences that may result from having sex."[28]

Television, Sex, and Antisocial Behavior

What are the consequences of all the "telesex"? Two studies have "found correlation between watching higher doses of 'sexy' television and early initiation of sexual intercourse."[29] In other words, teenagers will more likely engage in sexual promiscuity if they spend a great deal of time watching prime-time television. That's frightening because "in the prime afternoon and evening hours the three largest networks broadcast a total of more than 65,000 sexual references each year. The average American now watches 14,000 references to sex in the course of a year."[30] The average teenager watches twenty-one hours of television per week.[31] If illegitimacy is the greatest social and moral crisis facing America, as stated by Patrick Fagan and Charles Murray; and if a heavy dosage of television viewing is going to produce a higher rate of sexual intercourse among teenagers; and if teenagers are watching high doses of television; then it is only reasonable to assume that within a few years America will face a social and moral catastrophe unknown in our history.

George Comstock, a professor at Syracuse University, analyzed 275 studies and concluded that "10 percent of antisocial and illegal behavior can be linked to television."[32] Epidemiologist Brandon S. Centerwall told *Newsweek* magazine his speculation that "without television there would be 10,000 fewer murders per year, 70,000 fewer rapes and 700,000 fewer assaults."[33] It's worth noting that the number of forcible rapes has steadily risen in America since 1970. The seed of immorality sown in the '60s culminated with 37,990 forcible rapes during 1970. By 1980 the tree of immoral behavior had grown up, producing 82,670 forcible rapes during that year. The full fruit of immorality was produced by 1992. There were 109,060 Americans forcibly raped that year.[34]

In 1956 the motion picture industry had a code by which it lived. It simply said, "No picture shall be produced which will lower the moral standards of those who see it [hence] the sympathy of the audience shall never be thrown to the side of crime, wrong-doing, evil or sin. . . . The sanctity of the institution of marriage and the home shall be upheld. No film shall infer that casual or promiscuous sex relationships are the accepted or common thing. . . . Complete nudity, in fact or in silhouette, is never permitted, nor shall there be any licentious notice by characters in the film of suggested nudity."[35]

From the '60s to the '90s, there has been a rapid downward spiral of moral values in the United States. A decision was made by the Supreme Court to remove prayer from the schools in 1962. That act seemingly opened a door for a host of evil forces to invade the land. An entire generation was made vulnerable to a horde of demons that would play havoc with the heart of an entire generation. Then, in the '70s the Supreme Court went a step further. Abortion was made legal in America. The new morality had taken root in the country by 1973, and Americans began to kill their babies while they were still in their mothers' wombs. Freedom to choose took precedent over freedom to live. In 1988, the Supreme Court acted again. Freedom of speech ruled over the rights of decency. Larry Flynt was permitted, without consequence, to vulgarize one of America's most well-known conservative preachers. And, now, the Supreme Court of the land is consistently being faced with decisions about assisted suicide. Life is quickly losing its value in the nation. When that happens, God's judgment is certainly around the corner.

3
FAMILY BREAKDOWN

Our inner cities are filled with children having children, with people who have not been able to take advantage of educational opportunities, with people who are dependent on drugs or the narcotic of welfare. . . . If a single mother raising her children in the ghetto has to worry about drive-by shootings, drug deals, or whether her children will join gangs and die violently, her difficult task becomes impossible. It doesn't help matters when prime-time TV has Murphy Brown—a character who supposedly epitomizes today's intelligent, highly paid, professional woman—mocking the importance of fathers, by bearing a child alone, and calling it just another "lifestyle choice."[1]

VICE PRESIDENT DAN QUAYLE
1992 Family Values Speech

THE NEXT GENERATION TASTES THE FRUIT

1960: THE SEED IS SOWN—5,829,000 children in the United States live in a home with only one parent.

1970: THE SEED TAKES ROOT—8,438,000 children in the United States live in a home with only one parent.

1980: A TREE COMES FORTH—12,466,000 children in the United States live in a home with only one parent.

1994: THE FRUIT IS PRODUCED—18,590,000 children in the United States live in a home with only one parent.[2]

JUDGMENT IS PENDING

FAMILY BREAKDOWN

---★---

When I returned home from the office one afternoon in 1996, the television was tuned to the evening news. Nicole Brown Simpson's famous 911 call was being broadcast. Apparently O. J. Simpson was in a rage of jealousy and Nicole feared for her life. As I listened to O. J. Simpson's voice, I immediately identified with his feelings of rage. It had been so long since I had experienced those feelings that I had forgotten what they were like, but as I watched and listened, it was almost as though I were transported back more than thirty years in time.

Don't misunderstand me. I've never physically abused anyone. I've never hit a person of the opposite sex. But I was quite familiar with the rage that produces that kind of abuse. Before I became a Christian, a deep sense of jealousy and insecurity would overtake my emotions and thought processes instantly. I didn't want it to be that way. I was insecure, and I didn't understand why I felt the way I did. It was only after I came to have a personal relationship with Christ through faith that I began to experience His victory over those emotions.

Many factors contributed to the rage I felt as a teenager. Some of them came from cultural surroundings: It was emotionally difficult growing up in the '60s. American values were changing rapidly. We traded the foundational Rock of God's Word for the shifting sands of relativism. That produced deep insecurity within many of us. Other factors that created deep uncertainties in our lives came from our own choices. No one could be blamed for the mess in the hearts of an entire generation except us, the boomers. We made the decisions. Or even more personally, I must say that "I made my own bed, and I had to sleep in it."

When I heard Simpson's voice on the news, I realized that those feelings could have destroyed my life. If I had not found God's source of peace and security as a university student, those feelings of anger and jealousy could have easily erupted into physical abuse. After becoming a Christian, I began a long search to discover what made me feel the way I had felt as a young person. I don't propose to have grasped it all. But I have come to understand some basic truths that have enabled me to more clearly deal with my own feelings.

I realize that I made moral decisions that had a negative emotional impact on my life. My emotions were intertwined with my will. The decisions I made (good or bad) ultimately influenced how I felt about myself and the world around me. Also, the cultural surroundings played a vital role in my attitudes and actions. Again, I had a choice to make—conform to my social environment or be transformed by God's power within me. That led me to the keen awareness that only Christ could really make me a new person on the inside. I didn't have to be a slave to the fear, anger, and jealousy that raged within my soul, because Christ is the great liberator of the human heart.

IN THE CENTER OF THE STORM: THE FAMILY

Unfortunately, many of my contemporaries have not come to the same faith relationship with Christ, and they've carried much of the '60s cultural baggage with them throughout their lives. That has produced not only a storm raging in the hearts of individuals, but a storm raging in the soul of a nation. The American family stands in the center of the storm, which is leaving a trail of social devastation and destruction. Divorce in American life has progressed from rare to common to fashionable. It has become a part of the cultural landscape in the United States. As the family goes, so goes the nation.

Every institution in the nation has been affected by the '90s divorce culture. During 1993 Barbara Dafoe Whitehead wrote a response to the media flap over former vice president Dan Quayle's famous "Murphy Brown" speech. It appeared in the liberal *Atlantic Monthly* and was entitled "Dan Quayle Was Right." Her article ignited a heated debate about divorce in American culture, which resulted in her writing a book on the subject. Whitehead says, "Divorce is now part of everyday American life. It is embedded in our laws and institutions, our manners and mores, our movies and television shows, our novels and children's storybooks, and our closest and most important relationships. . . . Divorce has become an American way of life only as the result of recent and revolutionary change."[3]

Whitehead pointed out that divorce began to skyrocket in the '60s at an unprecedented rate. She said that after 1960 the divorce rate "doubled in nearly a decade and continued its upward climb until the early 1980s, when it stabilized at the highest level among advanced Western societies. As a consequence of this sharp and sustained rise, divorce moved from the margins to the mainstream of American life in the space of three decades."[4] In 1994, 2,362,000 couples got married, and 1,191,000 couples got divorced.[5] A rise in the rate of divorce from the '60s to the '90s meant a rise in children living in single-parent homes. In 1960, about 5,829,000 children lived with one parent. By 1994, 18,590,000 children lived in a single-parent household—a 300 percent increase.[6] That has proven to have dire consequences.

DIVORCE'S CULTURAL RAMIFICATIONS

Unfortunately, the divorce culture gained such rapid momentum in the '60s and '70s that it affected every major institution in American life, including the one that could have been a shelter in the midst of the storm—the church. By the mid '70s, the boomers' attitude of selfishness began to find a place within the church and institutionalized itself there. A new generation of preachers began to proclaim a gospel of "God wants you to be healthy, wealthy, and wise." The prosperity gospel was immediately embraced by the boomers, who were already prone to a self-seeking type of faith. The new and modern preaching of prosperity overtook the message of the Cross. Many Christians seemed more interested in their esteem than Christ's humility. Signs, wonders, health, wealth, and self-esteem became predominant themes in many circles by the '90s. They replaced the age-old biblical principles of death to self, brokenness, sacrifice, and servanthood. Today a message rooted in self-centeredness rather than Christ-centeredness plays havoc with Christian families.

Divorce in the Church

By the mid '70s, churches were beginning to experience the first pains of the cultural revolution of the '60s. I had been traveling and ministering throughout Europe during the early part of the '70s, but I felt a deep need for a place to call home. My wife and I returned to the United States and moved our international ministry offices to Texas. I was shocked at the moral permissiveness that had crept into the American church.

I became a member of a growing congregation where the pastor had a strong Bible teaching ministry. But it wasn't long before I experienced firsthand the effects of the national decline in moral values and its effect upon the church. A teenage girl reported to me that she had come upon the pastor of my church romantically embracing his secretary. At first, I couldn't believe it, and I encouraged the girl not to spread rumors that could be harmful to the pastor and the church. I knew that I had to find out the truth about her accusations. When a colleague and I confronted the pastor and secretary, they confessed that the girl's testimony was accurate.

Within a few weeks, the pastor left his wife and the church. Shortly thereafter he married the secretary. He then became associate pastor at a new and fast growing congregation. Its pastor had recently confessed to church elders at a previous church that his "marriage had collapsed" and that he "became immoral in [his] personal conduct." He resigned that church and began the new congregation. He was a dynamic speaker, and the new church grew rapidly. Within five months after his confession, he divorced his wife. Six months after the divorce, when he was at the second church, he married another woman. The new church continued to grow under the two divorced pastors' leadership.

My former pastor eventually began a mission church. Both churches became two of the largest evangelical churches in our city. By the time the '90s arrived, the pastor who had confessed to the elders was one of the most well known media preachers in America. That could only have happened in an age where the boomer mentality dominated the church. The culture of divorce had penetrated the conservative evangelical community, and it seemed to bother very few people. An "it happens to us all" attitude had apprehended a generation of boomer Christians.

By the time the '80s concluded, American newspaper headlines carried stories of televangelists who had cheated on their wives. Perhaps that's why Whitehead observed, "Two important features characterized American divorce in the twentieth century. One was that divorce became a mass phenomenon. The second was that secular opinion replaced religious thinking as the source of expertise on marriage and divorce."[7] Whitehead's observation was a sad commentary on the church at one of the most critical junctures of American history. The church held the solution to the looming moral and social crisis, but it, to a great extent, traded God's answer for the permissive attitudes of culture.

Divorce and Fatherlessness

Divorce has become so ingrained in American culture that it's a generally accepted part of life today. However, it has brought with it so many personal, social, and even criminal problems that many social scientists fear what could happen if the trend isn't reversed. Of course, the greatest devastation has taken place in the lives of the children of divorce. James Collier wrote, "Between a soaring divorce rate and an equally soaring rate of children born to unwed mothers, it is now the case that the majority of our children will spend at least a portion of their childhoods in single parent homes. . . . This is an extremely unusual circumstance— perhaps unique in human experience. In no known human society, past or present, have children been generally raised outside of an intact nuclear family."[8]

Obviously, there have been short periods of modern history where societies have experienced this phenomenon of fatherlessness within the culture. During World War II fathers were away from home in 3 to 4 million families. An estimated 20 to 25 percent of the nation's families had fatherless children during the war. Yet in 1990 it was estimated that "36.3% of all the children in the nation lived apart from their biological fathers."[9] However, there are two major differences between fatherless children in the '40s and fatherless children in the '90s.

Being a fatherless child in the '40s was a temporary situation. Fathers had gone away to war, and the children had a reasonable hope that their dads would return. But the children of the '90s have only a usually futile hope of their dads returning. Divorce is final. That has left a sense of hopelessness in the hearts of this generation of young people. Second, fathers left home in the '40s because they had to. They had no choice but to go away to war. Fathers today, in large part, leave home because they choose to. That has left a deep sense of rejection in the hearts of young people in this generation. David Blankenhorn, president of the Institute for American Values, summed it up, "The 1940s child could say: My father had to leave for a while to do something important. The 1990s child must say: My father left me permanently because he wanted to."[10]

Divorce has left emotional scars on an entire generation of young people. In 1983 the American Academy of Pediatrics characterized the clinical symptoms of divorce in children. They noted such things as "irritability, separation anxiety, sleep problems, and regression in toilet training as common behaviors for children under three; while tantrums, combativeness, poor school performance, and hyper aggressiveness figured in the conduct problems of older children. Adolescents commonly manifested anger, antisocial behavior, and somatic complaints."[11] A decade later the Academy stated the problems associated with the children of divorce in an even stronger manner. They spoke of aggression in boys and depression in girls as "the most troublesome."[12]

One schoolteacher wrote to San Antonio columnist Roddy Stinson:

> During my years in the classroom, I have seen example after example of children who started school "ready to learn" and did fine—until their parents divorced. Then they broke into pieces. Yet there is never any public discussion of this educational phenomenon. Why? Because our political leaders are divorced. Our business leaders are divorced. Our educational leaders are divorced. Our media commentators are divorced. Even our ministers are divorced. . . . But we don't talk about it. We don't read about it. And we DON'T DO ANYTHING about it. Meanwhile our children continue to be sacrificed on the altars of "do your own thing," "go your own way" and "personal fulfillment."[13]

Not just the children suffer because of divorce; those being divorced also experience trauma in a number of ways. One of the most alarming discoveries of researchers is that suicide is much more likely among those who have been divorced. Researchers Larson, Swyers, and Larson pointed to one scientific study that stated, "In fact, divorce now ranks as the number one factor linked with some of the highest suicide rates, outstripping many other social and economic predictors (Burr et al., 1994). Consistent with earlier research, the rate of suicide for divorced individuals is much higher than the rate for married individuals (Stack, 1992). Combining all races, ages, and sexes, the suicide rate for the divorced is approximately triple that for the married."[14]

In addition, these researchers also pointed to a 1977 study that reviewed two years of data from the National Center for Health Statistics and showed "the premature death rate from cardiovascular disease, for both white and non white divorced men, was double that of married men."[15] They also cited the premature death rate for "pneumonia for white divorced men was more than seven times that of their married counterparts," and "the premature death rate due to hypertension . . . was double for divorced men compared to their married counterparts."[16] There's no question that the divorce culture has affected the lives of those going through it psychologically, physically, and economically.

OUT-OF-WEDLOCK BIRTHS

But family life has been hit hard by more than the storm of divorce. The seed of immorality sown in the '60s has produced an attitude in which many boomers have attempted to redefine the family. A shift of opinion and belief about having children out of wedlock took place between the '60s and the '90s. For example, the Family Research Council commissioned a survey in 1993 that found that most Americans believed that a "woman should be able to have a child out of wedlock without anyone passing judgment," and that "70% of young adult Americans, ages eighteen to thirty four, believe that a woman has the right to bear a child outside marriage."[17] Because of changing attitudes and values of Americans, the number of births to unmarried women grew from 665,747 in 1980 to 1,289,592 in 1994—close to a 100 percent increase.[18]

When Dan Quayle challenged the premise that out-of-wedlock childbearing is good in his family values speech in 1992, he was politically scourged by the media. The vice president used the illustration of Murphy Brown bearing a child out of wedlock. Many laughed at him and attempted to make him look idiotic. The *Murphy Brown* television series poked fun not only at Vice President Quayle, but at anyone who believed in the traditional family. One of the characters on the program said, "I was raised to believe that if you had a child out of wedlock you were bad. Of course, I was raised to believe a woman's place was in the home, segregation was good, and presidents never lie."[19] The parallel was obvious: Anyone who believed that out-of-wedlock childbearing was wrong was sexist, racist, or completely naive.

But Dan Quayle was right. The producers of *Murphy Brown* were wrong. The data overwhelmingly support the former vice president's argument. The consequences of the boomers' philosophy has produced a level of illegitimacy previously unknown in this nation, which has plundered the moral and social landscape of America. Cheryl Wetzstein, national affairs correspondent for the *Washington Times,* cited research compiled by the National Fatherhood Initiative that showed risks for children in single-parent homes:

- Lower scores in math and reading, higher dropout rates, and more incidences of violent misbehavior, suspension, and expulsion in school
- Emotional and antisocial problems, as well as difficulties creating stable positive peer relationships
- Teen suicide
- Drug abuse and cigarette smoking
- Physical and sexual child abuse, especially when the child lives with a biological parent and stepparent
- Poverty[20]

James Collier stated succinctly the reason today's attitude change is problematic: "The nuclear family is one of the most basic of all human institutions, a system of doing things so fundamental that until this century it occurred to very few people that life could exist without it."[21] The '60s attitudes have been firmly ingrained in American culture. We're already reaping their fruit in homes throughout the land. We're walking a dangerous path upon which society has never before traveled. Danger signs appear everywhere. Only God knows where it's all headed.

4

SEVEN CULTURAL KILLERS

The family is the cornerstone of our society. More than any other force it shapes the attitude, the hopes, the ambitions, and the values of the child. And when the family collapses, it is the children that are usually damaged. When it happens on a massive scale the community itself is crippled.[1]

PRESIDENT LYNDON JOHNSON
at Howard University, 1965

POISONED FRUIT

1960: THE SEED IS SOWN—There were 393,000 divorces granted in the United States.

1970: THE SEED TAKES ROOT— There were 706,000 divorces granted in the United States.

1980: A TREE COMES FORTH—There were 1,189,000 divorces granted in the United States.

1994: THE FRUIT IS PRODUCED—There were 1,191,000 divorces granted in the United States.[2]

JUDGMENT IS PENDING

SEVEN CULTURAL KILLERS

★

The family is as vital to the health of a nation as the immune system is to the health of the human body. It's the first line of defense. The health of the nation will be determined by the well-being of the family, and the fitness of the family is ultimately determined by the character of individuals. When people turn from the absolute truths of God's Word, the foundation for building a secure family erodes. Then the character of the nation begins to disintegrate. The traditional family, the most fundamental unit of American society, has never faced an onslaught against it as great as the one it's encountering at the close of the twentieth century.

Even those who are deeply committed to making their marriage successful find it difficult in times when everything in society seems to work against families. Even the phrase "family values" has been so politicized and depersonalized today that some people aren't sure what it means. Americans, who desperately need a clear definition of sound family values, find themselves abused by political strategists attempting to make gains for their party or their candidate. Perhaps the most glaring example of this kind of political seduction took place within the 1996 presidential campaign. Dick Morris, chief political strategist for President Clinton's reelection campaign, determined to make family values the chief issue in the campaign. After a poll showing that the values issues could win the election, Morris concluded:

> The inference was clear. We had to get the values voters back. At a strategy meeting in July, Penn [Mark Penn, Democratic Pollster] explained it rather harshly to Clinton. "If someone is single, we can count on their vote. If they've been married and divorced, separated, or widowed they'll vote for us, but not quite as heavily. Once voters marry, we begin to lose them. Once they have children, they're likely to be for Dole." This was a damning analysis.[3]

The political strategists and pollsters knew that American families were desperate and hurting. People were searching for answers and looking to our leaders for help.

It was good for the strategists and pollsters to come to grips with the crisis facing the American family and propose solutions, although ultimately the solution cannot be a political one (we'll get into that in the second half of this book). The country desperately needed a solution. But the problem Morris faced in promoting a values agenda became evident during the Democratic National Convention. A tabloid magazine ran a story in which it exposed Morris's ongoing relationship with a prostitute. The prostitute even claimed to have listened to conversations between Morris and the president. Morris left the convention in shame and humiliation and was relieved of his responsibilities.

He later wrote a book about his relationship with the president. In his book, he defended his promoting family values at the same time that he was hiring a prostitute. He said,

> Many have questioned my advocacy of a values agenda at the same time as I was seeing a prostitute. My sexual conduct was indefensible, but that is now a matter between myself and my loved ones. My personal failings should not prevent me from helping to get power into parents' hands to control TV images aimed at their children, to keep their children from becoming addicted to tobacco, or from giving them more time off from work to be good parents. We all have our personal demons. But we need not let our struggles with them prevent us from doing whatever good we can manage to do in the larger scope of our lives.[4]

It was a typical boomer response. Morris basically was saying that we must separate our personal lives from our public lives. The problem with his argument is that character is most obvious in our personal lives. The greatest evidence of a person's character will be discovered in the manner in which he treats his family. When personal character no longer matters to our leaders, then the nation is in serious trouble. Leaders, by nature, are to be followed. They are role models. They send a clear signal to the nation by the way they live their lives.

America has a character crisis. It could be said that there is not only a crisis of character in the nation, but also a deliberate attempt to redefine character. Shortly after Morris resigned his position as President Clinton's chief strategist, he was honored at a breakfast hosted by Tina Brown, editor of *The New Yorker.* Syndicated columnist John Leo said about the event, "This was a ghastly moment—one of the nation's leading magazines celebrating one of the nation's leading sleazeballs immediately after revelations about his gross behavior."[5] Parts of the American media seem to have inverted moral values and are attempting to convince the public of its new values.

Not long after the revelation about Morris's seeing a prostitute, it was discovered that he had previously secretly seen another woman for six years and that they had a child out of wedlock. When his book came out, he made a tour of many of America's talk shows. While being interviewed on *Oprah Winfrey,* he was challenged by a person in the audience. She said that Morris had betrayed the voters' trust by seeing a prostitute and having had a secret relationship with another woman when at the same time he made family values a major issue in the campaign. Again, he rationalized his involvement in the family values issue by stating that he stood for families in public policy making.

CULTURAL KILLERS

This attitude of "do as I say—not as I do" has left Americans in a spiritual and moral desert. People are thirsting for truth upon which they can build their lives and families, but they are only able to see a mirage. It looks like water for thirsty souls, but turns out to be only a figment of our imaginations. Not only do politicians need to stop delivering the message that words and actions don't have to be consistent with each other, but the church especially needs to practice what it preaches. Families find themselves struggling with mounting pressures. Many are fainting in the desert. Others don't make it. It's tough for families today. It's easy to understand why many want to give up. But it's not just that we are receiving mixed signals from our leaders. The entire culture has been built on a faulty premise during the last thirty years. Consequently, so much strain has been placed on the family that its failure is almost predetermined.

Since the '60s, a number of distinct "cultural killers" of the family have emerged. Some of these family assassins are inner attitudes. Others are actions and activities that have appeared in the last thirty years. A few are secret assassins, and others are more obvious. But all have been deadly. These cultural killers have been so ingrained in society that they have left a generation of X'ers with a sense of hopelessness. Today's young people face unique challenges as they prepare for marriage.

The Institutionalization of Selfishness

Seven "cultural killers" roam the neighborhoods of America and wreak havoc within homes. *The institutionalization of selfishness* is at the top of that list. The boomer generation was spoiled by unprecedented prosperity and parents who had gone through a time of economic depression. Biblical values such as sacrifice and service were replaced with new concepts of personal success and individual rights. Consequently, a self-centered generation emerged with attitudes that are destructive to the institution of the family. By the '90s these new ideologies were intertwined in every aspect of American life.

Marriage is the most fundamental human relationship in society, and it requires love, commitment, and sacrifice. Selfishness has no place in marriage. If two young people come together to commit themselves to love each other until death, then they will have to work hard on their relationship. Love isn't a funny feeling; it's the giving of one's self. When two people grow up in different environments with different habits, and they begin to live together, sharing the most intimate moments with each other, then it's going to take a great deal of sacrifice on each one's part.

However, within the last thirty years we have produced an entire culture centered in self. We've been taught to place our personal dreams, aspirations, and plans before anyone or anything else—including a spouse or children. That attitude ingrained in American culture has become a killer to marriages. This attitude is most easily seen in this generation's view toward children. Whitehead pointed out that prior to the '60s the basic cultural point of view was that "parents had a moral obligation to place their children's interests in the marital partnership above their own individual satisfactions. This notion was swiftly abandoned after the 60s. . . . If divorce could make one or more parents happier, then it was likely to improve the well being of the children as well."6

But the reverse has been true. A tremendous amount of evidence shows children have been severely damaged by this selfish spirit that has engulfed Americans. Whitehead continued to say,

"Divorce has hurt children. It has created economic insecurity and disadvantage for many children who would not otherwise be economically vulnerable. It has led to more fragile and unstable family households. It has caused a mass exodus of fathers from children's households and, all too often, from their lives. It has reduced the levels of parental time and money invested in children. In sum, it has changed the very nature of American childhood."[7]

The Success Syndrome

The second "cultural killer" of marriages is the *success syndrome*. This attitude is a direct outgrowth of the institutionalization of selfishness. When a nicer car, bigger house, or better economic status takes precedent over time with the family, then the marriage is headed down a deadly collision course. A good marriage not only takes work, but it also takes time. It takes time to build good communication. It takes time to teach children right from wrong. It takes time just to express our love and feelings for one another.

Patrick Fagan of the Heritage Foundation stated in a 1996 study on the social breakdown in America, "On average, parents are available 10 hours less per week to their children than they were a decade ago, and a full 40 percent less today than in 1965." He went on to say, "Adequate time with parents is critical for the development of every child, especially for their self esteem and confidence." Fagan pointed to a 1990 *Los Angeles Times* poll that "found that 57 percent of all fathers and 55 percent of all mothers felt guilty about spending too little time with their children."[8]

In previous generations, families lived an entire lifetime in one house. An automobile's primary function was transportation. But today, a house and one's car have become symbols of success. In many cases, they aren't just a practical help to accomplishing the tasks of ordinary life. They have become badges to display one's status. This attitude has produced an unprecedented entrance of women into the workforce. That has obviously meant time away from home and new stresses on family life.

Americans have prospered financially over the last thirty years, but have entered a period of "depression" when it comes to the time factor. And no matter which way one views marriage, it takes time to build a strong, healthy marriage and family life. I should be careful to note that I realize not all women are in the workforce because they desire status symbols or they want more things. Many are forced to work because of difficult situations. My mother worked because my father was very ill the last ten years of his life and she was forced to be the breadwinner. Many women have found themselves abandoned by their husbands, and they have courageously entered the workforce to provide for their children. However, there exists a tremendous amount of strain on families when both the husband and wife are working. Furthermore, two parents working has become the norm rather than the exception. All too often, the reason is more for status than survival. That has left marriages in America in a more difficult position than our society has ever known.

"Everyone Is Doing It"

A third cultural killer is the attitude of *"Everyone is doing it. Divorce can't be all that wrong."* It used to be that within society there was a belief that marriage was permanent. But divorce has become the norm today and permanence the oddity. Divorce has become acceptable within American culture—and in many cases expected. Therefore, when the going gets tough in the marital relationship, the easiest way to solve the problems is to dissolve the relationship.

Our ministry recently produced a video about spiritual revival and moral renewal in Scotland. We interviewed a number of historians about what had transpired during times of spiritual awakening from the 1600s through this century. The Rev. Sinclair Horne, head of the Scottish Reformation Society, told us that during the days of the Reformation in Scotland there was a call in the land to "raise up the fallen standard of the Word of God." Similarly, in America today the biblical view of permanence in marriage has been lost. We need a fresh call to raise up the fallen standard of God's plan for the family if America is to be renewed. Marriages are in trouble today. God's standard has fallen into disrepute. Divorce has even become chic. If a couple does not have a strong commitment to marriage, the chances are that the relationship won't survive.

Psychological and Emotional Baggage

Another assassin of marriages today is the *psychological and emotional baggage* that many couples have brought into their relationships because of their own sexual impurities. The boomers exchanged traditional biblical morality for a new morality, and the effects can be staggering.

Insecurity and jealousy gripped my life before I became a Christian. Those feelings had been produced by a boomer's lifestyle of the new morality. Even though I turned away from an immoral lifestyle when I came to know Christ, my former immorality left emotional and psychological scars on me. Some of the greatest difficulties that my wife and I have faced in our relationship were produced by the baggage of my previous immoral lifestyle. It has only been by God's grace working within me that I have been able to rid myself of that baggage. Thousands of others just like me have found victory. However, the boomers and generation X have largely never come to grips with the severe consequences of sexual impurity. The prevalent attitude appears to be a continued acceptance of the new morality. As long as that point of view dominates American culture, it will be difficult for marriages to survive.

Pornography

It is not only inner attitudes and feelings that have produced assassins of marriages today. Outward factors within society have also wreaked havoc within the land. One of the fastest growing and yet most destructive influences on marriages in the last thirty years is *pornography*. Syndicated columnist Cal Thomas pointed to a 1991 study by the Los Angeles police department. It showed that "pornography was used in two-thirds of the child molestation cases over a ten year period. The police department in Louisville, Kentucky reached a similar conclusion in 1984."[9]

Pornography is destroying the moral fiber of our communities, our children, and our families. Yet its growth has been phenomenal in the last thirty years. *U.S. News & World Report* said, "Porn has become so commonplace in recent years that one can easily forget how strictly it was prohibited not long ago. The sociologist Charles Winick has noted that the sexual content of American culture changed more in two decades than it had in the previous two centuries."[10]

But technology promises to make pornography even more widespread. *Playboy* magazine's website averages about 5 million hits per day.[11] Unless Americans have the moral courage to put a

stop to the proliferation of all the "web sex," we may find ourselves on the verge of moral disintegration. A generation of spine-
less men who refuse to stand against the current growth of
pornography will place their wives and daughters in even greater
danger than already exists. Pornography stands as the greatest example of what has gone wrong in America. When man loses
moral law, he begins to live according to his base nature. He acts
out of animal instincts rather than by God's principles. Women
will find themselves treated as pieces of flesh to gratify the base
desires of men rather than treated in the manner the Bible describes as "heirs together of the grace of life" (1 Peter 3:7 KJV).

In my interview with James Dobson (chapter 9), he notes that
teenage boys have access to all of this web sex and are the ones
most likely to view it. In later years they then bring a terrible concept of sexual intimacy with them into the marital relationship.
The marriage in which the husband developed his sense of sexual normalcy from pornography is headed for disaster. Yet Americans are filling their minds with pornographic garbage and lining
the pockets of people like Larry Flynt with millions of dollars. If
this rapidly growing trend isn't reversed, then marriages in America will face such difficult times that it's questionable whether the
nation will ever again be able to exist in the same manner as was
previously known.

American Mobility

Mobility within American society is another factor that is
producing a devastating impact upon marriages today. Its impression can be seen on two fronts. First, it takes time to develop intimacy and a deepening relationship within the family. A global
economy has caused people to be on the move more than at any
other time in history. We can travel farther and faster than was
ever imagined by previous generations. Businesspeople increasingly find themselves taken away from their families for commer-
cial purposes.

I have been an itinerant evangelist and conference speaker for
twenty-one years. I know how difficult it is to be a husband and
father and yet be thousands of miles away from home. I also know
that if there's not a really deep commitment to the family, then it's
almost impossible for the marriage to stay intact. Marriage takes
time and energy. When time is taken away from the family, then

the marriage is made vulnerable. When I traveled away from home in the days when our children were small and my wife was unable to go with me, I needed to go to great lengths to maintain my family priorities. Sometimes I was exhausted when I returned home, but I knew that I needed to have some special times with my wife and children. If a person who is required to travel doesn't understand the huge commitment it takes to make his marriage work, then he will find his marriage in trouble quickly.

But tremendous strain has been placed upon marriages in our mobile society in a second way. Temptations that are unique to present-day culture face the traveling person. One of the areas in which pornography is most accessed is in hotels throughout America. I've traveled in cultures that are very hostile toward Christianity. Many times my life has been in danger because of the political systems within the nations where I've gone. But I've repeatedly said that the most dangerous place in which I have ever traveled is America. Pornography is available at the push of a remote switch on a television set in hotels across America.

A Christian business friend of mine gave me great advice before I began my itinerant ministry. He said, "The moment you arrive in your hotel room, you need to immediately unplug the television." That was some of the best traveling advice ever given me. I've seen Christian leaders lose their intimacy with God because they didn't exercise enough discipline to turn off the television set. There have been devastating effects upon marriages because businessmen haven't been disciplined in their travels. Mobility within American culture has produced great temptations. Those traps can lure a person into destructive actions that have the ability to destroy his marriage.

Television

I would like to mention one final destructive force in American culture—*television*. The boomer generation was the first to grow up on television. Since the '60s, television has become one of the most predominant features of American households. William Bennett, former U.S. secretary of education, wrote, "In 1990, more than 98 percent of all households had at least one television set. More American households have televisions than have indoor plumbing."[12]

Television has produced difficulties in marriages in two ways.

First, it's perhaps the greatest thief of family time. It has stolen precious time that it takes to develop deep, intimate relationships. Bennett noted that the "average teenager spends 1.8 hours per week reading, 5.6 hours per week on homework, and an average of 21 hours per week watching television, or about 3 hours per day."[13] When the prime time for husbands and wives, parents and children to interact is spent in front of the television set, then communication breaks down.

I once asked a Christian leader whose marriage had failed, "How could this have happened?" His response was simply, "We quit communicating." I'm convinced that television has had a devastating effect upon communication within the family. It has become a narcotic that deadens our senses and prevents us from communicating on the deepest levels. Daniel Goleman reported in the *New York Times* that "watching television has many of the marks of a dependency like alcoholism or other addictions." He said, "One study found that self-described addicts watch 56 hours a week; the A. C. Nielsen Company reports the average for adults is just above 30 hours a week."[14] It's virtually impossible to develop intimate communication while working forty hours and watching television thirty hours the same week. Any kind of long-term relationship will be rooted in deep and consistent communication. That means if the sanctity of the home is to be restored, then someone is going to have to turn off the television.

But television has also affected the moral fiber of the country. Prime-time television has set itself up against biblical and family values. In the book *Watching America,* the authors state that "75 percent of that [Hollywood] elite describe themselves as 'left of center' politically, 97 percent are pro-choice, and 51 percent find adultery and extramarital relations acceptable behavior." One of the authors, Robert Lichter, found that "two thirds of Hollywood's creative elite believe that TV entertainment should play 'a major role in social reform.'"[15] Thus we find an anti–biblical and family values agenda being thrust on marriages that are already struggling. Prime-time television continually portrays extramarital and premarital sex as good. Its mark is being left upon a generation that consistently spends more time in front of the tube. Andrew Fletcher of Saltoun said in the eighteenth century, "If a man were permitted to make all the ballads, he need not care who should make the laws of a nation."[16]

In fact, Robert Lichter remarked about sex on television, "Sex has gone from prohibited to pervasive since the mid 1970s. Today's typical viewer sees about 10,000 scenes of suggested sexual intercourse, sexual comment, or innuendo during one year of average viewing. . . . In fact, marital sex is as rare these days as recreational sex used to be. Seven out of eight acts of intercourse on prime time are extramarital."[17] One cannot help but escape the fact that the rise of viewing immorality on television has been parallel to the rise of divorce in America.

Not only has Hollywood presented an alternative morality to the American public, but it has also attempted to redefine the family for America. The homosexual community has gained clout in Hollywood and is attempting to thrust its new morality on the average citizen. During April 1997, *Newsweek* magazine reported that only five years ago LIFT (Lesbians in Film and Television) had its first party. *Newsweek* stated that LIFT now has nearly one thousand members.[18] Dannielle Thomas, president of Inter Act Management, said, "It's a great time to be a gay woman. Five years ago, we would whisper about being lesbian. Now, in the boardrooms of Hollywood, we're talking about it openly, even making jokes."[19]

But is there actually an agenda by some Hollywood producers to promote a different kind of family to today's young person? It would certainly seem so. *Newsweek* stated that Jamie Tarses, the newly installed head of ABC Entertainment, and Dean Valentine, president of Disney Television, were approached by Ellen DeGeneres, the star of *Ellen,* about having a show with Ellen discovering herself to be a lesbian. The ABC and Disney officials agreed. Interestingly, Tarses had "championed the lesbian wedding on 'Friends'" in her previous job at NBC.[20]

THE CHALLENGE

Families are struggling today as never before in our history. Secret assassins within American culture are ready to destroy any marriage without a solid foundation. More obvious forces are also fighting forcefully against the sanctity of marriage. Without a moral renewal and spiritual awakening, the situation can only get worse. When families disintegrate, society is in deep trouble. The social order cannot stand without strong families. We've produced a culture of divorce. Such a culture will ultimately lead to a culture of death.

5
THE CULTURE OF DEATH

The foundation of our independence and our Government rests upon our basic religious convictions. Back of the authority of our laws is the authority of the Supreme Judge of the world, to whom we still appeal for their final justification. . . .

It seems perfectly plain that the authority of law, the right to equality, liberty and property, under American institutions, have for their foundation reverence for God. If we could imagine that to be swept away, these institutions of our American government could not long survive.[1]

CALVIN COOLIDGE
September 21, 1924

THE FRUIT PRODUCES DEATH

1960: THE SEED IS SOWN—There were 288,460 violent crimes committed in the United States.

1970: THE SEED TAKES ROOT—There were 738,820 violent crimes committed in the United States.

1980: A TREE COMES FORTH—There were 1,344,520 violent crimes committed in the United States.

1992: THE FRUIT IS PRODUCED—There were 1,932,274 violent crimes committed in the United States.[2]

JUDGMENT IS PENDING

THE CULTURE OF DEATH

---★---

When America traded the solid foundation of God's Word for the shifting sands of relativism during the '60s, it opened her citizens to dangers previously unknown. The new foundation has led to a culture obsessed with death. The pattern has been quite clear. An entire generation rejected biblical values and principles during the '60s. Indecency and immorality were brought out of the closet and paraded down Main Street. Eventually that led to the institutionalization of immoral behavior. From the centers of entertainment to the courts of justice, depravity has become an acceptable manner of life.

The first institution to crumble under the heavy weight of licentiousness was the family. The breakdown of the nuclear family has given rise to all kinds of social disorders, including abortion, assisted suicide, teen suicide, and a dramatic increase in violent crime. The apostle Paul wrote almost two thousand years ago about two "laws" at work within society—the "law of sin and death" and the "law of the Spirit and life" (Romans 8:2). He clearly stated the consequences of both laws, "For if you live according to the sinful nature, you will die; but if by the Spirit you put to death the misdeeds of the body, you will live" (Romans 8:13). As a people, we have chosen the law of sin, and it has produced a bountiful crop of death. Freedom without boundaries has triumphed over life. America has been left at the brink of God's judgment.

James Lincoln Collier concluded his book *The Rise of Selfishness in America* with a succinct statement of what has transpired in the nation:

> America was once more than simply a place, more than simply a nation. It was an idea—an idea so powerful that it inflamed the imaginations of men and women around the world, and led them everywhere to topple emperors and kings. The world no longer ad-

mires the United States. It envies our prosperity and our freedoms; but it does not admire us. Yes, immigrants continue to swarm in, but that is mainly for the abundance of things that we have. They do not come because of an idea. And Liberty weeps to see what we have done with her gift.[3]

OUR SELF-CENTERED FOCUS

What has America done with its gift of freedom? We have abused that precious gift for the pursuit of our selfish pleasures. When man places his own interests above the interests of others, then disaster becomes the order of the day. Not only will marriages experience chaos and disorder, but society will be devastated by the deadly consequences of selfishness. Former United States education secretary William J. Bennett pointed out,

> While population has increased only 41 percent since 1960, the number of violent crimes [author's footnote: this includes murders, rapes, robberies and aggravated assaults] has increased more than 550 percent. . . . The rate of violent crime in the United States is worse than in any other industrialized country. The homicide rate is more than five times that of Europe, and four times that of Canada, Australia, or New Zealand. In addition, the rate at which rapes occur in the United States is nearly seven times higher than it is in Europe.[4]

Most authorities agree that the rise in violence in America is directly related to the breakdown of the family. A secure and stable family is the best medicine to cure the cancer of crime in our communities. Without security within the home there will never be security within the community. But many of today's young people have lost that sense of security. According to the National Center of Health Statistics, "In 1980 one in five births was nonmarital; in 1992 almost one in three births (30.1 percent) were to unmarried women."[5] Those children will have to overcome huge obstacles in order to live a productive life in society.

"The numbers are stark and incontrovertible," wrote Patrick Fagan, senior policy analyst at the Heritage Foundation:

> The United States is on an undeviating path toward becoming a nation of fatherless families. . . . The rise in crime . . . is tied to the disintegration of marriage. From the very beginning, children born

outside of marriage have life stacked against them. While many single mothers work wonders and raise their children well despite the obstacles they encounter, for many others the challenge is too great and their children suffer the consequences.[6]

Senator Daniel Patrick Moynihan struck a similar chord when he cited Karl Zinsmeister, who said, "There is a mountain of scientific evidence showing that when families disintegrate children often end up with intellectual, physical, and emotional scars that persist for life. . . . We talk about the drug crisis, the education crisis, and the problems of teen pregnancy and juvenile crime. But all the ills trace back predominantly to one source: broken families."[7]

The Parent Gap and Crime

Parents too often don't have adequate time for their children, who desperately need love and supervision, along with acceptance and guidance. When the family breaks down, the children turn to the next closest place that will embrace them. Too often they find their acceptance in gangs in their communities. Professor James Alan Fox, editor of the *Journal of Quantitative Criminology*, has repeatedly warned of an "impending youth crime wave." He says that "as many as 57 percent of children in America do not have full-time parental supervision, [but are] either living with a single parent who works full-time or in a two-parent household with both parents working full-time. While some children do enjoy suitable, substitute supervision provided by friends and relatives or in day-care, far too many do not."[8]

One of the most disturbing indicators of a culture consumed with death is the rate of homicide among children. J. Tom Morgan summarized the rate of homicide of children under age four in 1995. He said that homicide in this age group "had reached a forty-year high. It is now the leading cause of death among this age group. . . . Most of these deaths were perpetrated by parents or caretakers."[9]

The rise of violent crime has been dramatic. It's quite interesting that this increase has paralleled the rise in divorce and the forsaking of biblical values within American society. We can't build enough prisons to incarcerate those committing crimes against society. Often criminals go free because there isn't enough room to house them. We've produced a culture in which violence and crime have become such a normal part of the American way of life that many social historians are referring to the present generation as having produced a "culture of death." We've become a society where militias are arming themselves, children are killing children, gangs control neighborhoods, and drive-by shootings are common. One commentator has described it this way: "If our society does someday expire, the notation on the autopsy report will accurately characterize the cause of death as a self-inflicted wound."[10]

The Family Research Council cited a 1984 report by Gary Bauer, who was at that time undersecretary of education. The report told of crime in America's schools. The facts were startling: "Three million high school students were victims of in-school crimes each month. . . . One out of every 10 high school students had been a crime victim the previous year. . . . Each month 1000 teachers required medical attention because of in-school assaults and 125,000 were threatened."[11] But Robert Maginnis, policy analyst for the Family Research Council, said that "10 years after the Bauer report, the problems are worse. America's schools are battlegrounds where children are too often physically harmed and deprived of a good education. Teachers are more at risk than ever before."[12] Michael Resnick, spokesman for the National School Boards Association, agreed, saying, "Just as the incidences of violence are increasing, so is the severity of the violence, so that this is becoming a much more serious problem in terms of numbers, location, and severity."[13]

The Ultimate Lack of Connection: Suicide

Americans have also begun taking their own lives in a manner never known in American history. Suicide has grown rapidly in American culture, especially among young people. Suicide rates have more than quintupled among young men between ages fifteen and twenty-four since 1950.[14] Fewer than one thousand suicides were committed by persons between ages fifteen and twenty-four in 1950. By 1980, young people in that same age group had lost their moral and spiritual compass. That year, 5,239 of them took their own lives.[14] Suicide has become the third leading killer of young people. More teenagers and young adults have died from suicide than cancer, heart disease, AIDS, birth defects, stroke, pneumonia and influenza, and chronic lung disease *combined*.[15]

Public health officials and researchers find suicide a very complex issue to understand. However, they agree that since the '50s there has been a dramatic increase in young people, most of them males, killing themselves. The most alarming fact is that in a 1990 national survey of high school students, it was discovered that at least 276,000 high school students in the United States had made at least one suicide attempt that required medical treatment.[16] In past years in the United States, the elderly were more likely to commit suicide. However, young people have increasingly begun taking their lives.

There are no easy answers to why these trends have taken place over the last thirty years. However, I'm convinced that once society abandoned the Rock of God's Word, we made our young people much more vulnerable to destructive forces in their lives. Now our children are left with only shifting sand for a foundation in their lives. As storms blow across their lives, many don't seem to have the ability to withstand them. A number of these young people have grown up in stable families. Yet the culture has become so engrossed with death and destruction that even young people from the finest of homes struggle against forces that could devastate their lives.

A biblical foundation produces a recognition of our value, hope, and purpose in life. When the destructive winds of violence and death blow across our lives, we are able to withstand them. We know that we were created in the image of God. As long as there is a God who loves us, then no situation is hopeless. However, when we began to remove any expression of faith in God from our schools and institutions, then we left our young people wide open for a sense of hopelessness to grip their lives. A deep faith in the God of the Bible can give this generation of young people a sense of hope and purpose in their lives. One cultural study showed, "The practice of religion reduces the rate of suicide, both in the United States and abroad."[17]

When I was a high school student during the '60s, there were several times I considered suicide. Even though I had achieved academically, I felt hopeless. Those occasions were normally during times when a relationship with a girl had been severed. I was tender and desperately desiring love. When a girlfriend broke up with me, it seemed like the end of the world. In my eyes, there seemed to be no future. My mother sensed that something was wrong and talked to me. She told me that I couldn't give up. Her words gave me enough strength to continue with my life. But they didn't satisfy the emptiness in my heart.

I heard of God's love for me one night as a university student. That night I prayed and placed my faith in Jesus as God's Son and my Savior. After I prayed that night, I had a Rock upon which I could build my life. Since then, I have gone through many difficult experiences. But I've known that no situation is ever hopeless. Christ has given me the inner courage to face any and every circumstance of life. That's the ultimate choice that Americans have to make. It's a choice of life or death; heaven or hell; self-centeredness or Christ-centeredness. The choice we make will affect not only this generation but generations to come.

THE CHOICE

Perhaps never in all of American history has the choice of life or death been so clear. The information age and modern technology have opened the minds of Americans to a strange mixture of religions that offer life and yet produce death. The nation was shocked when thirty-nine members of the Heaven's Gate cult committed suicide in 1997. The cult had recruited on the World Wide Web, but the Heaven's Gate cult isn't the only weird new religious group on the web. Everything from Killer Cults to the Satanic Network can be found on the Internet.[18]

Americans by nature and history are a religious people. Our history is filled with revivals of the Christian faith and spiritual movements rooted in the Bible. However, when the boomer generation threw out that age-old foundation of God's Word, it left the hearts of people open to any kind of belief system. A deep void was left in the hearts of future generations. Just as we began to reap the full harvest of the seed sown in the '60s, the Internet was introduced to households across America. Undoubtedly, there's much good on the Internet. However, it has opened the door to ideas and beliefs that could be very destructive to a generation already speeding down a road leading to ruin.

The Internet is proliferating with cults prepared to suck the soul out of America. Tal Brooke, who edited a book called *Virtual Gods,* commented on the cults' use of the Net: "I think the Net can be an effective cult recruiting tool. It's like fishing with a lure—Little Johnny Latchkey gets behind the keyboard and hears someone say, 'I'm the dad you never had.'"[19] Rabbi Abraham

Cooper of the Simon Wiesenthal Center also pointed out that more than five hundred fringe religious and hate groups have sites on the Web.[20] If Americans don't quickly turn back to the solid Rock of the Word of God, the Net will provide ample spiritual ammunition for soldiers of darkness to ambush this generation. The result can only be death.

Life is becoming cheap in the United States. Americans seem to be choosing death over life with an alarming frequency. God laid a choice before the children of Israel in Deuteronomy 30:15: "See, I set before you today life and prosperity, death and destruction." It was a simple but profound choice: life or death, prosperity or destruction. Americans are increasingly choosing death and destruction. God described what constituted the choice in the next three verses:

> For I command you today to love the Lord your God, to walk in his ways, and to keep his commands, decrees and laws; then you will live and increase, and the Lord your God will bless you in the land you are entering to possess. But if your heart turns away and you are not obedient, and if you are drawn away to bow down to other gods and worship them, I declare to you this day that you will certainly be destroyed. (Deuteronomy 30:16-18a)

Sexual Promiscuity

Sexuality plays an important role in life and death choices that we make. Sex is a creation of God and intended to be something beautiful that produces life. God created us and knows fully that which contains life and that which produces death. He desires that we choose life rather than death. But it's our choice as individuals as well as our choice as a nation. The first commandment that He gave after creating man and woman was, "Be fruitful and increase in number; fill the earth and subdue it" (Genesis 1:28a). God created man and woman to live in a committed relationship as husband and wife. In the context of that relationship, He commanded us to reproduce and fill the earth. When we live in the context of that relationship (one man and one woman committed to each other until death), then sex becomes a joy and we live productively as families. Ultimately, society is benefited.

Homosexuality: the Lie

However, God left us a choice to make, and, unfortunately,

many Americans have been consumed with choices that can lead to death. One of those choices is about sexual commitments. Homosexuality is being propagated as an "alternative lifestyle" by the mainstream media, but God called it an abomination in Leviticus 18:22 (KJV). The first order of business on President Clinton's agenda when he was elected president of the United States in 1992 was to issue an executive order lifting a ban on homosexuals in the military. Ted Koppel on his ABC news program, *Nightline,* interviewed Lt. Tracy Thorne who planned to tell the world that he was gay.

Koppel's first question to Thorne was, "If you're going to tell folks that you're gay, there are easier ways to do it than coming on a network news program. Why this way, Tracy?"

Thorne responded, "I really think it's time for a change. I think the political climate is ripe, and I've just seen too much discrimination. I see thousands of people a year that are kicked out of the Navy for something that is beyond their control. It's what they're born as. It's what they are, the core of their human being."[21]

According to Washington D.C.'s Accuracy in Media, "Koppel failed to correct the false claim that the Navy is discharging thousands of people each year because they are homosexuals. The total of such discharges for all the services was less than a thousand in each of the previous three years, and the Navy alone accounted for about half the total. . . . Nor did Koppel challenge Thorne's assertion that people are born gay and nothing can be done about it."[22] That seems pretty unusual because Koppel is known for his hard-hitting questions of those who come on his program.

Homosexual activists have been consistently and blatantly furthering their agenda with a basic fundamental untruth. The foundation upon which they have built their argument is that homosexuals are born that way. I'm convinced that's one of the greatest lies thrust upon Americans in the last twenty years. Homosexuality is not a birth defect. It's a heart defect. It's not how we're born, but rather a manner of life that we choose. Sex researchers Masters and Johnson claim "an immediate 79 percent success rate for clients who want to cure their homosexuality, with 72 percent remaining cured after five years."[23] If such a high percentage of people can be cured of homosexuality, then it must be a learned behavior and not a genetic issue as the homosexual proponents would have us believe.

One reason the homosexual issue is of such great importance to the moral stability of America is that many scientists believe that the HIV virus, which results in AIDS, was introduced into the nation through homosexual behavior. Not all of those dying of AIDS were infected because of homosexual behavior. However, a substantial percentage of AIDS-related deaths stem from homosexual behavior. Before 1981 there were only thirty-one known deaths from AIDS. However, by the end of 1995, 315,918 people had died from AIDS.[24] According to the Centers for Disease Control, 55 percent of the 1994 reported AIDS cases of men were adults and adolescents who had sex with men; 25 percent were from injecting drug use; and 7 percent were from men who had sex with men and injected drugs. A total of 87 percent of the reported AIDS cases among men in 1994 came from men having sex with men and/or injecting drugs. Those three categories also make up 78 percent of all AIDS cases that include men and women.

Even though the statistics are alarming for the homosexual agenda, Americans seem to be willing to accept that agenda. It has been craftily set in motion and swallowed hook, line, and sinker by the mainstream media. The Family Research Council reported in 1996 that PFLAG (Parents, Friends & Families of Lesbians and Gays) has launched a one-million-dollar TV and newspaper campaign to promote a homosexual agenda. The campaign, "Project Open Mind," is expected to run in several major U.S. cities and press the homosexual agenda on the following fronts:

- Homosexuals in the military
- Homosexual marriage
- Homosexual adoption
- Civil rights for homosexuals[25]

The homosexual community would have Americans believe that they are to be pitied because they are the target of Christian persecution. In their media propaganda they link Christian leaders to terrible deeds inflicted upon homosexuals. According to the Family Research Council, "One of the two 30-second [TV] spots dramatizes gay-bashing, where a young man is chased by a group and then beaten; the other depicts a young woman holding a gun as she considers suicide. Visuals then cut to TV comments from the Rev. [Pat] Robertson and the Rev. Jerry Falwell and Sen. Jesse Helms (R-NC)."[26]

Homosexuality: the Truth

However, the realities of homosexuality are quite different from what is being portrayed by the media. Americans are being sent a message that homosexuals are simply clean-cut ordinary citizens. Stanley Montieth, M.D., author of *AIDS—The Unnecessary Epidemic,* said, "The tragedy today is that most people in the general population do not understand what the homosexual lifestyle really involves. . . . Homosexuals are brought into schools all across America—successful businessmen, successful lawyers and doctors, nice men—and, of course their whole plea is, 'Look, we're victims of homophobia. We're nice people and we just want to live our lives and be left alone.'"[27]

But most Americans would be appalled by the Gay Pride parade in San Francisco. Footage of the parade showed the following: "near-nude men in gyrating movements and grotesque costumes; men wearing women's clothes; women in cages, one waving a whip at the others; Lesbians with bare breasts; a man slapping his bare buttocks with a riding crop . . . simulated oral sex; kissing; kissing genitals; sign with God is gay."[28] Dr. Montieth states that "100% of homosexuals engage in fellatio, which is either insertive or receptive oral sex. About 93% engage in rectal sex, which is anal intercourse. . . . It's not a healthy activity. And it's because you tear the rectal mucosa that there's such a high incidence of disease in these cases."[29]

The rest of Dr. Montieth's description of homosexual activity is so utterly vulgar that I did not feel that I could identify it in a book of this nature. Homosexual activity is not quite the nice innocent-boy-next-door behavior that is being portrayed by the media. In fact, studies show that male homosexuals "average between 20 and 106 partners every year. The average homosexual has 300 to 500 partners in his lifetime. . . . Compared to heterosexuals, male homosexuals are more than 8 times more likely to have had hepatitis, 14 times more likely to have had syphilis and 5000 times more likely to have contracted AIDS."[30]

Abortion

Not only are Americans killing themselves because they have contracted AIDS due to their immoral behavior, but many are killing their own children primarily because of their immoral behavior. An epidemic of killing babies was unleashed in America in 1973 when abortion was legalized. Americans began to use their freedom as a license to kill. A woman's right to choose took precedent over a baby's right to live. Most of the abortion debate has nothing to do with extreme circumstances that could endanger a woman's life. In fact, according to statistics cited by William Bennett, "only 7 percent of all abortions fall into the category of threatened life of the mother, health of the child, and victim of rape or incest."[31]

According to the Alan Guttmacher Institute, more than 80 percent of the women who have abortions are not married.[32] That basically means that most of the abortions that are taking place are a result of immoral relationships. The crux of the abortion debate would stop if Americans turned from immoral lifestyles. Unmarried women wouldn't be having abortions if they weren't getting pregnant.

The Wrong Answer

Of course, most proponents of abortion and/or a homosexual lifestyle believe that the answer to these issues is greater use of the condom. There are, however, three basic flaws in that solution. First, the use of condoms doesn't address the root problem facing this generation. There is scientific research that says that promoting the use of condoms is not the answer to many of the social problems facing American young people. It's like putting a bandage on someone who needs heart surgery. Second, condoms are not 100 percent safe, even when used properly. Third, it's pretty unrealistic to think that teenagers are going to use condoms correctly in the heat of sexual activity. In fact, one study states that at least 50 percent of condom usage by sexually active youth is done incorrectly.[33] Finally, most sexually active youth don't use condoms consistently. According to a study by Dr. Thomas Fitch, the range of sexually active young people consistently using condoms varies from 5 to 40 percent.[34]

We have opened this generation to disease, death, and patterns of destruction. It's difficult for today's young person to determine right from wrong when those in authority are sending mixed signals. It's not just a political or ideological debate. It's a debate about life and death issues. Dr. Fitch says in his study, "I doubt most women know that most cancer of the cervix is caused by a sexually transmitted disease with little or no protection from condoms. (I found no articles in the world literature that show condoms are protective in females against the HPV virus). I doubt most teenage girls know that having sex at an early age puts them at greater risk for STD infection and later for cancer of the cervix and infertility."[35] Why do we risk the lives and health of our youth? The only answer is that we have attached ourselves to a culture of death and destruction. We have turned our freedom into a license for immoral behavior, and it's killing us.

Physician-Assisted Suicide

And now America is toying with the idea of physician-assisted suicide. It's being debated in our halls of justice and on the floors of our legislatures. All of this is indicative of a nation consumed with death. The standard for physicians used to be the Hippocratic Oath, which says that the doctor "will neither prescribe nor administer a lethal dose of medicine to any patient even if asked nor counsel any such thing nor perform act or omission with direct intent deliberately to end a human life."[36] That began to change in 1973 when abortion was legalized. Interestingly, the Hippocratic Oath has even been reworded to allow legal killing. A new version approved by the American Medical Association weakens this section to say that a doctor "will give no drug . . . for a criminal purpose, even if solicited."[37] It was only logical that killing the elderly, disabled, or weak would follow a license to kill babies in their wombs. Holland has already crossed that bridge. Some of the results there have been horrifying. A 1991 survey states that "as many as 1000 cases of euthanasia occurred without patient consent, and it documents more than 4,500 cases of excessive medication without patient consent.[38]

When life becomes so cheap that we kill the weakest in society, then we open ourselves to horrors unimaginable. Cathleen A. Cleaver of the Family Research Council said, "History warns that the institution of assisted-death gravely threatens to undermine the foundational ethic of the medical profession and the paramount principle of the equal dignity and inherent worth of every human person."[39] She was right. Much of what happened in Nazi Germany occurred because life had become cheap. Physicians often justified their actions with the same reasoning used today for assisted suicide. Cleaver cited Pediatrician Ernst Wentzler, who justified his participation in Nazi war crimes saying, "I had the feeling that my activity was something positive, and that I had made a small contribution to human progress."[40]

We made a choice thirty years ago. The only way to escape the consequences of our decision is for a new generation to stand up and make a different choice. If we don't have the courage or character to choose a new direction, then we ought to consider writing our national epithet as the century comes to a close.

SECTION TWO

The Road to Revival

6
REVIVAL IN THE CHURCH

Then he said to them all: "If anyone would come after me, he must deny himself and take up his cross daily and follow me." (Luke 9:23)

JESUS

The church world is full of Christian professors and ministers, Sunday school teachers and workers, evangelists and missionaries, in whom the gifts of the Spirit are very manifest, and who bring blessing to multitudes, but who when known "close up" are found to be full of self.[1]

L. E. MAXWELL

REVIVAL IN THE CHURCH

⎯⎯⎯⎯⎯⎯★⎯⎯⎯⎯⎯⎯

There will never be a spiritual awakening and moral renewal in the nation until we have dealt with the root problem facing this generation. A selfish spirit was planted in the hearts of an entire generation thirty years ago, and since then selfishness has been institutionalized. A generation of boomers rejected the Word of God as the basis of their authority, and then became gods unto themselves. Boomers bowed down to five gods who have self as their first name: self-will, self-righteousness, self-confidence, self-pleasing, and self-exaltation. This generation has rejected the one true and living God of the Bible and worshiped at the altar of self. We have indulged ourselves. We must tear down the altars of self and return to the God of our forefathers if we are to undergo a national revival.

We will never have spiritual awakening in the nation until we first see corporate revival within the church. The solution to the problem of self-deification lies within the church. However, the church seems to have embraced the self-idols, rather than forsaking them. When God gave His formula for the healing of a nation, He began by saying, "If my people, who are called by my name. . . ." The healing of a nation begins with the people of God. All too often, Christians point their accusing fingers at the non-Christian world surrounding them. However, the Bible says, "For it is time for judgment to begin with the family of God; and if it begins with us, what will the outcome be for those who do not obey the gospel of God?" (1 Peter 4:17).

The church needs to take a long, hard look at itself. We must ask God to search our hearts and see where we have worshiped at the altar of self. The time has come for Christians to fall on our faces in repentance. We must turn from worshiping self to worshiping God. Jesus was once asked what the greatest commandment of the Law was. He simply replied, "Love the Lord your God

with all your heart and with all your soul and with all your mind"
(Matthew 22:37). We need to turn from loving self to loving God
with all of our hearts.

The church to a great extent has left its first love. We have embraced the gods of the culture rather than the God of the Bible.
We have created unseen altars within our sanctuaries. Our worship services are geared to make us feel good rather than to embrace the old rugged cross. Our sermons teach us how to be
healthy, wealthy, and wise rather than humble, broken, and contrite. Our altar calls are for us to receive a blessing rather than be
a blessing. Our programs are geared to fill us with fun rather than
call us to the Cross. Consequently, we have produced a generation of Christians who have a passion for pleasure rather than a
desire for Christ. And the church stands powerless in perhaps the
most critical moment of the history of the nation.

The church must recapture the source of God's power if it is
to be an agent of change within the nation. However, it's not the
preaching about "the power of God" that releases the power of
God. In this crucial moment of time, many churches have begun
to proclaim signs, wonders, and healings rather than the death,
burial, and resurrection of Christ. The power of God isn't found
in "power encounters" or outward signs and wonders. Miracles
don't change the hearts of people. Multitudes followed Jesus because of the miracles He performed, but they never had a change
of heart. They were fickle. Jesus made one statement and the
crowds ceased following Him. He simply told them that no one
could follow Him unless the Father had drawn them, and the multitudes quit seeking Him.

THE POWER OF THE GOOD NEWS

The message of Christ proclaimed in the nation has the power
to change the moral fabric of American culture. Society will never
change until people in it have been changed in their hearts and
minds. Only one message given to the church has that kind of power. There's but one truth that can penetrate the deepest and darkest parts of the hearts of ordinary citizens in the land. Only one
word can bring forgiveness and healing to a guilt-ridden and broken nation, and yet at the same time produce a transformation of
the moral character of its people. The Bible says, "For the message
of the cross is foolishness to those who are perishing, but to us

who are being saved it is the power of God" (1 Corinthians 1:18).

Many Christians would never admit it, but many of us live as though the old-time, old-fashioned preaching of the Cross has no relevance today. However, I'm convinced that it's the most relevant message for American society at this critical moment. The root cause of moral decline in our culture has been the rejection of biblical authority and the rise of a selfish spirit in the land. The message of the Cross has the power to uproot and tear down the idols of self-will, self-righteousness, self-confidence, self-pleasing, and self-exaltation. It has the ability to turn a self-centered heart into one that is filled with God's will, Christ's righteousness, and confidence in the Savior. That timeless message makes us pleasing to God and ultimately exalts only the name of Jesus.

The message of the Cross has the power to melt and change the hardest of hearts. It can set those free who have been enslaved for decades by sin and moral wrong. It's the truth that can enlighten the darkest of hearts. The message of the Cross contains the power and the grace of God. By His grace we find forgiveness. By His power we experience victory over the selfish spirit. That's why we must proclaim one message—the Cross. It's the secret weapon that's able to change lives and ultimately transform our nation.

Changed Lives

In 1970, my wife and I began a street ministry in one of the most crime-ridden areas of Chicago. We worked with drug addicts, runaways, and street gangs. Many thought those with whom we were working were hopeless. However, we had one simple but powerful message—"Jesus died on the cross to forgive our sins and change our lives. When we turn from our self-centeredness and trust in what He did on the cross, then we can find the true meaning and purpose in life." It wasn't a seeker-sensitive message. It wasn't wrapped in supernatural signs and wonders. It was simply the old-time, old-fashioned message of the Cross. We continuously saw the power of God demonstrated as we told that old, old story of what the Savior did two thousand years ago.

One day in 1971 a young woman came to my office in Chicago. She was part of a satanic cult that worshiped a triune god: Jehovah, Lucifer, and Satan. They believed that when Jesus taught us to love our enemies, He brought Jehovah, Lucifer, and Satan together. This young lady had been caught up in the cult for several years, but she longed to be free from it. She came to our office seeking help. I opened my Bible and began to present the message of what Christ did on the cross. As I was talking about the blood that Christ shed on the cross for our sins, the girl fell on the floor and began to scream. We started to pray for her, and she, all of a sudden, jumped up and ran out of the office screaming. It was a harrowing experience, to say the least.

For years, I often wondered what happened to that young lady. I prayed that one day she would come to know Christ, but I had no idea what happened to her after she left our offices. Seventeen years later I preached at the First Baptist Church of Edmond, Oklahoma. When I walked into the church that Sunday morning, one of the leaders said to me, "There's a lady here that would like to speak with you."

When I walked into the office, a middle-aged lady asked me, "Do you remember me?" She looked somewhat familiar, but I couldn't recall where I had seen her. Then she said, "I came to your office in Chicago in the early 1970s. I was involved in a satanic cult. As you shared the gospel of Christ with me, I began screaming."

I immediately reassured her that I remembered that encounter. She then told me an amazing story of freedom from the cult. She said that when she heard the truth of what Christ did on the cross, she knew that she needed out. However, Satan had such a hold on her heart that she could only scream when she heard the message. When she left our office that day, she knew that she had to find a way out of the cult. She ran away a couple of times, but others always found her and brought her back. Finally, she met a group of radical lesbians. They took her in and protected her. But one night in a motel room, she found a Bible placed there by the Gideon's organization. As she opened it and began to read the Bible, she recalled that I had shared the same message of what Christ did on the cross. She quietly prayed and placed her faith in Christ.

Jesus changed her life that night. She left the lesbians and found some Christians who could help her grow in Christ. She was living in Oklahoma and serving the Lord. She read in the local newspaper that I was speaking at the church, and she came over to tell me, "I just wanted you to know that I never forgot the mes-

sage you gave me seventeen years earlier in Chicago. That message is so powerful that I could never forget it. Because of that
message, I am a new woman." I can't tell you how much joy filled
my heart as I listened to her story.

Personal Testimonies

Later in the service that morning, the music director said,
"This morning is a special morning for me. I placed my faith in
Christ as a young boy when I heard the man who will speak to us
today talk about what Christ did on the cross. Christ came into my
life, forgave my sins, and changed me completely." I was overwhelmed as I sat on the platform that morning. I realized that only
one age-old message has the same power to set a Satan worshiper
free and also transform a Sunday school child and make him a
leader among God's people. I silently prayed and asked God to
never let me lose sight of the power of the message of the Cross.

In 1989, I led a seminar at the Lausanne Congress on World
Evangelization. The congress brought together Christian leaders
from around the world. After my seminar, a number of leaders
had gathered and were speaking with me. After they left, a lady
walked up to me and said, "Are you the same Sammy Tippit that
was arrested in Chicago in 1971 for telling others about Christ in
a nightclub district of Chicago?"

"Yes, I'm the same person," I said. In 1971, many people were
coming to Christ in the area, and the clubs were forced to close
early because of the power of the message we were proclaiming.
Some police came out of a club and arrested a friend and me. Later the city of Chicago admitted to false arrest and dropped the
charges. "But how did you know about that?" I asked.

"I was a dancer in one of those clubs. One night you gave me
a gospel pamphlet, and I took it home and read it. It had Scriptures about what Christ did on the cross and what He could do
for me. Later, I went to a rally and heard you speak. I never forgot
the message, and soon thereafter I placed my faith in Jesus. He
came into my life and changed me. Now I'm married, and my husband and I are missionaries. I saw your name on the program, and
I just wanted to come and say, 'Thank you for telling what Christ
could do for me.'"

Whether a person is a Satan worshiper, a boy in a Sunday
school class, or a dancer in a night club, the power of the mes-

sage of the Cross is the same. It has the power to change a Satan worshiper into one who worships the Lamb of God who takes away the sins of the world. It can make a Sunday school lad a leader in the Christian community. It turns a provocative night club dancer into a humble missionary serving humanity. I've seen this wonderful message of the Cross change the most vile criminal behavior into sweet service for God and mankind.

The first time I traveled to Northern Ireland, I prayed with a lady who was living with the leader of a terrorist gang. She heard the message of the Cross and turned to Christ that night. Her pastor told me that she immediately left the terrorist group and eventually married a man who teaches in a Bible college in America. Recently, I received an E-mail from a couple that had been involved in drugs in the 1970s. The man had been in an institution for juvenile delinquents because of his use of drugs. He heard the message of the Cross when I spoke in the Washington, D.C., area. God changed his life that night through that message. He's now married, has children, and serves as a deacon in his local church.

THE POWER OF THE CROSS

I could fill this book with stories of people whose lives have been dramatically changed by the message of the Cross. The apostle Paul said, "I am not ashamed of the gospel, because it is the power of God for the salvation of everyone who believes" (Romans 1:16). Why, then, are so many Christians afraid to boldly tell the grand old story of what Christ did for sinners? It's the only message that can change the moral outlook of this generation. It's the only message where God promises to release His power. It's the only message where a guilty and broken generation can find peace and forgiveness. It's the message that can change the moral climate of America. The power is in the proclamation of the message—not the packaging of the message.

American Christians seem preoccupied with how we package our faith rather than how we proclaim it. We've produced a generation of pastors in which many are more knowledgeable of the principles of being a good CEO than they are of being a good soldier of the Cross. The sad part of all of this is that the message of the Cross is the one that can speak directly to the issues of the moral and spiritual crisis we're facing today. Christ's death upon the cross provides forgiveness for those who are guilty. It provides freedom to those who are slaves to the passions and desires that they know to be wrong. The Cross produces reconciliation for those filled with bitterness and hatred. It is the covenant upon which a solid marriage can be built.

But it's not just the proclaiming of the Cross that produces power to change people's hearts. We live by the Cross. When God told Solomon that He would heal the land and forgive the people, He laid out the conditions for the healing of the nation. The first condition that had to be met was that God's people had to humble themselves. It's not a proud and powerful church that will restore the nation, but one that is humble and contrite in spirit. It's not a church of self-motivated and self-willed people that will impact society, but a people who have been to the Cross and tasted of Christ's brokenness. It's a people who can say with Christ, "Not my will, but Thine be done." Those who will be the instruments to transform culture are those who can honestly say, "Without You, O Jesus, I could do nothing."

This great truth is somewhat of a mystery. It doesn't seem to make sense. We are naturally inclined to think that we must achieve in our own power if we are going to make a difference in society. We gather our talents and abilities and attempt to change the world. However, that only leads to pride. And pride ultimately leads to a fall. If I've learned one lesson in the last ten years, it has been this: God can do more in one moment than I could strive with all my resources to accomplish in a lifetime. It's not my great abilities that He wants. It is my availability that He desires from me. *He* has the ability. He wants us to be available to His will. That means I must live by the Cross.

The cross was an instrument to inflict death in the first century. It wasn't thought of as a beautiful piece of jewelry. No steeples and stained glass windows declared the beauty of the cross when Jesus said, "If anyone would come after me, he must deny himself and take up his cross daily and follow me" (Luke 9:23). The disciples knew well what that meant. It meant death: death to self, death to their ambitions and aspirations, death to their feeble attempts to win the world, death to their pursuit of pleasure, and death to their pride and arrogance. But later they also learned that life came from the cross: the resurrected life of Christ, a life of victory, a life of abundance, eternal life, and a life of purpose and meaning. It was an exchange: their lives for His life. They found His life by losing their lives.

The cross spells death to the selfish spirit. Selfishness has engulfed the nation and somewhere it has to be put to death if America is to be restored. But judgment begins in the house of God. We must begin to recognize the selfishness that has been so ingrained within the church. If the church is going to rise to the occasion, then it must bow before the cross. We need to tear down the altars of self if we are going to be light and salt to a dark and hurting world.

All for God

Approximately one hundred years ago there was a man mightily used of God. He housed, clothed, and fed thousands of children who were orphans. He made it his practice to never ask men for money. He trusted in God alone to provide for the needs of the children. Someone once asked George Mueller what was the secret to his service for the Lord. He responded, "There was a day when I died," and as he spoke he bent down until he could almost touch the floor and continued, "Died to George Mueller, his opinions, preferences, tastes, and will; died to the world, its approval or censure; died to the approval or blame even of my brethren or friends; and since then I have studied only to show myself approved unto God."[2]

Where are the Muellers of this generation? Where are the men and women who care nothing of reputation or fame? Where are those who have so died to self that they live only for God and to serve their fellow man? Where are those who are emptied of self and filled with Christ? Where are those who live for the applause of heaven rather than the temporary pleasures of the day? Where are those who have surrendered their wills and desires to God? God can use a mighty army of men and women who have been to the cross daily. He will use those who have died to the opinions of men and live only for the approval of God. Otherwise, we will never see God's glory in the land. Revival costs. It costs everything. The church will never see an awakening by telling everyone how to prosper. We'll experience revival when we understand that following Christ means losing everything.

Self-Dependence

One of the greatest struggles that I constantly face in my life and ministry is the battle with dependence upon my own talents and abilities. When I was sixteen I had the opportunity to study at the United Nations in New York City. I traveled with about thirty other selected students from my home state, Louisiana. While in New York City I entered an international oratorical contest. I not only won in the group from my state, but eventually was awarded "Most Outstanding Youth Speaker in North America."

Two years later I became a Christian and felt that God had a call on my life to the ministry. I surrendered my life to that call. Not long after that, I traveled to the Astrodome in Houston to hear the world-renowned evangelist, Billy Graham. After listening to Graham speak, I wondered why there was such a big deal about him. He was a decent speaker, but nothing extraordinary in my opinion. When he came to the close of his message, he began to invite people to join him at the front of the platform to pray to receive Christ into their lives. I became concerned and began to pray for Billy Graham.

"Oh, God," I said, "please help him not to be too discouraged if no one comes to the platform to pray with him."

Was I ever in for a surprise! It almost felt like an earthquake because so many people were going to the front of the platform to pray with Dr. Graham. I couldn't believe what I was seeing! He was good, but certainly not great, yet multitudes listened and responded to his very simple message about Christ. I am ashamed to admit what I begin to think: *If that's what happens when he speaks, man, what's going to happen when people hear me? The whole world will come to Christ!*

Was I ever in for a double surprise! Not long afterward, I had the opportunity to speak at an evangelistic meeting. I prepared. I practiced. Then I spoke. I had a wonderful introduction and an inspiring conclusion. I laid out the message logically. I inflected my voice at just the right moment. I lowered it for the right effect. Then I came to the close of the message. I asked people to bow their heads and pray with me. I then invited people to the platform just as Dr. Graham had done. Do you know what happened?

You guessed it. Nothing! I couldn't understand what went wrong. Later in my Christian life I learned that it is not man's eloquence and ability that God uses. All of that can just compound the idol of self in a one's life. God is looking for men and women whose strength is in the Lord, whose ambition is to please Him, whose love is to obey the Savior, whose service is to mankind, and whose glory is in the Cross. When He finds that kind of Christianity in America, then I'm convinced that the winds of revival will begin to blow across the land. It's not by our power, but by His Spirit that a mighty flood of revival will sweep across the land.

REVIVAL BY GOD'S POWER

Revival is not a discovery of some new truth. It's the rediscovery of the grand old truth of God's power in and through the Cross. If revival is to come to America, then we must lay the ax to the root of selfishness that has grown up in the nation in the last thirty years. It must begin in the church. It will begin with you and me. It begins by going back to the Cross. Dr. A. T. Pierson summed it up well, as he looked at the necessity of "laying the ax at the root of the tree of self, of which all indulgences are only greater or smaller branches. Self-righteousness and self-trust, self-seeking and self-pleasing, self-will, self-defense, self-glory,—these are a few of the myriad branches of that deeply rooted tree. . . . Until the ax, then, is laid at the root of the tree of self, and our natural life gives place to the life of the Spirit, all our virtues are only taught practices grafted upon a corrupt bottom."[3]

7
TOM ELLIFF
ON CHURCH REVIVAL

Dr. Tom Elliff is the president of the Southern Baptist Convention and pastor of First Baptist Church of Del City, Oklahoma. Dr. Elliff has been calling the Southern Baptist Convention to pray for revival in the nation.

"The answer is the church being revived, and the church experiencing awakening. The church must display the true character of the church. . . . Our present problem is that we have an unrevived church struggling to have a reputation of a revived church. Our reputation is not the issue. The issue is that we need to be revived."

TOM ELLIFF
ON CHURCH REVIVAL

SAMMY TIPPIT: Could you define revival?

TOM ELLIFF: Sammy, revival begins with God, not man. The following is revival in my most simple definition: It's the sovereign moving of a Holy God to bring His people to a fresh sense of His presence and a deeper surrender to the lordship of His Son, Jesus Christ.

ST: Many pastors and churches are struggling just to keep their heads above water. What would you say to them about revival?

ELLIFF: We have an option as Christian leaders. We have an option to become obsessed with ecclesiastical machinery, or we have the opportunity to become overawed with God's majesty. I heard someone say one time, "As long as men had machines to move mountains, they would not turn to God." The truth is that we have many churches and pastors trying to do just that. They're attempting by the cleverness of man and through organizations and drive to do what can only be done by the power of God. When revival comes, I think they set aside their preoccupation with machinery, and they stop trying to move mountains with bulldozers. They begin to realize they have a God that is big enough if He so chooses and desires to move those mountains on the basis of prayer and faith.

ST: It seems like time is a big problem in the American church. Churches are so caught up in doing many things. How big of an issue is time to a church that is working with machinery rather than seeking God? What role does the time factor play in revival?

ELLIFF: Time is a creation of God. He is outside of time. We measure time by things God created, the earth spinning on its axis and revolving around the sun. Because it is a created entity, we can assume that there is a sense in which time is under the curse (resulting from man's fall) just like everything else that was intended for man and the glory of God. But when it comes under the curse, then time becomes a problem. That's why I believe the apostle Paul said that we are to redeem the time. In other words, time left by itself with no other agenda will naturally run to evil. You can see that in the old illustration "an idle mind is the devil's workshop." I believe that those who have hearts for revival must make a deliberate decision to redeem the time. The busyness of man and the preoccupation with machinery are symptomatic of the need for revival. But where there is a need, there is always an answer. The apostle Paul said, "My God will supply all your need according to His riches and glory by Christ Jesus." The busyness of man is symptomatic of a deeper sickness, which is the lost sense of God's consciousness in our nation.

ST: When I was in India a few years ago, a pastor shared with me that attendance in their prayer meetings dropped when the general population started having television in their homes. Do you believe the entertainment of Americans has affected the church in America in the same way it did in India?

ELLIFF: Sure. You know that it has. Entertainment is mindless. So, you bring home a weary worker, and you give him the opportunity to think about nothing. It's an intruder. It's like having a guest in your home that constantly is talking. He's constantly cursing. If I said that I was going to bring this person over to your house, and he was going to let out these following expletives, talk to your kids about beer, drugs, and immoral lifestyles, you would say, "I don't want that." But that is precisely what TV is doing. It's become another member of the family, and sometimes the dominating member of the family.

ST: Television is just one of the modern assaults on the believer's purity. What is the relationship of revival to purity within the life of the believer and the church?

ELLIFF: From my experience and also from biblical principles, I believe purity and holiness are both a prerequisite and a result of revival. The apostle Paul through his own experience said that the closer he got to God, the more aware that he was of sin. The more aware of sin he was, the more conscious he was to confess his sin and turn to God. You see a cycle here of deep conviction of sin because of a lack of purity in the life of the believer. Then there's a calling out to God for revival, which brings him to a deeper level of purity. The truth is that the great enemy of revival in our nation is the lost sense of purity. The author of Hebrews tells us, "Looking diligently lest any man fail of the grace of God; lest any root of bitterness springing up trouble you, and thereby many be defiled" (Hebrews 12:15 KJV). He then gives an illustration of Esau. What has happened is that venues of impurity used to require effort, and they drew attention to persons going to them. Thus, they were avoided by Christians. But they are now moved from the streets and dark allies into the homes and into the motel rooms via TV. We have an amazing drift in our nation.

ST: The number of unmarried couples living together has increased from 1960 to 1994. There has been a 900 percent increase—from over 400,000 to over 3,600,000.

ELLIFF: You know that over 50 percent of the people getting married today have lived together—with each other or others before marriage. Over 50 percent don't believe that [the institution of] marriage will succeed.

ST: How much of that has affected the church?

ELLIFF: An unrevived church is affected by the world. We are called to be salt and light, and an unrevived church is powerless before the world. It's only when we have a keen sense of God, when our lives are filled with God, that we change the world. Until then the world will change us.

ST: What about the relationship of revival and evangelism? You don't want the world's attitude in the church, but you do want to reach the world for Christ. How do we relate revival and evangelism?

ELLIFF: In the first place, we are to be an evangelistic people. You can look at the last words of our Lord, and you can see what is on His heart. We're commanded to evangelize. He modeled that for us when He taught His disciples to evangelize. We are to be an evangelizing church. That is a command that's upon the church whether or not we are living in a state of revival. It's commanded by God to live in a state of evangelism.

Evangelism is my response to the Lord. It's not my response to the lost. It's not my response to whether I believe hell is real, or that I believe heaven is wonderful. That may all be a part of it, my burden for the lost. But I should evangelize whether or not I feel a burden. Jesus said, "As the Father sent Me, so I send you." It's basically my response to the Lord. Now in addition to that, you cannot do evangelism unless you are where the lost are. Jesus came from heaven to earth. We do evangelism when we go where unbelievers are and share the gospel with them.

I realize there are people who have a big difference with me. I have heard people take the passage in Acts 5 "No one else dared join them . . ." (v. 13). They believe that the church is supposed to be [just] for the saved, not the lost. That's twisted. Yes, the church is comprised of the saved. But a worship service is not only for the saved. If that was the case, the apostle Paul would not have given careful instruction to the Corinthian church about speaking in tongues because of what impression it left on the nonbelievers. He didn't want to confuse those people. You can argue a lot of things about evangelism, but you cannot debate the fact that it is a specific command to the church. My thought is this. One of the routes to revival is through evangelism. He said that as you evangelize, I am with you. If I want to be with Jesus, then I must remember that Jesus came to seek that which was lost and save them. I would have to say that one of the venues where I would most likely experience genuine revival is the venue of evangelism. Not only is it a path to revival, but it is also a product of revival.

ST: In the conservative evangelical Christian community there seems to be a tension between those who say we need to go deeper for revival and those who say we need to go outward for revival. How do you bridge that gap—or should it be bridged?

ELLIFF: I think it's a tension that will always be present because there are always people who are leaning to one or the other. You cannot escape the command to evangelize. Whatever God is looking for in this world, He's not looking for cloistered monks behind ivy-covered walls who are merely contemplating the greatness of God. He's looking for people whose lives are absorbed with His greatness and want to share that greatness with other people.

"Deeper Lifers" generally have shelves full of books on the fullness of the Spirit. It would be worth noting that most of those books are written by people who have not hidden themselves away someplace in some cave and written about it. They are written by people who are in the trenches. They are written by people who had to be filled by the Spirit just to do their work. What's happened is that we have gotten their books and gotten out of the trenches. The reason their truths will not impact us like they ought to is because they are "trench truths." When a man is out there on the forefront sharing the gospel with others, he is more keenly aware of his needs to draw on the strength of the Lord than he is in any other place in his life.

ST: Have you ever pastored a church where you experienced a touch of corporate revival?

ELLIFF: Yes, on more than one occasion. I was pastor of a church in Texas when God just swept across that church, and we found ourselves on our faces before God. I remember I was in a prayer meeting one time, and the phone rang. There were thirteen of us in the prayer room, and I got up to answer it. It was a call from a girl [in California who] worked at a home for unwed mothers. She had led a girl to the Lord, who subsequently went back to her home town in Colorado. There, while praying for her father she became burdened for her town. She believed God wanted to bring revival to the town. Not knowing what to do, she called her friend in California, who subsequently called me for help in arranging for the meeting. This girl asked if I would go preach there in a couple of weeks. I said, "Well, I don't think so. I appreciate this, but there are no churches involved with this. It's two weeks away, and I am really busy."

I went back to the prayer meeting and the vice president of the bank said, "I think you should go, and I will go with you." The pharmacist said, "I think you should go, and I will pay your way." Two weeks later, four of us showed up in this little town of Colorado, and the gymnasium was filled with people. There had been no advertisement. I gave an invitation and in fifteen seconds there would be eighty people at the altar. You would walk down the middle of the street at night, and lights would be on. You'd walk into a home and find yourself in the middle of a prayer meeting. There are Bible studies going on today that were started in the fever pitch of that revival meeting in 1970–71.

When I was pastor in Tulsa at Eastwood Baptist some years later, we suspended everything. There was no Sunday school, not any meetings. I said to the people, "Come to the church, and we are going to pray for revival." I remember one night God just came, and broke through in the meeting, and that church was never the same. God just manifested Himself in an amazing way. I remember another time in Applewood Baptist in Colorado. We had just come back from the mission field, and Life Action Ministries was there. God just moved in an amazing fashion. I can remember a number of occasions when God moved here where I have been pastor for eleven years.

ST: Is there anything practical that a pastor, a church leader, or a group of church leaders can do to open the door for God to send revival to the church? Or is it totally God's sovereign move? How does that work?

ELLIFF: It's God's sovereign move, but that does not rule out our responsibility to act in concert with Him. In the first place, the church is longing for a pastor with a transparent life. When the pastor stands up, the people need to know that they are seeing the depth of the pastor's heart. When he finds himself drifting or [finds he has] drifted, he needs to be willing to stand before his congregation in confession and repentance and restoration. I also believe that there needs to be from the pulpit a constant call to prayer. This should be accompanied with fasting and repentance. But the call to prayer should be sent out. There needs to be the call for revival, the call for awakening. I believe that the drum ought to beat on that issue.

On the practical side, pastors ought to knit their hearts together. They ought to pray for revival. Inevitably revival either comes on the wings of someone or ones who are willing to stand before a congregation with brokenness and absolute transparency and say, "This is what has happened in my life, and I need you to forgive me. My heart is completely for God." There is a great lack today of pastors being transparent before their congregations.

ST: Tell me what you are doing among Southern Baptists, in your own denomination, to encourage revival.

ELLIFF: Shortly after assuming this responsibility, I contacted each of our seminary presidents and asked them to host, for lack of a better term, "A Call to the Cross." I believe the Cross must be the message. If you look at the history of awakenings, they have been accompanied by strong preaching on justification and sanctification. Justification is the work of the Cross leading to salvation. Sanctification is the continued work of the Cross in our lives following our conversion. This year's convention theme is "To the Cross." I believe that we need to go right to the Cross.

A person must go forward to the Cross if he's not converted. But a Christian needs to go back to the Cross for sanctification. The Cross must be central. If you look at what the apostle Paul said, it must be central in our message. Jesus said, "If any man would follow Me, let him deny himself and take up his cross and follow Me." I need to die daily.

I issued a convention-wide "Call to the Cross." We sent out thirty thousand letters, and gave them a list of our seminaries and a list of dates to come. We said that there would be some singing, some preaching, and a lot of praying. I took with me Ron and Patricia Owen, Dr. Henry Blackaby, and Dr. Avery Willis, each of whom I believe has a pertinent and relevant message about the Cross. It's an amazing thing, a wonderful thing that every one of these seminaries' presidents said to us, "Come, and on that day we will suspend classes. We will open our doors to you." So, we asked pastors and church leaders to find the seminary campus or the date best for their schedule and to come join us.

These were wonderful moments, and the Lord just blessed it all. To this day I still receive correspondence from people who attended one of those convocations. The issue was the crucified life. Jesus said that "I tell you the truth, unless a kernel of wheat falls to the ground and dies, it remains only a single seed. But if it dies, it produces many seeds" (John 12:24). The issue of death to self is pertinent. That is right at the heart of revival. This was my call, and I continue to issue that call to our denomination.

ST: What is the difference between awakening and revival? Define how you view those things.

ELLIFF: I believe that what we need in our nation could be more adequately termed an awakening. On a few occasions in our history—when our nation was at the brink of moral, political, spiritual, and social disaster; when it looked as if there was no turning back; and it looked as if we would go the way of all other nations; on a very few occasions, God has stepped in and brought an awakening to our nation. When I think of revival, I think of revival in a personal sense. When I think of revival happening in a corporate sense, it's that which happens in churches. I think as these tributaries join together to make rivers, they empty into a larger ocean that leads to a national awakening. My prayer is that both people and churches would be revived. But my great prayer is for a national awakening. I think that is a critical issue. I believe that the issue is the church must really be the church that God intended. That's what happens in the time of awakening.

ST: There are a lot of cultural trends that run counter to awakenings. For instance, there's been a breakdown of the nuclear family since the 1960s. There has been a major rise today in suicide and teen violence among young people. We have tremendous racial divisions. What happens in awakenings? Are these trends reversed?

ELLIFF: I was at a meeting with about 125 national leaders of various Christian groups. We were meeting in Washington, D.C., and the main topic was pornography on the Internet. They were talking about how to combat child pornography on the Internet. I'll tell you what I told them. You can deal with this as long as you want. But my message to you is that child pornography, as tragic, awful, and perverted as it is, is merely symptomatic of a bigger issue. And the bigger issue is the lost sense of God-consciousness in our nation.

I am not narrow enough and hope I am not foolish enough to believe that we do not need to speak out against racial division, the breakdown of the nuclear family, the rise in teen suicide, and the rise in teen violence, etc. [But] as long as we fight those issues, we're merely treating the symptoms. It's like giving an aspirin to a man with TB. Yes, you have calmed his fever and cough, but he is dying of TB. When I take a glass of water, and then I drop into that water a capsule of red food coloring, suddenly that water becomes red. What did that water have to do to become red? Nothing. It just had to be there. The reason that our society has lost its sense of God-consciousness is that [Christians] have conformed to the society. The great issue is that the church must be true to the character of the church. There won't be that powerful church unless there is an awakening.

ST: There are groups in Hollywood that often portray Christians as radical extremists. Can that be changed? Have we lost our moral integrity and our moral authority?

ELLIFF: Jesus said the servant is not greater than the master. So, why should we go around being shocked that a lost world thinks a life of holiness is radical and extreme? The answer is to be overwhelmingly good. The world just can't stand in the face of good. But as long as we put people on TV to argue the issue with someone and say, "We're not extreme," then we've missed the solution. The answer is the church being revived, and the church experiencing awakening. The church must display the true character of the church.

I have had personal experience with being called a radical. The guy who calls me a radical extremist will never call me that again if, during a flood, I am moved by the love of God to rescue him, bring him in, and feed him. When the church starts being the church, then we ought not to worry what they do to us because they did that to our Lord. We are not bigger than our Lord. Secondly, that's not our battle. Our present problem is that we have an unrevived church struggling to have a reputation of a revived church. Our reputation is not the issue. The issue is that we need to be revived.

ST: Why did Southern Baptists pass a nonbinding resolution to boycott the Disney corporation?

ELLIFF: Free speech is both a constitutional right and a wonderful privilege enjoyed by our citizens. But with every privilege comes responsibility—in this case, the responsibility to use the privilege of free speech in a manner that lifts and strengthens the moral standards of our nation. The Disney corporation has flagrantly and persistently abrogated their responsibility in this instance. While flying the "family friendly" flag they have brought subsidiaries under their umbrella which produce material of graphic sexual and violent content. Additionally, through their productions, hiring and insurance policies, and openness to providing their facilities as locations for gay and lesbian celebrations, they are openly pushing an agenda which is absolutely contrary to the biblical definition and standards of marriage and family. While Disney and similar corporations may be free to follow these practices, Southern Baptists are equally free to send them a message by exercising the stewardship of our patronage. More important than "bringing Disney down" in this instance is "bringing Southern Baptists up" to the biblical standards of morality. My neighbor is free to place in his yard whatever he desires. But if what he places there causes my property value to be diminished, I am free to speak out in protest. Southern Baptists are saying to Disney [and others], "We believe that the immoral garbage you are placing in the front yard of America is diminishing and demeaning to the worth of this great nation."

ST: Do you really think the American church can experience a revival or a national awakening? Why?

ELLIFF: Yes. The issue of an awakening depends on a holy and sovereign God. There is nothing too difficult for Him. Those who say we cannot experience revival are those whose focus is upon "who we are" instead of "who God is." And since revival is a God-initiated enterprise, then, of course, it is possible.

ST: Do you believe the prayer movements that have emerged in the last five years are a precursor to revival in the church today?

ELLIFF: I certainly believe they are symptomatic of the deep sense of need we are experiencing within our churches. People have become disappointed with the world. We tried it the world's way, and the world's way doesn't work. People are realizing that the world's way is not going to cut it. I think the calls to prayer from all these different corners are indicative of our perceived need for God. There are 131 different calls to prayer in the nation that we've been able to identify. I believe that God's people are beginning to cry out to God. Regardless of the motive, I believe that we are calling out to God. That crying out is an acknowledgment that we can't do it on our own anymore.

ST: Is there any final message that you have to Christians in America?

ELLIFF: The burning message on my heart is that we must come to the Cross. The apostle Paul said, "God forbid that I should glory, save in the cross." Jesus said that "we must take up our cross." Paul said, "I die daily." I would call believers to the Cross. The Cross must be central. We must understand that what Jesus did on the cross was not just saving sinners to go to heaven. But, also, the power of the Cross was availed to conquer every sin I am facing in my life today. I must not go on living in solemn and silent resolution that I have to be held captive by bullish sins which diminish my effectiveness in serving God. I can bring those sins to the Cross and get victory. When I come to the Cross, I abandon my agenda and take God's agenda for this world. So, I would say, "Come to the Cross." That is the message that I have burning in my heart.

8
PRINCIPLES OF FAMILY RENEWAL

For this reason a man will leave his father and mother and be united to his wife, and the two will become one flesh. This is a profound mystery—but I am talking about Christ and the church. However, each one of you also must love his wife as he loves himself, and the wife must respect her husband. (Ephesians 5:31–33)

A sensitive, insightful spirit, a responsive, positive attitude, a teachable, willing heart are bottom-line essentials for a marriage.[1]

CHARLES R. SWINDOLL

PRINCIPLES OF FAMILY RENEWAL

---★---

When I was a freshman at Louisiana State University in Baton Rouge, Louisiana, I heard the message of God's love. I heard more than just a man telling me what Christ could do in my life. I sensed that something deeply spiritual was taking place. That evening I prayed and placed my faith in Jesus. He came to live in my life by His Spirit. Since that day I've never been the same. The desire of my life has been to please God and to make His love known to a lost and hurting world.

Three years later, I met and married a young lady who was also new in her walk with God, a beautiful young lady called "Tex." Debara Sirman was called "Tex" because she had moved from Texas to Louisiana with her family during her senior year of high school. She ran for freshman class secretary at Southeastern Louisiana University and advertised, "Vote for Debe 'Tex' Sirman." I met her during that time and called her "Tex." The name has stuck with her for thirty years now.

Tex had a heart for God. She carried her Bible to class with her, and every free moment she was reading the Scriptures. At church she wept for her friends who needed Christ. A tender and pure love for God and for people was obvious in her life. At the same time the fire of the love of God was burning deep within my soul. I had been trained and skilled in oratory and was ready to tell the world what Christ had done for me. One day Tex and I were talking about our dreams and aspirations. We both sensed that God's will was that we join our lives together in marriage. We loved each other deeply. We decided to separate for a period of time to see if this really was God's will. But the more we were apart, the more we knew that it was God's will for us to be together.

LIFE LESSONS

I asked her to marry me, and on June 8, 1968, we joined our

lives together in the holy act of marriage. We committed ourselves before God and before man to love each other in the good
times as well as the bad times; in health as well as in sickness; and
in poverty as well as wealth. As I think back on those days, I realize we were so naive. We really loved each other, but we didn't
have any idea what we were getting into. God had placed a call
on our lives that would take me into places from the highest
crime area of Chicago to countries held in the clutch of communism. During the next thirty years, I would walk into a revolution
and also witness the aftermath of an attempted genocide in a nation.

We had one thing going for us. We both had made a commitment to God and to each other, and we really meant it. That commitment has held us together when extraordinary difficulties
would seem to tear us apart. Out of the commitment that we
made to God, we found grace in our times of failure. Out of our
commitment that we made to each other, we found strength to
persevere during the storms that would blow across our lives.

The first three years of our marriage couldn't have been
thought up by a novelist. We loved God and gave our lives to
spreading His love to our generation. He had given us grace and
abilities, and we wanted to use them for His glory. We were a
team. Not long after we were married, I was preaching in a small
church in Monroe, Louisiana, and revival broke out. The church
couldn't contain the people attending, and we moved to the university campus. Then the facility on the university couldn't hold
the people attending. That necessitated that we move to the civic
center for the final evening. We concluded the meetings with several thousand people in attendance.

An atmosphere of spiritual revival permeated the youth of the
city. The local news covered what was happening. The entire city
buzzed about what was taking place. Tex and I felt that God
might be calling us to "march" across America and call America
back to God. Five other young people felt that they should join
us. Thus, for the next four months, Tex and I marched with five
other young people from Monroe, Louisiana, to Washington, D.C.
We distributed Bibles all along the way. God opened incredible
doors for us to call America back to God.

I had the opportunity to present a Bible to Alabama Governor
George Wallace and challenge him to follow Christ. I preached in

the midst of demonstrations at the University of Georgia when students took over the administration building. Student government leaders came to our group and asked us to pray for peace on the campus. Shortly afterward, peace and order were restored to the campus. In Atlanta, we were on a talk show with then national television host Art Linkletter. During a volatile moment of history, Tex and I walked across this great nation of ours calling our colleagues and peers to Christ. After four months, we arrived in Washington and held a prayer and fasting vigil with Arthur Blessitt.

Settling In

At the conclusion of the time in Washington, we began to pray about where God would have us to settle into ministry. Tex told the Lord that she was willing to go anywhere, but she made a "special request" that it not be New Orleans! We had ministered previously in the famed French Quarters. It was the pits! But we felt that God would have us minister in a major U.S. city. We finally decided on Chicago. We had never even seen Chicago. But we sensed that God was leading there. We had no idea that New Orleans was a piece of cake compared to Chicago.

We moved into a district called "Uptown." It was a very high crime area in the early 1970s and was filled with competing street gangs. While in Chicago, we faced some of our most difficult circumstances in our lives. I had guns put to my head, was threatened with knives, was challenged by Satanists, and was ultimately arrested for presenting the gospel in Chicago's famed nightclub district. The city of Chicago later admitted to false arrest and dropped the charges. But the arrest was a milestone in my life and in our marriage. The day that I went to court, Tex went to the hospital to have our first child, Dave.

Up until that time, we did everything together. We battled together with the forces of darkness. Together, we shared the love of Jesus with lonely and hurting people. We stayed out late at night together ministering to hippies, yippies, and anyone else searching for meaning in life. The *Chicago Tribune,* the *Chicago Daily News,* and one Northside Chicago newspaper carried major feature stories on our lives and ministry. We were extremely close. We were living out our dreams and we loved it. And we loved each other!

Drifting Apart

But after Dave was born, something changed in our relationship. We began to drift. Part of it was due to the physical circumstances. But most of it was simply because of my selfishness. When Dave was born, Tex could no longer be out on the streets with me ministering to people. She was changing diapers, feeding our newborn child, and, in general, being a good mother. The worst part of our drifting was that I didn't even know that we were drifting apart. I became insensitive to her needs.

In the next chapter, James Dobson says that life doesn't naturally bring us together, but rather there's a tendency for a couple to drift apart. He said that we have to invest time and energy in our relationship to make sure that we don't drift apart. Sadly, I didn't do that. I loved God and I loved Tex. But somewhere along the way, I substituted loving the ministry for loving God. I began to allow my life to be consumed with loving a lost and dying world and forgot to love my closest neighbor.

The first time that Tex began to voice her needs and hurts was in 1973. Dave was almost two years old. We had gone to Berlin. A communist youth world festival in communist-dominated East Berlin had 100,000 hard-core communist youth gathered to be trained to evangelize the world for atheism and communism. Two friends of mine, Fred Starkweather and Fred Bishop, and I attempted to infiltrate the meeting and give the gospel. It was a very dangerous venture, and we had no idea what to expect.

We stayed in a mission house in West Berlin, the free side of the city. Every day the three of us got a twenty-four-hour visa and traveled to East Berlin to present the gospel to the communist youth. Tex and Dave remained at the mission house. Tex prayed for us, but the immense tension from the danger took its toll on her. We left every morning not knowing if we would be arrested for spreading the gospel in this communist meeting. We returned elated because many gave their lives to Christ. God intervened and protected us in an incredible way every day. For the three of us it was like living on a constant mountaintop. But for Tex it was like living on a roller coaster. She lived with a sense of fear all day, and then we would come storming into the house full of joy late every night. The pattern was repeated for the entire week. Loneliness and confusion began to settle into her heart—loneliness because we were gone most of the time and confusion because she wanted to be excited about what God was doing but was unable to feel the same enthusiasm that we experienced.

The greatest problem was that I was totally oblivious to Tex's needs even though she verbally told me she was hurting. I could only see the historic opportunity that God had afforded us to preach the gospel to thousands of atheist youth. Had I been caught up in God rather than the *"ministry of God,"* I'm sure that I would have been able to reach those young people and meet Tex's needs as well. But I lost sight of God and fixed my focus on the opportunity. Consequently, we continued to drift apart.

God blessed us with our second child, Renee. But Tex and I kept on drifting for five to six years. We both loved God deeply. We wanted His will for our lives. We had given ourselves completely to His service, but the more we drifted, the deeper we seemed to hurt each other. I became very controlling. When we disagreed, I knew how to win the argument. I had been trained and skilled in debate. I always won. Therefore, Tex began to clam up. She knew that she couldn't win the argument even if she was right. So, why should she even share her hurts and differences with me? I immersed myself more and more into the ministry and she continued to withdraw.

It began to affect everything in our lives. We were not experiencing the joy of sexual intimacy that we once knew. That became very frustrating to me. But we no longer were able to communicate on a heart level. All of our communication became superficial. Something was wrong, but we didn't know what. And we didn't know what to do about it.

Turning Around

Finally, one day I was having a time of prayer. I sensed that something was deeply wrong in my life. I felt that my ministry had outgrown my character. I felt that if I was going to be used of God to my fullest potential, then I had to escape the cycle that I had gotten into. I thought that I needed to go somewhere where no one knew me. I needed to get back in touch with God. I prayed that God would show me what to do. Not long after praying that prayer, I received a call to become the pastor of the Hahn Baptist Church in Hahn, Germany.

Hahn is a rural community that at that time was made up of a large American military community. When I received the call from the church, I knew immediately that it was God's plan for our lives. Tex was a faithful and loving wife, willing to follow me anywhere, even though we had lost our intimacy with each other. We packed all our belongings, gathered the kids, and moved to a small mountainous area of Germany. We didn't know it when we left the United States, but we would experience a personal revival that would change our lives, family, and ministry.

I began preaching through the book of Genesis verse by verse. It was an exciting time of seeing church growth and making some of the closest friendships that we would ever know. One Sunday morning I was scheduled to preach on Genesis 22 where Abraham was to offer his son, Isaac, on the altar to God. I had studied. I was prepared to minister to the people the context, meaning, and application of the Scripture. However, on the Friday evening before that Sunday, something happened to change our future.

Everyone was asleep that Friday evening when I heard a noise in our son's bedroom. I got up and went into his room and found him in convulsions. I called for Tex and she ran into the room. We prayed for him, but he continued convulsing. We rushed him to the hospital. The doctor on duty was one of the men in our church. We prayed with the doctor for Dave. Tex and I wept and prayed the entire night. I knew that God was trying to say something to me, but I didn't know what.

The next eighteen months were extremely difficult. The doctors placed Dave on medication, but he reacted to the medications. We prayed and asked God to heal Dave, but he was not healed. We didn't know what to do. We were desperate and hurting. One evening Tex said to me, "We need to talk." She began to weep as she said, "I was having a time alone in prayer with God today. I was reading in the Bible about the holiness of God. He showed me that I've harbored bitterness in my heart because of some of the things that happened in our marriage. I need to ask your forgiveness."

I was devastated. If we had not been going through Dave's illness, I probably would not have been open to what she had to say. But God had gotten my attention. I can only describe what transpired next in spiritual terms. Somehow, I saw my "self." I saw my insensitivity, my pride, and my selfishness. I realized that I had not loved Tex the way that I committed myself to love her. I had failed her and failed God. I was so devastated that I went to the deacons and leaders of the congregation and asked for some time off.

Tex and I left the kids with some friends and found a place where we could get alone and spend time sharing our hearts with each other. We opened up and told our hurts honestly. I wept and wept. I saw that I had not only hurt Tex, but that I had deeply grieved God. I had misplaced priorities. I had made an idol out of my ministry. I had only been concerned about what was happening in my life and had ignored Tex's needs. I was a broken man.

But in the midst of that brokenness, God worked deeply in both of our hearts. We experienced a renewal of our love for each other. We began to communicate on a deeper level than we had ever known in our marriage. I began to rearrange my priorities. I've been amazed at how much ministry I can do and yet have ample time to communicate intimately with Tex when the priorities are straight. As a matter of fact, we've seen God do greater things in our ministry since we rearranged our priorities than before that evening. God's grace was applied to our lives and our marriage. I quit trying to be right and started listening. Tex started opening up once again. We began to dream together once more. And God healed our son. We eventually had to return to the United States because of his sickness. But the doctors in the States were able to successfully treat his condition until he was completely healed.

That doesn't mean that we've not had any problems since that experience in Germany. It simply means that the paradigm in our marriage changed. We now have a solid foundation upon which we can build our relationship. The root problem of most marriages is selfishness. The self life has to be brought to the Cross and dealt with thoroughly if two people are going to continue to grow in their relationship. God showed me my self in Hahn, Germany, in 1980 and applied the Cross to the self life.

I'm convinced that my marriage was saved. If you had asked me before that experience if I had a good marriage, I would have said, "Of course I do." I would have then compared our marriage to others. But the tragedy is that it's not very difficult to make your marriage look good today when you compare it to others. I have friends who were just like Tex and me. They loved God and they loved each other when they first were married. Yet, somewhere along the way, they lost that intimacy with each other. They developed wrong priorities in life. Some of them lost their marriages.

FOUR PRINCIPLES OF RENEWAL

I have gleaned four principles from my experience in Germany and also from a study of the Scriptures on marriage and the family. I'm convinced if we are to see renewal in our marriages, then we must apply these simple but profound truths.

Commitment

First is the principle of *commitment.* Paul said in Ephesians, "For this reason a man will leave his father and mother and be united to his wife, and the two will become one flesh. This is a profound mystery—but I am talking about Christ and the church" (Ephesians 5:31-32). He compared the relationship of the husband and wife to that of Christ and the church. Christ loved the church all the way to the end. He didn't give Himself for the church only until He had to face the cross and then decide to quit. No! He loved the church all the way to the point of death. He refused to give up when it got tough. He loved the church so much that He was willing to go through hell. He loved the church all the way to death, even death on a cross.

One of the things that Tex and I had going for us in our marriage was that we believed that divorce was never an option. We would have never experienced the deep work of renewal in our marriage if there had been an escape hatch. We knew that we had made a commitment to each other and that it was the same kind of commitment that Christ made to the church. He loved the church all the way to the end. If there is to be a renewal of our marriages, then our commitment to one another must be sacred. The words "until death do us part" must once again have real meaning.

The relationship of Christ to the church is a covenant relationship. A covenant relationship to the ancient people was until death. Two people entered a covenant by giving themselves and all that they had to each other. Often they exchanged weapons, signifying that all of their power belonged to the other. They exchanged clothing, signifying that all of their possessions belonged to the other. And sometimes blood was shed, signifying that they were giving their lives to each other.

The New Testament is the story of the "new covenant." Christ gave all for us, and He calls us to give all for Him. This covenant is not a superficial commitment. It's one that led Jesus to the cross. This is the kind of deep, meaningful relationship that God desires for a husband and wife to have. It's the deepest and most intimate of all human relationships. It's the foundation upon which all other relationships within society are built. Many Americans and even American Christians have lost that kind of deep commitment to God and to our families. If there is to be revival in the land, then we need to return to the keeping of our covenants.

Communication

The second principle is *communication.* The renewal began in our marriage when we began to communicate with each other. I'm convinced that 75 percent of the problems in marriage could be solved if couples just learned to communicate with each other. Any healthy relationship will be built on honest and transparent communication. Therefore, a healthy marriage will always have open lines of communication.

I've had to learn some things in order to establish effective communication with Tex. First, I've had to learn the *art of listening.* I was always quick to give my ideas, but slow to listen to Tex's thoughts. Renewal couldn't come to our marriage until I learned to listen. I needed to listen not only to what she was verbalizing, but also to the deep cry and needs of her heart. Before God did a deep work in my life at Hahn, I was always forming my response to Tex's disagreement with me while she was still attempting to tell me how she felt. Consequently, I wasn't really listening to her. God had to allow me to go through deep pain and suffering before I really began to listen. It's been amazing how deeply we've learned to love each other since I began listening.

Also, *communication takes time.* I often hear people say that they have quality time with their family even if they don't have quantity time. We need quality time, but we also need consistent quantity time of communicating the deep things on our hearts if we are going to continue to grow in our love for one another. Tex and I try to take some time every day to communicate with each other what's going on in our lives. We try to get away from the telephone or anything that could distract us. Often we go for a three-mile walk together, and we spend most of that time sharing our hearts with each other. Other times, we go out for a cup of coffee and just talk.

When things are really tense, we'll go out to a nice restaurant for a meal. We'll discuss our differences over a meal. A public place keeps us in check so that we don't raise our voices. That allows us to communicate in a reasonable manner with each other. But we need regular uninterrupted daily times of opening our hearts to each other.

We also attempt to take a day or two away from home once every three to six months. During those times we try to dream together. We tell each other the things that are really important to us. We spend time talking about and praying for our children. We set goals for our lives. We discuss the ministry. We talk about our friendships. We come away from those times together renewed and refreshed in our relationship.

Correct Priorities

The third principle that has enabled us to renew our relationship is *correct priorities.* For a long time I rationalized that my ministry should take priority over my relationship with Tex. I did that because I equated ministry with God. I didn't understand that service to God is different from God Himself. It's easy for people in Christian ministry to become workaholics. It's the ultimate sacrifice. We develop an attitude of belief that "I'm doing this for God. Therefore, it's OK to neglect my family."

I've discovered that such reasoning is normally a cover-up for the truth. The real truth is that we often want to climb the ladder of religious or professional success. Therefore, we sacrifice our families, not for God, but rather for our own egos. When Tex and I experienced renewal in Germany, God showed me that I had misplaced priorities in my life. Those wrong priorities could be traced back to an attempt to inflate my ego. It really had nothing at all to do with God.

When I came to grips with the truth about my own motivations, I knew that I had to rearrange my priorities. I developed a deep conviction that my priorities had to be: *God, first; my family, second; and my work, third.* By God, I mean my personal walk with God. I needed to maintain my personal devotional time and fellowship with Him before I did anything else. Without Jesus be-

ing first, I could never love my wife and children the way I needed to love them. Out of intimacy with Him, I am enabled to love
Tex and our children the way I ought to love them. I become sensitive to their needs and learn to meet those needs. Out of that
kind of relationship with my family, I am then freed to work at
maximum capacity. I've discovered that I can accomplish more in
my work in less time because I am enabled by God to work at my
highest efficiency level. When I have correct priorities I'm enabled supernaturally to be all that He created me to be.

Living Near the Cross

Finally, the greatest principle that has brought renewal to our
marriage is *living near the Cross*. When we build our lives around
the Cross, two things occur. First, the "self life" is constantly crucified. Self is the greatest hindrance to any relationship. When we
only think of what we want rather than the needs of the other,
then there are going to be immense problems within the relationship. We must die to self. The apostle Paul said, "I have been crucified with Christ and I no longer live, but Christ lives in me. The
life I live in the body, I live by faith in the Son of God, who loved
me and gave himself for me" (Galatians 2:20). When Christ is living in and through each person in the relationship, then there's
going to be a growing intimacy between them.

Second, when we live near the Cross, we experience the
depth of the grace of God. What Christ did on the cross can be
described simply as *grace, amazing grace*. When we build our
lives upon what He did on the cross, we drink regularly from the
well of grace. I know one thing for sure about any marriage—
there will always be a need to drink from the well of grace. No
matter how much we love and care for each other, we will fail
each other—not just once, but many times. But God's grace is
able to cover a multitude of wrongs. When we live by the Cross,
then we are able to reach out in love and forgiveness. There are
no bitter waters in the well of grace. Only love, forgiveness, reconciliation, and intimacy are found there. The Cross is the greatest expression of grace ever known to mankind. We must build
our marriages around the Cross if we are to grow in our love and
intimacy for one another.

I know that what God did in my marriage, He can do in any
marriage where these principles are applied. I know that there

are many complex issues and situations in marriages throughout this nation. But I also know the power and grace of God is able to meet every need of our lives. If we will build our lives and relationships upon His truths, we can know and experience revival in our families. It doesn't depend on our abilities, but on His power that works within us.

You may need to take a retreat with your spouse and begin to listen to the needs of his or her heart. Or you may need to get alone with God and ask Him to search your heart. Ask Him to allow you to see your self in the light of the Cross. That's where renewal begins.

9
JAMES DOBSON ON
PERSONAL AND FAMILY RENEWAL

Dr. James Dobson is the founder and president of Focus on the Family. Millions of people throughout the world listen to Dr. Dobson's radio broadcast. He has become one of the most influential figures in helping families in this generation.

"We have to find our values, orientation, principles, and belief system in what was written [in Scripture]. Without that foundational grounding we're unable to withstand the influence of television, the movies, the media, our politicians, and even our neighbors. It's very difficult to go upstream against the river, but we must do it, and we must help our children do it."

JAMES DOBSON ON
PERSONAL AND FAMILY RENEWAL

SAMMY TIPPIT: How has your view of Focus on the Family changed in the past twenty years?

JAMES DOBSON: When I organized and began Focus on the Family on March 26, 1977, I started with an assumption that's no longer valid today. I began with an understanding that most of the people who listened to me on the radio and read my books had a basic knowledge of the fundamentals of the Christian faith. They knew who Jesus Christ was and why He came to the earth. They grasped why He died on the cross and why His blood was the only remedy for the disease of sin. We took for granted that most people comprehended these and other basic biblical truths. I assumed that I did not have to repeat those principles in my own teachings.

As the years have passed, I've realized that we can no longer operate on that assumption. I can no longer assume that the people who are listening to our program because of their interest in family-related issues have any comprehension of our Christian faith. The culture has changed that much. Therefore, in recent years I've begun including much more of the basics of the Christian faith in our work and broadcasts. Our emphasis has had to change. Our mission statement here at Focus on the Family is to cooperate with the Holy Spirit in spreading the gospel of Jesus Christ to every person on the face of the earth and to do that through [our ministry that provides] support for the family and the institution of the family.

ST: You mentioned the changes that have taken place. Some social scientists are saying that the boomer generation has institutionalized selfishness. Do you believe this to be true, and, if so, how has the family been affected?

DOBSON: Although that's a generalization, I do believe that it's basically true. It was certainly valid in the 1970s and, to some degree, in the 1980s. Some people today are recognizing that this kind of selfishness is empty and meaningless. But it's still very deeply ingrained in the culture. It's had a devastating effect on the family. When mothers say that their children are going to have to fend for themselves, that it's their turn as women to seek fulfillment on their own; when men bury themselves in work to the degree that they ignore the spiritual and emotional needs of their children; then it's devastating to the next generation. Selfishness is always destructive in human relationships, and it has had a profound effect on the family in our time.

ST: After the fall of communism in Romania, I was in Romania and a Christian leader said to me, "We've gotten communism out of the nation, but I find it difficult to get communism out of me." It's easy to internalize these cultural attitudes that develop within society. How do we in the '90s get the '60s attitudes out of us?

DOBSON: Culture can be likened to a raging river. We're all in its rushing currents, and we hardly even realize that we're being carried downstream. The natural progression is [to go] with the flow and not against it. Those who try to oppose that "strong rush of the cultural current" find that they struggle every inch of the way because its influence is so pervasive. The culture today has forgotten most of what the Judeo-Christian culture stands for. The only way I know to counteract that destructive influence is to go back to the fundamentals, to the Scriptures. We have to find our values, orientation, principles, and belief system in what was written there [some] two thousand years ago. Without that foundational grounding we're unable to withstand the influence of television, the movies, the media, our politicians, and even our neighbors. It's very difficult to go upstream against the river, but we must do it, and we must help our children do it.

ST: What do you see as the greatest need in marriage today? I know there are a lot of needs, but what would you put your finger on as the greatest single need?

DOBSON: Sammy, there are so many needs that it's very difficult to answer that question. That's almost like asking, "What do you see as the greatest health need of people who are fifty years of age?" They need exercise and a good diet. They need a healthy environment in which to live. They need clean air, clean water, and plenty of vitamins. The kinds of answers that I would give parallel one's health.

We need Christ-centered homes that are based on transcendent truths. Moral relativism is a lie. Selfishness is terribly destructive, and [many of] the other principles that our culture teaches us are wrong. We need care and concern for one another. Another important need is relief from fatigue and time pressure, which squeeze out everything that is meaningful in a relationship. When you can't take walks together, talk together, relax together, or even have enough time and energy to interact sexually together, then the relationship begins to deteriorate. Let me give you an example. Someone described to me a wonderful illustration of two rowboats on a choppy lake. The natural tendency of the rowboats in that situation is to drift apart. The lake will not keep them together. If you don't row vigorously and invest energy to remain in the same area of the lake, then one person will wind up at the north end and the other at the south.

I wish life naturally brought us together. It typically does not do that. It usually takes us apart. Therefore, if marriage is important to us, and the family has significance in our lives, then we've got to row like crazy to remain together and overcome the natural forces that will take [us] in opposite directions.

ST: Let me ask you some specifics about this. The first one is that we're living in a time of great mobility within the American population. It's probably greater than any other time in American history. How does the family survive in the context of such a fluid society?

DOBSON: That kind of mobility is very difficult for individuals to handle, and, therefore, it's difficult for families. We are very dependent on permanent, warm, long-term relationships with each other. Moving often disrupts those associations. It's interesting to me as a psychologist to look at how God made human beings. He could have constructed us in any way He wanted. He could have made us independent, strong, confident, assertive, and not needful of one another. He could have compared us to grizzly bears, leopards, or pythons who have few social needs. Instead, He chose the word "sheep" to describe how He sees us. He made us inadequate, vulnerable to each other, and absolutely dependent on the Shepherd. He created us as a people who desperately stand in need of emotional bonding.

Therefore, anything that isolates us from one another produces great stress in our lives. Women, especially, need relationships with other women. They need lifelong friends. When a husband and wife move to a new community, it's usually the wife who suffers the most. She struggles until she can rebuild her network. But men also need other men. We are made that way. God made us vulnerable not only to each other, but also to Him. If He'd have made us so independent, I don't think we would have sensed our great need for a relationship with Him. So, those things kind of go together.

Where you have a highly mobile society and you have people running to and fro, then the extended family is scattered. You might have two sisters, one who lives in North Dakota and the other in Oregon. They're unable to depend on each other in the same way they would have if they lived next door or around the block. When people live in a community for two or three years and don't know the people who live across the street, then greater stress is placed on the husband/wife relationship. That relationship has to meet all the social needs, some of which ought to be met in the context of a community. I believe that factor contributes to many divorces. People have a deep soul hunger and expect their mates to satisfy it. With all the pressures of living, men are often unable to meet all of the needs of their spouses. That frustration eventually leads to disillusionment and conflict.

ST: So, you think they need to develop some good strong relationships and friendships as soon as possible after they've moved into a new community?

DOBSON: Men and women who think their spouses can meet all of their emotional needs are asking for trouble. There needs to be a network around us to supplement what occurs at home. Paul instructed us not to forsake the assembling [of ourselves] together. We need one another as Christian brothers and sisters. We need accountability to people outside the marriage. We need the church fellowship, and frequently in this culture people have a hard time finding that kind of fellowship.

ST: I know that you have a very busy schedule, and you mentioned "time" just a moment ago and the important factor that it plays in the relationship. How do you and Shirley

maintain open, honest, and transparent communication?

Dobson: I wish that I could say that the stresses of living are everybody else's problems—that Shirley and I have completely resolved them, and therefore we don't struggle with the same cultural river that I was talking about previously. But we do. There are tremendous pressures on us as the leaders of Focus on the Family. Our ministry has grown very large, and Shirley has her own work with the National Day of Prayer. We have found a way to preserve what is too precious to lose. And your readers can do it, too. They can find time for one another. They can set aside days of recreation, and they can give priority to one another. It's not easy for anybody, but it can be done and it must be done.

For example, we have enjoyed skiing through the years, and we love to just talk and be together. There's no one on the face of the earth that I would rather go to dinner with than Shirley. We very frequently will go away from Focus on the Family for one to two months. We'll take writing trips to London, Edinburgh, or some place where we will not be recognized. We try to regenerate our batteries and get in touch with one another in the Lord again. You can do it too, but I don't want to imply it's easy, because it is not.

ST: Let me turn a corner and ask a question in another direction. I know that you were on President Reagan's pornography commission. There's been a dramatic increase in the spread of pornography in the last twenty to twenty-five years. How has that affected the family? What can we do about it?

DOBSON: Pornography is another snake-in-the-grass, Sammy, that is frequently not recognized. It's not often preached against because it's all through the church. But obscenity has had a devastating effect on the family. If people could read the mail that comes to Focus on the Family, they would be heartbroken. It comes primarily from wives whose husbands are addicted to this kind of material and expect them to imitate what they've seen in these depictions. When marriages break up, people don't admit that pornography had a key role to play, but frequently it's at the core of their problems. It is so pervasive now. All businesspeople who stay in major hotels have it right there in front of their noses. It's there when they turn on the television set. It can hardly be avoided.

The material that we had to witness in 1985 and 1986, when the commission was in operation, was extremely disturbing. But now everything from child pornography to all the perversions (including homosexual violence and bestiality) is available to any twelve year old with an inexpensive computer and a modem. They can pull that information down and [print] pornographic pictures on high-density printers. They can have in their hands things that are one hundred times worse than the pictures in *Playboy* magazine, as bad as that is.

It's everywhere today. My greatest concern is that the largest group of users and purchasers of hard-core, violent, and perverse materials are teenagers, mostly boys. They get addicted to it as young people and remain hooked after they're married. And for the most part, the church seems unaware of that danger.

ST: What is the relationship between moral renewal in society, renewal in the church, renewal in the family, and personal renewal? How do you see that they relate to one another?

DOBSON: There is a direct connection between what people believe and how they behave. The first leads inevitably to the second. Therefore, when millions of citizens lack a framework for moral judgment, their selfish rebellious nature is unchecked. Instead of conforming to an eternal standard of behavior, "each man does what is right in his own eyes." That usually leads to violence, lawlessness, immorality, and social upheaval, which are the natural by-products of a dead or discredited faith.

The second president of the United States, John Adams, recognized this link between belief and behavior almost two hundred years ago, when he said, "Our constitution was made only for a moral and religious people. It is wholly inadequate to the government of any other." Adams's statement is highly relevant to our day. Unless the majority of the people want what is moral and healthy for themselves and for their country, it won't be possible to build enough prisons, hire and train enough police officers, or pass enough laws to protect society from licentiousness. In a democracy, the citizens will have their way. That's why the dramatic change in theology we are now seeing, this "falling away from the truth," may carry within it the seeds of our own destruction.

ST: Let's talk about that falling away. The church has had its share of scandals, and they have been centered in the breakdown of the family. Why do you think that's happened within the church? What encouragement could you give to Christian leaders regarding their families?

DOBSON: My greatest concern is not with the occasional scandal that shows up here and there in the press. Those are terrible events that devastate individual congregations and pastors. It's a tragedy. The greater scandal is the apathy of the church. There's a lack of concern about the moral issues in society at large. There's unconcern for fellow Christians, brothers and sisters around the world who are being persecuted today. There have been more Christians martyred in the twentieth century than in the other nineteen centuries combined. Yet you hear very little about it. You don't hear these atrocities addressed from the pulpit. Likewise, we hear little about the scourge of gambling, which is at an epidemic proportion. It's unusual in many pulpits to even hear a pastor talking about premarital sex and how dangerous and sinful it is. In some churches, parishioners rarely hear that "the wages of sin is death." Young people don't often know that what happens in the backseat of a car matters to God and can ruin their lives.

I don't want to tar the church with a broad brush here, because there are many, many churches out there that are standing for truth in a day of moral relativism. But many churches seem to have forgotten what Christianity is all about. It's not about tapping into the power of God for more successful living. It's not discovering how to make life more meaningful. It's not about seeing if God can help us be successful in business or even have a better family. All those things are by-products of a relationship with Jesus Christ. Christianity is about repentance and forgiveness from sin. It's turning from our wicked ways and calling upon His name. It's living for Him, changing the way we think and believe. It's trying to implement the principles of Scripture in the culture and attempting to influence as many other people [as possible] to accept this relationship with Jesus Christ. There seems to me to be tremendous apathy in the church at that point.

ST: What role do you think renewing the American family plays in this overall renewal in society or even renewal

within the church? In other words, God has given you this target of the family, in speaking to the issue of the family. There's much talk about revival and renewal. Where does the family fit into a spiritual revival?

DOBSON: Honestly, Sammy, I don't believe spiritual renewal is brought about by family renewal. I believe we must have spiritual renewal first, and that in turn improves family life. Family health will come from a deeper commitment to Jesus Christ. That is why our mission statement here at Focus is to cooperate with the Holy Spirit in spreading the gospel of Jesus Christ to as many people as possible, and to accomplish that by helping to make families stronger and more stable. It doesn't say our purpose is to hold families together and then spread the gospel of Jesus Christ. It's the other way around. Our purpose is to bring people back to the Cross and to the blood of Jesus Christ. If we help get people right with God, everything else falls in place, including improved relationships within the family.

ST: Let me ask you one more cultural question. It seems as though we've developed a culture in which divorce is almost fashionable. What will it take to change this attitude within the nation?

DOBSON: That links directly to what I just said. When there is a genuine sorrow for sin; and when we have come to the point that we are sick of ourselves and of our efforts to solve our own problems; when we recognize that there is no other answer but prayer and throwing ourselves on the mercy of the Cross; then other things, including the family and marriage, will be improved. That's why I really believe the only answer for the problems that plague Western civilization is repentance, forgiveness, and commitment. There are no other solutions. If there were other answers, we would have found them. Our government has spent four trillion dollars since the 1960s attempting to eradicate social ills, poverty, sexually transmitted diseases, and other problems we face. But they're all worse than they were then. We're not going to solve them that way. We must revitalize the church. National revival is the only hope. The only way to have a national awakening is through the prayers of God's people.

ST: Do you have any final word that you would like to say? Is there anything else on your heart?

DOBSON: I turned sixty years of age not long ago. That experience has had a profound impact on me. It's made me look again at every component of my life and reexamine everything I thought was important. As I watch the sand running out of the hourglass of my life, all the things that I was chasing when I was twenty-seven years of age (professional and financial success and perhaps fame or notoriety) have become meaningless and insignificant. I hope the Lord gives me ten, fifteen, or twenty more years. However long I'm here, it's but a moment in the perspective of eternity. As I approach the end of my time on this earth, I realize that there are only two things that really matter. The first is being acceptable to the God who made me and hearing His words someday, "Well done, thou good and faithful servant." The second is to seek to take as many people to heaven with me as I can, beginning with my own family. Those are the only two value systems that will stand the test of time. Everything else will be consumed by God's refining fire. If younger people could grasp those ideas and concepts, and begin to live by them daily, it would revolutionize their lives.

10
KEYS TO PERSONAL REVIVAL

Will you not revive us again, that your people may rejoice in you? (Psalm 85:6)

Expect a revival when there are dissensions, jealousies, and evil rumors among believers. These things show that Christians have grown far away from God, and it is time to think seriously about a revival.

Revival is needed when there is a worldly spirit in the Church. The Church has sunk down into a low and backslidden state when you see Christians conform to the world in dress, parties, seeking worldly amusement, and reading filthy novels. When the Church finds its members falling into gross and scandalous sins, then it is time to wake up and cry to God for a revival of religion.[1]

CHARLES FINNEY

KEYS TO PERSONAL REVIVAL

━━━━━━━━━━━ ★ ━━━━━━━━━━━

A merica is only as good as its inhabitants. When ordinary citizens accept moral darkness as a way of life, the future of the nation is then destined for days of depravity. However, when God's people awaken to the power of God's renewal, then hope begins to shatter the darkness. The light of God's Word will always be greater than any corruption within culture. The church in America is like a sleeping giant that's slumbering at the midnight hour. She is the keeper of the key to renewal within the land. She has the lamp that can light the way on a dark night. However, she must be awakened at this critical moment of history. She seems to be in a deep sleep; only a loud voice will awaken her.

America is a nation constituted as a government "of the people, by the people, and for the people." Common ordinary people can change the destiny of the nation. But it begins with individuals—with you and with me. We first experience personal renewal and allow God to work deeply within our own lives. Spiritual awakening and moral renewal within the nation are a result of what God has done in the lives of common ordinary Christians. As a fountain of personal revival begins to flow in our lives, it will soon merge with the streams of renewal within our families. Those streams will then join into one mighty flowing river within the church. As the rivers of revival begin to join together, then society and our culture will be affected. A culture of death will be transformed into a culture of life.

The bottom line of moral and spiritual renewal in the land is personal revival in individuals' hearts. We are to be renewed in our own walk with God. We live by biblical convictions. We repent of how we've conformed to the culture and accept our own personal responsibility for following the pack rather than standing up for what's right. But, most of all, we understand that the rise of selfishness within the nation is directly related to the rise of selfishness in our own individual lives.

PERSONAL RENEWAL GOD'S WAY

God has given very clear directives for personal renewal. It begins with His people. The Bible states clearly where revival begins, "If my people, who are called by my name . . ." (2 Chronicles 7:14). Revival begins with His people. Therefore, some very simple but important questions must be addressed if you are to be a participant in renewal within the land. First, do you know for sure that you have eternal life? Has there ever been a time in your life when you turned from your own self-centered ways and placed your faith in Christ? Revival is a renewal of the life that is already within you. If you don't have the eternal life that's promised in the Bible, then it's impossible to be revived. You have to be born of God's Spirit before you can be renewed by His Spirit.

If you don't have the assurance that you have a personal relationship with Christ, then let me encourage you to do the following. First, be honest. Admit that you've failed God. Confess to Him in prayer that you've sinned. Be willing to forsake the cause of your sin problems—your self-centeredness. You may not feel that you have the strength to do that, and in reality you don't. That's why Christ died. He gave His life on the cross to save you from your sins and set you free from the bondage of selfishness. Place your faith in Him. Believe in your heart that He died for your sins and that He is risen from the dead. Right now, you can call upon His name and He will save you. He will forgive you. He will come and dwell within your heart as you place your faith in Him.

If you don't have the assurance that you have God's eternal life, then pray this prayer silently. It's not so much the words that are important, but the attitude of your heart. If these words express the attitude of your heart, then stop right now and pray,

Dear God, I know that I've failed You. I've sinned. I've been a very self-centered person, and I ask You to forgive me. Right now, I want to turn from my selfishness, but I'm so weak. I can't do it by myself. I need You. I need Jesus to come and dwell in my life. I believe in You and in Your Son, Jesus. I believe that He died for me. I believe that You raised Him from the dead.

*Come into my life and save me from my sin and self-centered-
ness. Thank You for hearing my prayer. Thank You for sending
Jesus into my heart. I love You, and I'll live for You as You give
me the strength to follow You. I believe that You will give me the
power and strength to live for You. In Jesus' name, Amen.*

If you prayed that prayer sincerely and in faith, then have confidence that God heard and answered your prayer. He said that He
hears and answers prayers that are prayed according to His will
(1 John 5:14, 15). It's His will that you turn from your self-centeredness and place your faith in Jesus as your only hope and salvation.

Spiritual awakening and moral renewal begin with God's people. Your religious affiliation and church membership don't make
you God's child. You cannot depend upon your parents' faith because God has many children, but He doesn't have one single
grandchild. You need a personal faith in Christ. Only God and you
know if you've truly placed your faith in Christ to save, forgive,
and transform your life. But if you have allowed Him to do that,
then you've taken the first step toward revival in the nation. It begins with His people "who are called by His name."

Humility Before God

The Scripture also says that His people must "humble themselves and pray and seek [His] face" (2 Chronicles 7:14). Biblical
and historical revivals have always arrived on the wings of the
prayers of God's people. When God gets ready to intervene in the
affairs of the history of a nation, He always places a longing in the
hearts of His people to pray and seek His face. God always initi-
ates a prayer movement before He allows His light to shatter the
darkness. But the darkness will first be shattered in our personal
lives before it can be shattered in the nation. Prayer has a way of
allowing God to bring His light into our darkness. Personal revival
and renewal began within my family when I started praying. I
knew something was wrong, and God impressed on my heart that
I needed to be somewhere where no one knew me. I needed to
find a place where I could meet with God. When Tex began to
seek the face of God in her private devotional time, He showed
her His holiness. That led to brokenness in her life and ultimately
mine, also. But it began with prayer in both of our lives.

That's why I'm convinced that Dr. Bright's call to prayer and fasting (mentioned in the following chapter) within the nation is vitally important. Prayer is essentially the expression of a humble heart. It's saying to God, "I need You. I can't be the person that You want me to be without Your strength and power." It's saying, "You are the center of my life. You're everything to me." But a life of prayerlessness is basically the manifestation of a proud heart. It is, in essence, saying, "I don't need You, God. I can live in my own strength." Prayer isn't the only factor in personal or corporate revival, but it's certainly the first step toward personal renewal.

During the time that I experienced personal revival and family renewal in Germany, I determined that the most important thing that I could teach the people in our congregation was how to have a personal time alone with God. Because the church was primarily made up of American military personnel, I knew that they would eventually be scattered around the world. Some would have to go on remote duty assignments. I wanted those men and women to know how to walk with God no matter where they were stationed. The church set a goal that every member of the congregation would develop a quality time alone with God.

Personal and Corporate Growth

Our church experienced incredible growth. Most of it was a result of what was happening in the personal lives of our people. We didn't have a great church growth strategy in place. But as Christians began to experience revival in their lives, they began to share God's love with their friends, colleagues, and neighbors. Our church became a spiritual hospital for the brokenhearted and spiritually sick. Couples on the verge of divorce began coming to the church and trusting Jesus to heal their marriages. Young people turned to Christ. Families were restored. Hearts were healed, and lives were changed. Our building couldn't contain the people coming to the church. We went to multiple services on Sunday morning and had to move to the high school gymnasium on Sunday evenings.

It all began with individuals who learned to pray and seek God's face. Actually, it began with a pastor's wife who came to her husband and said, "Sammy, I was having my time alone with God and studying about God's holiness. He spoke to my heart." It just takes one person to hear what Moses heard God say when he was alone in the wilderness with God: "Take off your sandals, for the place where you are standing is holy ground" (Exodus 3:5b). When He speaks to the deep parts of our lives, we will never be the same, and those around us will never be the same. We must evaluate our personal prayer lives and the priority that prayer takes in our churches. If revival comes, then it will be ushered in by those who have prayed and sought the face of God.

Bill Bright, founder of Campus Crusade for Christ, told me of how God had moved deeply in his life when he was at a conference with Henrietta Mears. Out of that meeting with God, a fire began to burn in his heart to reach the youth of the world with the gospel. In the following chapter, he details what transpired in that meeting. I'm convinced that we need men and women in this generation who have sought the face of God in such a manner that it results in a movement that will reach this generation with the gospel.

REPENTANCE

Prayer, however, is only the first step toward personal renewal. There must also be deep repentance in our lives. The Bible says, "Repent, then, and turn to God, so that your sins may be wiped out, that times of refreshing may come from the Lord" (Acts 3:19). Prayer and repentance have been characteristic of every great spiritual awakening. Times of spiritual refreshing follow times of repentance. But what does it mean to repent? According to *Vine's Expository Dictionary of New Testament Words,* the Greek word used is "metanoeo," which signifies "to change one's mind or purpose."[2] Hence, when we repent we change our minds about the direction of our lives.

Repent is a word that American Christians seldom use. However, it's a word that God often uses to place the church back on the path to pleasing Him. John the Baptist prepared the way for the coming of Christ by preaching repentance (Matthew 3:2). When Jesus ministered to the people, He preached repentance (Luke 13:3, 5). After Jesus ascended to the right hand of the Father, Peter preached repentance to those who had crucified the Savior (Acts 2:38). Paul told King Agrippa that he preached repentance to the Jewish and non-Jewish world (Acts 26:20).

In the letters to the seven churches of Asia in Revelation chapters 2 and 3, God gave His formula for revival to each church. He said to the churches of Ephesus, Pergamum, Sardis, and Laodicea that they must repent if they were to please God. The message of repentance has been a hallmark of the New Testament church.

Honest Confession of Sin

When God sends times of refreshing to His people, it's always preceded by repentance in their hearts. There are several characteristics to repentance that results in revival. First, there is *honest confession of sin*. There can be no repentance, nor can there be forgiveness, when we are denying the sin that creeps around in the secret closets of our lives. We can't keep the closets of our hearts cluttered with spiritual skeletons and expect to experience spiritual renewal. We must get brutally honest about things in our lives that don't please God. Many believers live in total defeat because of an unwillingness to come clean about things in their past that continue to haunt them.

I'm convinced that much of the Christian counseling business would cease if Christians began to get honest with God and with themselves. We will continue to be haunted psychologically and emotionally if we refuse to be candid about the wrongs in our lives. Many of us have somehow developed the idea that time will heal our self-inflicted wounds that were caused by past sins. Time doesn't forgive. Nor does it heal. Forgiveness and restoration take place when we take responsibility for our wrongs. Too many Christians in America are living unnecessarily with broken and scarred emotions. We can be healed if we are straightforward about our sins. Only the blood that Jesus shed on the cross can cleanse us from sin. But the Bible says that we must confess our sins if we are to know His forgiveness and cleansing (1 John 1:8–9).

Specific Repentance of Sin

The second characteristic of biblical repentance is that it be specific. When God told the churches of Asia to repent, there was something specific from which they needed to repent. The Ephesian believers needed to return to their first love. The Christians in Pergamum needed to turn from false teaching, quit eating food sacrificed to idols, and cease participating in sexual immorality. Believers in Sardis were outwardly alive but inwardly apathetic. Laodicean Christians were only lukewarm in their commitment to Christ. Each group of believers needed to change its mind about

something specific that did not please God. Thus, repentance includes honest confession and also specific confession of sin.

The American church has too much general confession of sin
and not enough specific repentance. Too often we pray, "Please
forgive my sins," but we never truly come to grips with what our
sins are. Thus, there can never be a genuine change of attitude
about our sins. It was only when I said to Tex, "It was wrong for
me to cut you off when we disagreed," that I could truly repent. It
was a lot easier to confess, "I know that I'm not the husband that
I should be." How could I repent of that? The truth is I'll never be
completely the husband that I should be. No one can be. We all
fall short. That confession wouldn't make me a better husband.
Nor would it bring healing and restoration to our marriage. It was
only when I said from the depths of my heart, "I have been so
selfish and egotistical that I didn't really try to listen to what you
were saying," that I could begin to experience repentance (a
change of mind). When I became brutally honest and specific
about my sin, then I was able to repent. God brings healing and
forgiveness as a result of such confession.

Remorse Over Sin

*Repentance is characterized by a sense of remorse about
that which is wrong in our lives.* The apostle Paul wrote, "yet
now I am happy, not because you were made sorry, but because
your sorrow led you to repentance" (2 Corinthians 7:9). He went
on to say in the following verse that "godly sorrow brings repentance." However, much of American Christianity centers around
feeling good. The attitude of many American Christians is that if it
makes you feel good, then it must be OK. Many Christians believe
that pain and suffering are to be avoided at all costs. But for me, it
was when I experienced deep sorrow over the illness of our son
that I became open to God's searching my heart and showing me
the wrong in my life. That sorrow led me to deep repentance. I
realized that I had offended the One who is absolute holiness. I
knew that I was dirty and He is absolutely pure. I came to grips
with the horror of my sin. I realized that it was my sin that nailed
Christ to the cross. I was devastated and broken over my sin.

The psalmist said, "The sacrifices of God are a broken spirit; a
broken and contrite heart, O God, you will not despise" (Psalm
51:17). God is looking for Christians whose hearts are genuinely

broken over their sins. His grace and forgiveness will be amply supplied to such a heart. It's actually His grace that enables us to turn from our sins. Many Christians don't seem to have the ability to overcome certain sins. But when we experience genuine sorrow over the wrong that has been committed, then God supernaturally applies His grace to the heart of the one who has repented. His grace then enables us to turn our backs on the attitude or action that was wrong.

I must, however, offer a word of caution at this point. Sorrow that leads to true repentance is the result of seeing that we have offended the Creator of the universe—not in the fact that we were caught. It's not sorrow over the punishment that may be bestowed upon us, but rather sorrow over the wrong in our lives. It's agreeing with God about the nature of our wrong. It's realizing that our sin was what caused Christ to go to the cross. When we see the horror of our sin, we become broken men and women. That results in turning from the sin. When Tex told me in Germany that I had done things that hurt her, I saw for the first time that I had deeply grieved God and wounded the person on this earth that I loved most. That brought about a change of heart and a change of action in my life.

A Christian friend of mine from the former Soviet Union visited me a few years ago. I was speaking at a large conference of Christian leaders in the United States. He attended the meetings with me, and I asked him what he thought of the meetings. I'll never forget his observations. He said, "The main difference in your meetings in the United States and ours is that you laugh a lot while we weep much." He was right. Much of our preaching, ministering, and worship is more entertainment than it is coming face-to-face with a holy God. Don't misunderstand me. Joy is a great part of the Christian experience. It's a fruit of the Holy Spirit. I believe that God desires joy to be characteristic of the Christian. However, I'm afraid that we've substituted entertainment for joy in our hearts. We've produced an entire industry of Christian comedy. And we've forgotten how to weep. We don't weep over our sins. We don't weep over the lostness of those closest to us. We don't weep over the condition of the nation. We've lost the ability to weep.

Recently, I preached at the Emanuel Bible College and Seminary in Oradea, Romania. It's the largest Bible college in Eastern Europe. A number of the students come from the former Soviet

Union, and many of them came to Christ through evangelistic crusades I held in the early and mid '90s in Siberia, Ukraine, and Moldova. The rector of the school, Dr. Paul Negrut, told me an amazing story about one of the students from Siberia who had come to Christ through my ministry. The young man gave his testimony one evening when Dr. Negrut was speaking in Arad, another city in that region of Romania. The young Siberian student said that the last Christian in his village had been killed by the communists fifty years earlier. But right before he was killed he wept and prayed, "O God, I pray that You will raise up a new generation of young people who will once again bring the gospel to this village." Nearly fifty years later this young man heard me preach in a nearby Siberian city and received the gospel. When he went back to his village and began to tell the people, some of the elderly people told the young man of the prayer of that martyr.

I'm convinced that the freedoms that have come to the former Soviet Union came because God saw the tears of men like that martyr. They never lost the ability to weep—weep over their sins, weep over the sins of their communities, and weep over their nation. God honored their prayers. But American Christians have forgotten how to weep. We see no sorrow in the land over the destructive practices of sin because there's very little sorrow in the lives of Christians over our own patterns of sin. We'll never know the fullness of joy that comes in times of revival until we first know the sorrow that comes from seeing how greatly we have wronged God in our own lives. Too often, we're so busy being entertained that we fail to take a serious look at the sin that's wrecking our own lives.

Reconciliation with God and Others

But the bottom line of true repentance isn't just that we're sorry for our sin. The goal of repentance is reconciliation with God and our fellow man. It's not just turning from sin, but it's turning to God. It's reestablishing deep, intimate fellowship with God and with those we have wronged. When we have sinned against God, then we confess it to Him. But when we have wronged someone else, then we go to that person or persons and confess our wrong and seek forgiveness. We'll never know the joy of walking in fellowship with God when we have never corrected the wrongs against others that we have committed.

When Tex and I were ministering in Chicago during the early 1970s, I was invited to speak at a church in southern Illinois. God moved in that church in a wonderful manner that week. Many came to know Christ. Christians were renewed in their walk with God. One of the deacons told a testimony on the final Sunday evening. He said, "When I first moved to this community, I was a fairly new Christian. I desperately needed a job. I applied at the place where I'm now employed. The application form that I filled out said that if you were caught lying about your qualifications, it would result in automatic dismissal. I needed the job really bad, and I lied about my qualifications," he told the congregation. "For years this has haunted me. Every time I attempted to develop an intimate time alone with God, His Spirit reminded me of the lie on my application. But I was afraid to make it right with the company. I was afraid of the consequences. Finally, this week, I decided that I wanted to be right with God more than I wanted a job."

The deacon began to weep as he said, "I went to my supervisor and told him what I had done several years earlier. The supervisor told me that he would have to bring the matter to higher officials in the company. He came back later, and told me that they were going to give me another chance because of my record at the company." With tears of joy he then told the congregation, "This week, I've found an intimacy with God that I haven't known in years."

That's true joy! And most Christians have substituted fun for knowing the joy of having intimate fellowship with God. He desires that we walk in fellowship with Him and with one another. Sometimes when I look at the realities of church life, I become discouraged. So many churches across America are riddled with strife, division, and broken relationships. The nation will not experience spiritual awakening until the church experiences revival. The church won't experience revival until Christians begin to be reconciled to one another and in some cases make necessary restitution. It will begin within the family and work its way out into the church and community. When this kind of repentance begins to take place in our lives, families, and churches, we can begin to live with great expectancy of a mighty move of God across the land.

But once we have brokenness, confession, and repentance, then we understand that we can't live the Christian life in our own power. If we don't understand this simple but profound truth, then we will find ourselves lapsing back into the same old habits and ways of life. Every day we draw from God's well of living water. By faith we appropriate the power and fullness of the Holy Spirit to enable us to be the people that He wants us to be. Confession and repentance is what Dr. Bright refers to as "exhaling." It's getting rid of the junk on the inside of our lives. But then we also "inhale." We invite the Holy Spirit to take control of every area of our lives.

In practical terms we do that through prayer. As we begin to experience renewal, we learn to walk in the sufficiency and strength of the Holy Spirit. Each morning when we awaken, we yield every area of our lives to God. We give Him our relationships, our time, our future, and our resources. We ask Him to take control by His Spirit, and by faith we depend completely on Him to make us all that He wants us to be that day. At any point in the day that we find ourselves acting or reacting in a manner that contradicts the fruit of the Spirit, then we need to immediately confess it to God and repent. We then need to appropriate the fullness of God's Spirit in our lives. We learn to walk and live out our lives in this manner. Only then will we be salt and light to a dark and hurting world.

VICTORY THROUGH THE SPIRIT

The Holy Spirit is the originator of revival. Revival is God's Spirit moving and restoring God's people to a simple and pure walk of faith. Spiritual awakening is an outpouring of God's Spirit upon a community or nation. We learn to live in utter dependence upon Him. When God broke me and brought me to repentance and reconciliation with Tex, I had to learn to depend upon God's Spirit daily. In some areas of our relationship I had not exhibited the fruit of the Spirit. I had to learn to trust God to make me an "overcomer" in those areas. I've learned that when I trust Him for His enablement, then I am victorious over the sin. However, when I attempt to live in my own power, then I fall flat on my face. Personal revival begins when we allow the Holy Spirit to search our hearts and bring us to repentance. But revival can only continue in our lives as we learn to walk daily in dependence upon Him. He is our victory. He is the mighty stream that flows out of our hearts to a world around us that needs Christ.

11
BILL BRIGHT ON THE NEED
AND THE MEANS OF REVIVAL

Dr. Bill Bright is the founder and president of Campus
Crusade for Christ. Bill Bright's commitment to Christ has
been multiplied into thousands of lives around the world.

*"There [has] to be a time of repentance,
brokenness, and humbling ourselves
before God. The biggest problem every
person has, going all the way back to
Adam and Eve, is pride. I don't know of a
better Christian discipline that deals
with pride than fasting with prayer."*

BILL BRIGHT ON THE NEED
AND THE MEANS OF REVIVAL

SAMMY TIPPIT: Dr. Bright, a few years ago I was speaking to a national student conference with Campus Crusade. I spoke about the revival in Romania. After that meeting you came up and asked me what it would take to see a spiritual revival in America. Now I want to turn that question around and ask you: What will it take to see revival in America?

BILL BRIGHT: I believe God has shown me as a result of three forty-day fasts in 1994, 1995, and 1996 that the only way we will have revival is [if] the Christians repent and return to their first love. I don't know a better way to do that than by fasting with prayer. In 2 Chronicles 7:14, God's Word says, "If my people, who are called by my name, will humble themselves and pray and seek my face and turn from their wicked ways, then will I hear from heaven and will forgive their sin and will heal their land." That was a promise to Solomon which we can claim. Also, at another time King David said he humbled himself through fasting. The prophets also humbled themselves through fasting. It's a lost Christian discipline that needs to be recaptured.

ST: You said that you prayed and fasted three times. What precipitated that?

BRIGHT: The apostle Paul said in Romans chapter 1 that his letter was from Paul, Jesus Christ's slave who was chosen to be a missionary and sent out to preach God's good news. In 1951 my wife and I signed a contract with Jesus to become His slaves. That probably was the most important commitment I ever made. I know it was the most important apart from my salvation. A few days later, God began to give me a vision for the world, which we now call Campus Crusade for Christ. I had this desire to be a holy person. I wanted to be a man of God. The concept of spiritual breathing—exhaling by confession and inhaling by appropriating the fullness of the Spirit—became a very important emphasis in my life and ministry.

In 1962 the United States Supreme Court ruled that there was no need for God in schools. That was the essence of the ruling, though they wouldn't admit that. There could be no prayer and no Bible reading. Later, you couldn't even put the Ten Commandments on the classroom wall in school. Our nation began to disintegrate. I've become very concerned and realized that only God could help us. He showed me that in order to seek His face in a meaningful way, I needed to fast. I had to sort out my schedule so that I could have forty days to fast. On July 5, 1994, I began to fast for revival in America, the world, and for the fulfillment of the Great Commission. About the third week, God began to impress on me that He was going to send a great revival: the greatest our nation has ever experienced, and the greatest harvest of souls that our nation has ever known. First, there had to be a time of repentance, brokenness, and humbling ourselves before God. The biggest problem every person has, going all the way back to Adam and Eve, is pride. I don't know of a better Christian discipline that deals with pride than fasting with prayer.

ST: So would you say the purpose of fasting then is to humble yourself before God?

BRIGHT: Yes. The purpose of fasting is to seek God's face, and that includes humbling yourself. But it's more than just humbling yourself. It's a matter of intimacy with Him. I can say that those three forty-day periods have been the most wonderful times of deep spiritual intimacy with God that I've known, except in dramatic moments when God in unique ways met with me.

ST: Your life has been an inspiration to millions of evangelical Christians. How have you personally maintained a fresh, renewed walk with God over the years?

BRIGHT: When we relinquish all of our rights and choose to become slaves to Jesus, we experience intimacy with God. We know we are children of God, heirs [of] God, and joint heirs with Christ. We are crucified, buried, and raised with Him. We're seated with Him in the heavenly places. Yet, Paul discovered that there is something about being a slave to Jesus that is so liberating. When you become a slave to Jesus and you relinquish all of your rights and all of your possessions, you then experience that fresh walk with God. For instance, when the Templeton prize, a million-dollar award, came, I didn't even have to pray about what I would do with it. I already knew that God wanted me to use it [to promote a nationwide movement of] fasting and prayer to promote world evangelism.

Therefore, I keep my heart fresh by getting on my knees every morning when I first awake. If my wife, Vonette, is with me, then we do it together. We did that today. In so many words we say, "Lord, You know we are Your slaves, and You live within us. We invite You to walk around in our bodies, speak to our minds, love with our hearts, speak through our lips, and seek and save the lost through us just as You did two thousand years ago."

Then I get on my knees alone and read the Word. I don't think it's possible to live in the joy of the resurrection and the fullness of the Spirit unless you are regularly in the Word—reading, studying, memorizing, and meditating. It is the holy, inspired truth of God. I read the Word, and all day long I walk and talk with Him. At the end of the day, Vonette and I just say, "Lord, thank You. We are so grateful that You have been with us today. You have lived within us." We spend time just praising and worshiping Him. It is a twenty-four-hour time of fellowship. There's a constant prayer, "Lord, keep my heart aflame for You and never let me leave my first love." People ask me, "How can we pray for you?" and my response is, "Pray that I will never leave my first love." Nothing else is really important.

ST: As a new Christian I heard you speak on confession of sin. God did a mighty work of cleansing in my own life at that time. How important is confession of sin to personal revival?

BRIGHT: Someone can't even think of getting revived without getting rid of the garbage. The book of First John is so crucial. We are told that "God is light; in him there is no darkness at all. If we claim to have fellowship with him yet walk in the darkness, we lie and do not live by the truth" (1 John 1:5-6). It is impossible to have fellowship with God if there is sin in our life. The chapter continues, "If we claim to be without sin, we deceive ourselves and the truth is not in us. If we confess our sins, he is faithful and just and will forgive us our sins and purify us from all unrighteousness" (vv. 8-9). We need to understand that the word "confess" means "to agree with." If I agree with God concerning my pride, jealousy, lust, dishonesty, or whatever it might be, I will do three things. First, I will acknowledge what I am doing as sin. Second, I claim the truth of Scripture and Christ's death on the cross and the shedding of His blood for my sin. I accept that by faith. Finally, I repent. The word repent means "changing my attitude, which results in a change of action." If I truly repent, I don't continue to live in sin. There's no way one can walk in the joy of the resurrection if there is sin in his life.

I like to refer to this relationship as spiritual breathing. We exhale by confessing our sin. We inhale when we appropriate the fullness of the Holy Spirit by faith. We are all commanded to be filled with His Spirit as a way of life. Ephesians 5:18 says, "Be filled with the Spirit." God's promise to us is if we ask anything according to His will, He hears us. If he hears us, He answers us. By faith I can know that my life is free of sin if I confess that sin and truly repent. I can know I am filled with the Holy Spirit by faith if I have truly surrendered my life totally to the Lordship of Christ. The Holy Spirit came to glorify Christ. I can walk all day long in the wonder and the power of the Holy Spirit by faith. If there is no unconfessed sin in my life, then by faith I am filled with the Spirit and surrendered to the lordship of Christ.

ST: I would like to see if you would give me a definition of three terms that you have used: (1) brokenness, (2) confession, (3) repentance.

BRIGHT: They are all closely related. . . . The Scriptures say, "A broken and contrite heart, O God, you will not despise" (Psalm 51:17). I think other good words are surrender, full surrender, or yielded. All basically mean what Paul stated in Galatians 2:20, "I have been crucified with Christ and I no longer live, but Christ lives in me. The life I live in the body, I live by faith in the Son of God, who loved me and gave himself for me." In a sense, the Christian life is not what we do for God, but what we allow God, Himself, that dwells in us, to do in and through us. Christianity is a joyful adventure. It's not a drudgery as many Christians think.

ST: As I have done research for this book, I've discovered that many social scientists have concluded that my generation, the boomers, has institutionalized self-centeredness. How does brokenness take place in our lives? Is that some-

thing that is sovereignly done by God, or is that something we seek after? In other words, how is that brokenness initiated in a self-seeking generation?

BRIGHT: The first thing I would recommend for every believer is to study the attributes of God. We need to understand that the God we worship is the God who created the heavens and the earth. Astronomers say there are 100 billion galaxies or more. This planet Earth is a grain of sand in the vastness of our galaxy, and our galaxy is only a grain of sand in the vastness of all creation. The God that created everything is the One referred to in Philippians chapter 2 as a slave. This mighty God came to Earth as a slave. God became a man in order to die on the cross for our sins. Now, there is something that helps me recognize that Bill Bright is just a little nobody. It's when I have the right concept of this great, holy, magnificent, sovereign, creator God. . . . That does something for me. When you understand this great act of love, you then deal with this whole idea of pride.

The Scripture makes it very clear that God is not happy with proud people. He humbles the proud and exalts the humble. A man is a fool when he thinks he is something when he really is not. If I were a brilliant man, there's no way I could say, "Look at me. I am brilliant," or "I am eloquent." If a person should be eloquent or gifted in many ways, and think that he has a lot of which to be proud, then that man is truly a fool. If he understood who he was in relation to the God who created him, he could only do what Isaiah did in chapter 6 when he saw the Lord. Prior to that, he had been finding fault with others. But, then, he began to see his own unworthiness. When people are exalting themselves it is because they have not seen the Lord. You cannot have an experience of seeing the nature and character of the Lord and ever get carried away with your own importance.

ST: You have mentioned this, but maybe you can expand on it a little more. Once a believer has been broken of self and cleansed of sin, where does he find the power to live for Christ and maintain a pure walk before God?

BRIGHT: It's only through the enabling of the Holy Spirit. In John 16, Jesus explains to the disciples, "But I tell you the truth: It is for your good that I am going away. Unless I go away, the Counselor will not come to you; but if I go, I will send him to you.

When he comes, he will convict the world of guilt in regard to sin and righteousness and judgment. . . . But when he, the Spirit of truth, comes, he will guide you into all truth. He will not speak on his own; he will speak only what he hears, and he will tell you what is yet to come. He will bring glory to me" (John 16:7-8, 13-14a).

Everything that happens in the Christian life, starting with the new birth, is under the direction of the third person of the Trinity: God the Holy Spirit. I can't understand Scripture unless I am filled with the Holy Spirit. The Holy Spirit inspired holy men of old to record holy truths. It's only individuals whose minds are controlled by the Holy Spirit that can truly understand God's Word. I can't pray apart from the Holy Spirit. It is the Holy Spirit that makes intercession for us with groanings that cannot be uttered. I can't witness apart from the Holy Spirit. Jesus said that we would receive power after the Holy Spirit has come upon us to be His witnesses. I can't demonstrate the fruit of the Spirit apart from His empowering. The fruit of the Spirit is "love, joy, peace, patience, kindness, goodness, faithfulness, gentleness and self-control" (Galatians 5:22-23a). Everything that I do in the Christian life involves the third person of the Trinity. It is He who empowers and produces revival, because His role is to glorify Christ. Revival comes when there is a visit from heaven, by the Father, Son, and Holy Spirit.

ST: As I read the biographies of some of the men and women of old, there often has been a crisis experience that brought them to the point of complete surrender to Christ. Was signing the contract to become a slave of Christ a watershed for you? Or was there another time that you can point to?

BRIGHT: I think it was more of a series of things. I went through a period when the Lord allowed me to feel that nobody trusted me. There were critics of me that had misrepresented facts and given the impression to some Christian leaders that I was not an honest person, that I was not trustworthy. The accusations went back to some business dealings; they were not true. I was a new Christian in business at the time, and I chose to let the Lord fight for me. But I never defended myself. Because I never defended myself, some people concluded that the criticism must be true. I went through this period of difficulty for about five years, and yet

I had a great joy and peace in my heart.

Everywhere I went the enemy was saying to me, "You are perceived as a crook. You are a dishonest person and you are perceived as such." Of course, that hurt me. But I went on serving the Lord and leading people to Christ. Then one night my name was introduced as a candidate to be a deacon in my home church. I was sitting on the back row with my new bride. A couple of members of the church made a motion that my name be removed because they felt I was not worthy to be a deacon in the church. The pastor of the church knew all the facts, and he called the committee to his counseling room. He told them, "I know all about this. This is a terrible attack on a man who is totally innocent, and I insist that his name remain on the list."

He and the committee went back to the congregation. When it was announced that my name was to stay, there was a standing ovation that went on and on. It was like the Lord said to me, "I have set you free from all this feeling." I had gone through this for years. Yet the Lord sustained me, purifying me, and then He let me see how much I was loved. God vindicated me. I have often said that no man can be used of God unless he goes through a furnace experience under tremendous heat and pressure where he has to say no to self and yes to Christ.

ST: At the JAMA [Jesus Awakening Movement of America] conference you told me about an experience early in your life and ministry. I believe you were in a room with Henrietta Mears and some others. God just moved in your life in an extraordinary way. What happened?

BRIGHT: In 1947 I had just come back from Princeton Seminary. I was at a conference in Forest Home with Dr. Mears. I was the dean of the junior high conference, and I was in business at the time. My pastor's son and I walked Dr. Mears from the lecture hall to her cottage on the ground. She had delivered a good message. There was not anything unusual about it. She was just a very gifted, inspirational, and godly speaker. But it wasn't that unusual. We arrived at her cottage and she asked us to come in, and we began to chat.

Suddenly, without any understanding why, the Holy Spirit came upon us. I had not had an experience like that. I didn't know how to respond. I was just filled with joy and praise. I was overwhelmed with the sense of the presence of God. I felt that if

I couldn't praise God, then I would burst. My pastor's son said coals of fire ran up and down his spine. Dick Halverson was a very defeated, frustrated Presbyterian minister who served at a small church in Collenga, California, at that time. He came that evening to seek counsel from Dr. Mears. She counseled literally hundreds of pastors. There were hundreds that went into the ministry under her direct leadership. The moment he opened the door, before anyone talked to him, God changed him in a split second. He became overwhelmed with the presence of God. We were all on our knees praising the Lord. That night we were so ecstatic with the joy of the Lord that we wrote the rules for "Fellowship with a Burning Heart," which was a call to the youth of the world to surrender everything and follow Jesus.

ST: A couple of years ago Nancy Leigh DeMoss spoke at your international staff conference. God moved, and the remainder of the program was suspended. What happened?

BRIGHT: Nancy is kind of like a daughter to me. I knew her father before he was married. When she was twelve years old she was the most mature twelve year old that I had ever met. In fact, I said that when she graduated from college I wanted her to be my assistant. She is a very godly, Spirit-filled woman. However, what really happened was not dependent upon Nancy. She would probably say the same.

During the time of fasting in July, the Lord impressed me that there was going to be a revival. We had various ministry gatherings before we met in the large meeting hall. When we arrived at our staff training, revival began to break out in several of these groups, especially among the high school people. They got up and confessed their sins. These were all staff. There was a time of repentance and great joy. The other ministries had times of fasting and waiting upon God. There was this great sense before we gathered in Moby Gym, where all of us were together, that God was going to visit us in a special way. Then Nancy gave a marvelous Bible-centered message, which was the key that opened the floodgates. We spent hours where hundreds of our staff went to the microphones and confessed their sins. It was usually the sin of pride, and from that other sins followed. Almost always they spoke of pride. That brings us back to the importance of fasting. So God used Nancy, but all praise and credit belongs to the Holy Spirit, who is working through many, many people.

ST: Were the characteristics basically transparency, brokenness, confession, repentance, and appropriating God's fullness and victory?

BRIGHT: Yes, all of that. There was great confession. When this took place, several people would gather around their friends. There were a half dozen, and sometimes there were so many that they were smothered by people praying with them for victory. It was truly a prelude to the revival which I anticipate God will send to the whole church.

ST: Is there any last thing that you would like to say about revival?

BRIGHT: God does more in a split second than we can do in a lifetime. It's wasted effort to try to do anything apart from total dependence upon the lordship of Christ and the anointing and enabling of the Holy Spirit. At the same time, one can't walk in the fullness of the Spirit unless they are feasting upon God's Word. It's like the two wings of a plane. If you take one wing away, the plane will not fly. You can't live in revival power or even a Spirit-filled life unless you are filled with the Spirit and unless you are spending time in God's Word.

12
A CALL TO NATIONAL AWAKENING

*If my people, who are called by my name, will humble
themselves and pray and seek my face and turn from their
wicked ways, then will I hear from heaven and will forgive their
sin and will heal their land. (2 Chronicles 7:14)*

*This work of God, as it was carried on, and the number of true
saints multiplied, soon made a glorious attention in the town; so
that in the spring and summer following, anno 1735, the town
seemed to be full of the presence of God: it never was so full of
love, nor so full of joy. . . . There were remarkable tokens of
God's presence in almost every house. . . . This remarkable
pouring out of the Spirit of God, which thus extended from one
end to the other of this county, was not confined to it; but many
places in Connecticut have partook in the same mercy.*[1]

JONATHAN EDWARDS

A CALL TO NATIONAL AWAKENING

W e are presently living with the rotting fruit of the reversal of the spiritual and moral values that our forefathers held so dear. The consequences have been devastating. America, as it has been previously known, is a dying culture. The principles that made this nation great are now scorned in many of our institutions.

I would resign myself to accept the death sentence placed upon this nation by our own rebellion if I did not know that God is able in one moment to change our moral and spiritual paradigm. An inversion of moral values has been ingrained within the major institutions of American society. We no longer view ourselves in light of our Judeo-Christian heritage. We see ourselves as a pluralistic society. Bible-believing Christians are often portrayed as the enemy rather than those who hold pertinent and important truths for our culture. Christians in former times helped build the moral infrastructure of America, but now many find themselves facing legal difficulties because of their adherence to absolute truth. The media's continual portrayal of believers as evil right-wing bigots has been tragic. But even more appalling has been the lack of courage among Christians. Many of us have been satisfied to sleep through the revolution.

I'm convinced that the only hope for America is a spiritual awakening that results in moral renewal throughout the land. It is to this end that this book was written. The choice has become very clear. The line has been drawn in the sand. Either we choose God and His ways, or we continue on a collision course headed down a highway of death and destruction. It's a simple choice: life or death, revival or ruin. But it's a choice we must make. If America is to survive as a free nation in which good triumphs over evil, it will be because we have returned to the old-time, old-fashioned principles that made this nation great.

Most Americans don't have any idea what a national spiritual renewal is. Even though there have been two major spiritual awakenings in our history, the last one took place more than one hundred years ago. Minor revivals have occurred since that time, but none have been so widespread as to affect the moral climate of the nation.

Spiritual awakening is not a panacea for our problems. It's not a cure-all for the deadly consequences of our rebellion against God's authority. It doesn't mean that there won't be any more crime in our streets or divorce in our homes. But it does mean that we won't have a culture of divorce or a society absorbed with death. The paradigm changes when a national awakening occurs. The principle outlook upon which we view life changes from the shifting sands of relativism to the Rock of the absolute truth of God's Word. It means that we have a solid foundation when the storms of life pass across our nation.

A spiritual awakening is basically a grass-roots movement of common, ordinary people combined with a divine intervention of God in the history of a nation. Dr. Tom Elliff, president of the Southern Baptist Convention, defined revival in my interview with him (in chapter 7): "When I think of revival, I think of revival in a personal sense," he said. "When I think of revival happening in a corporate sense, it's that which happens in churches. I think as these tributaries join together to make rivers, they empty into a larger ocean that leads to a national awakening." Revival takes place on a personal level and ultimately affects the spiritual and moral lives of our families and churches. As churches are renewed, they become shining lights in a dark and decaying world. God intervenes in His own time, and the nation is renewed morally. A movement that possesses the seeds of life overtakes the tree of death that was planted previously in the hearts of the people of the nation. Such a movement, in my opinion, is the only hope for America.

THE POSSIBILITY OF NATIONAL AWAKENING

There are several reasons that I believe that a national awakening is possible in the United States. First, I have beheld the glory of God, and I know God can move in the affairs of countries. Before the collapse of communism, there was a great revival in a church in Oradea, Romania. This church had been a sleepy congregation during the dark days of Ceauşescu's evil dictatorship.

Christians were persecuted severely. Freedom to publicly proclaim the gospel was denied. There was also an inversion of moral values within the Romanian society. But a courageous pastor, Olah Liviu, began to call for repentance among the Christians in the congregation. Evangelical Christians were called "repenters." His message was simple and to the point: "The repenters must repent." The church entered into a "covenant of repentance." In the covenant, the people determined to turn away from the sins that were so prevalent in their culture. A grass-roots revival movement began with common, ordinary Christians and culminated with a national awakening.

I've traveled in Romania for close to twenty years and am convinced that the freedoms that came to that country at the close of 1989 were directly tied to the spiritual revival that began in that church. Tremendous church growth took place throughout that entire region of Romania during those days of revival. Many were converted to Christ. Churches throughout the region experienced renewal. "Repenters" repented. That entire northwestern region of Romania became a hub for evangelical Christianity. The grass-roots movement of Christians conforming to Christ rather than to culture was in full swing by the end of 1989. The seed had been sown years earlier by a humble, godly pastor.

Then, in one divine moment, God intervened in the history of Romania. It happened in another northwestern city of Romania—Timisoara, a university city where evangelical churches were experiencing rapid growth. Many were suffering for their faith. When an evangelical pastor was to be arrested, believers went to his home to try to protect him. The secret police fired into the crowd of Christian men, women, and children. When the blood of the martyrs began to flow into the streets of Timisoara, there was a release from heaven of the glory of God on the people of God and of the wrath of God on the evil Ceauşescu regime. An estimated 200,000 people gathered in the main square of the city to protest what had happened. People who had been brainwashed all of their lives with scientific atheism began to shout, *"Existe Dumnezeu! Existe Dumnezeu!"* (There is a God! There is a God!) This scene was multiplied in the major population centers of the nation.

I entered Romania at the conclusion of the revolution and couldn't believe what I saw. I never imagined that I would see anything like it in my lifetime. Ordinary people on the street gathered around me and began to shout, "There is a God! There is a God!" It was absolutely incredible. A few months later I went to Romania and preached the gospel in a stadium. Luis Palau went to Oradea and preached the gospel in another stadium. I preached in another city, Arad, a few months later. It was the first time in the history of Romania that the gospel of Jesus Christ had been proclaimed in a stadium. The stadium where I preached was located in that northwest region of Romania between Oradea and Timisoara. The stadium couldn't contain the crowds that gathered for the final service. Thousands of people sat on the ground and stood around the track because there were no seats left in the stadium.

God's Hand

There's only one explanation for what happened in Romania: God intervened in the affairs of the history of the nation. Western news agencies on the whole did not report the spiritual roots of the revolution in Romania. However, as a firsthand observer before and after the revolution, I'm convinced that two elements about what happened there cannot be ignored. First, there was a grass-roots movement of Christians who turned away from the sins of the culture. The seeds of change were planted in the hearts of Christians when Pastor Liviu called for repentance. That earned the respect of the non-Christian community. When the tragedy took place in Timisoara, the entire nation became incensed. Second, in God's own time, He chose to step into the affairs of the history of the nation. In one moment, God changed things. That doesn't mean that everything became a bed of roses in Romania. Decades of lies and moral decay had been practiced in the country. The system had been built over a period of many years and would not be torn down overnight. But the pattern changed in the country. The nation would not be the same. It will never again view life in the same way.

What transpired in Romania gives me great hope for America. It may be difficult for many Americans to believe a national spiritual awakening can occur in our country. But my eyes have seen the glory of God in a nation, and I'll never get over it. I know it's possible. I've seen it happen. The time has come in America for "the repenters to repent"! A grass-roots movement of Christians must turn from the sins of our culture. As long as Christians go with the present flow of moral values in American society, there's no hope for a national awakening. It begins with us.

Our Constitution

The second reason I believe a national awakening is possible is that we are a nation "of the people, by the people, and for the people." We don't need to have a revolution in order to change the direction of America. Our political system lends itself to a grass-roots movement. The people ultimately determine the destiny of this nation. We have no one to blame for the moral decline but ourselves. We can't even blame our politicians. We elected them. The Founding Fathers clearly laid the responsibility for the direction of America upon the shoulders of its ordinary citizens. The seeds of death and destruction that were sown in the sixties can be overcome by sowing seeds of life and righteousness today.

It's time for us to awaken to see our personal responsibility in this moral renewal. We must be the ones to change. We cannot expect to change the culture if we have conformed to it. The transformation of our society will only take place as we are transformed in our own hearts. Arkansas Governor Mike Huckabee said in my interview with him, "I can pray for God to change America, but it's ridiculous if I'm not praying for God to change me." The church in the final analysis holds the key to renewal. Revival must begin within the church and then flow out to the rest of society.

One of the most impressive aspects of my interview with Governor Huckabee actually took place before the interview. While waiting in the governor's office for our interview, my colleague, Joe Tower, and I began chatting with the receptionist. She told us of one of her most memorable days working in the governor's office. She had worked there long before Mr. Huckabee became governor. He had been elected as lieutenant governor after Bill Clinton resigned his position as governor because he had been elected president of the United States. Lieutenant Governor Jim Guy Tucker immediately became the governor of Arkansas. However, not only was President Clinton hounded by legal problems with his Whitewater land deal, but Governor Tucker was also investigated by the independent counsel, convicted of crimes, and sentenced to prison.

After his conviction, Governor Tucker had to resign his position as governor of the state of Arkansas. That meant that Lieutenant Governor Huckabee automatically became the new governor. However, the day that Governor Tucker was scheduled to formally resign, he huddled with his staff and reversed his decision. The national media were everywhere. Phones in the governor's office were ringing off the hook. Everyone wanted to know what was taking place. The receptionist was left in the dark about Tucker's decision. She was left stranded without anyone to help her answer all of the questions being asked.

She told us of the confusion in the office and about her frustrations. She didn't know what to do. Then she said that several men from then Lt. Governor Huckabee's office came walking into her office. They said, "Lt. Governor Huckabee heard about your dilemma. He sent us here to help you. What can we do to help?" The receptionist said, "Governor Huckabee was so nice. He was going through a very intense and difficult time that day. Yet he was concerned enough about a receptionist in the governor's office to send the people who were helping him down here to help me."

The reason that incident was of such great value to me was because of what the governor later told me in our interview. He had no idea what the receptionist had told us. However, one of the strongest points that he made in the interview was that we must not just talk about "family values," but we need to begin to discuss "my personal family values." He said to me, "I think it's very important that there is consistency with a person's public life and his private life. By private, [I mean] not only in home, but even within his own inner circle of friends and office personnel. I think there's got to be a consistency between when you're out there and the lights are on you, and when the doors are closed and you're alone with your staff. I believe there's got to be a consistency. If you're not genuine, then, to me, everything else is immaterial."

Governor Huckabee had integrated his faith into his personal life, and it made a difference in one person's life. That's precisely what's needed in America today. We are one of the most religious countries in the world—certainly the most religious nation among Western industrialized nations. The problem, however, is that we have not integrated our faith into our daily lives. Self-centeredness and the Cross can't rule in the same house. One or the other will reign. It's at this point that Christians need to repent. Enough people in this nation are Christians to reverse the moral decline in our society. However, it's time to integrate what we say we believe with how we live.

Christians in America

The Bible is even more specific when it states its formula for a national awakening, "If my people, who are called by my name, will humble themselves and pray and seek my face and turn from their wicked ways, then will I hear from heaven and will forgive their sin and will heal their land" (2 Chronicles 7:14). So, according to the Scriptures, national awakening begins with "my people, which are called by my name." The healing of the land begins with God's people, when His people choose to "turn from their wicked ways."

In my interview with Governor Huckabee, he stated that Christians cannot exempt themselves from the issues facing America today. He challenged believers to get involved in confronting the moral and spiritual issues facing society. I would add to his comments that our involvement will only produce the kind of fruit that we display in our personal lives. If our lives aren't exemplary of the character of Christ, then we will have little effect upon the nation as a whole. Therefore, it's imperative that we are in the process of being conformed to Christ rather than to culture if we are to truly affect the nation.

God's Prerequisite

The condition that God laid down for the healing of a nation begins with "If my people" and ends with "shall turn from their wicked ways." He then promised, "then will I hear from heaven and forgive their sin and heal their land." If we, the people, are willing to repent, then He, the Lord God Almighty, is willing to forgive our sins and heal our land. That's why I believe there's hope for America. There remains hope if we are willing to repent. Biblical repentance is "a change of mind, a change of attitude." We must be willing to change our minds, our attitudes about what constitutes right and wrong, good and evil. It can no longer be what seems good to me, but rather what God has said in His Word is right or wrong. If we want revival, we will turn back to His standard.

American History

But I, also, possess hope in my heart for a revival because our nation was born in time of historical awakenings and on at least two occasions experienced a divine intervention in our history. A major spiritual revival occurred immediately prior to the formation of the United States of America. Jonathan Edwards had been used of God and was seeing entire communities converted to Christ. Edwards described some of what was taking place by saying, "The Spirit of God began extraordinarily to set in and wonderfully to work amongst us. . . . A great and earnest concern about the great things of religion and the eternal world, became universal in all parts of the town, and among persons of all degrees and of all ages. . . . And the work of conversion was carried on in a most astonishing manner, and increased more and more. Souls did, as it were, come by flocks to Jesus Christ."[2]

Then in 1739 George Whitefield placed his feet on American soil. He had been used mightily of God to spread a great awakening in Britain. Sometimes he spoke to up to 50,000 people outdoors in Britain without any amplification. In God's appointed time, Whitefield arrived in America. Edward S. Ninde, a biographer of Whitefield, said, "And George Whitefield, born again in the Holy Club, was the chosen Apostle of the Lord in linking together these two awakenings that finally merged into the vast movement which changed the religious face of the English-speaking world. He came to America just in time to infuse new energy into the languishing work begun under Edwards, and to thrust it forward like a flaming torch into all the Colonies."[3]

Some of the estimates of the numbers of those hearing Whitefield preach were up to 80,000. Even if the figures were somewhat bloated, Arnold Dallimore in his biography of Whitefield says, "It is highly probable that these crowds, which were the largest of Whitefield's whole career, were also the largest ever reached by the unamplified human voice in the whole history of mankind. And this was the ministry of a youth of twenty-four!"[4] Thus, America was born during a time of spiritual revival and moral renewal. Spiritual awakening is at the very core of who we are as a nation. We were born as a nation with a deep sense of need and hunger for God. I don't believe we will ever be able to completely forget our heritage, and I know that God certainly has not forgotten it.

By the mid 1800s America again stood in the need of a great spiritual renewal. There had been a downturn in the economy, and spirituality was at a very low point. But one man, Jeremiah Lamphier, refused to allow the nation to slide into moral degradation. He began a prayer meeting at noon in the business district of New York City. At that first prayer meeting, no one came during the first thirty minutes. Finally six men came to the prayer meeting. The wind of God began to blow across their hearts and then throughout the nation. The move of the Spirit of God was so great that many church historians refer to that period of history as the "great prayer revival."

An incredible movement of prayer was birthed in the nation. In New York City the prayer meetings grew until 10,000 were in attendance. Thousands attended in other cities, and many were converted throughout Canada and the United States. A number of ministries began to flourish, including that of D. L. Moody and Ira Sankey during and following the revival.

RECENT MINOR AWAKENINGS

There has not been another major national spiritual awakening since that outpouring of God's Spirit in the 1800s. However, there have been a number of minor awakenings, the last of which took place in the late '60s and early '70s. It was during that time that I came to know Christ as my personal Lord and Savior. As a generation began to forsake God in the '60s, some Christian leaders became concerned for the radical changes that were taking place among America's youth. They began to pray for God to intervene in the lives of the youth. God answered their prayers. Thousands of young people all across America began to turn to God in the late '60s. The media dubbed this extraordinary movement of young people "The Jesus Movement."

Time, Newsweek, Life, and *Look* magazines all had feature stories about what God was doing in the nation among young people. William Cannon edited a book entitled *The Jesus Revolution* in which he interviewed a number of young leaders who were reaching youth across America with the gospel. My ministry was one of those featured in the book because we had a street ministry in Chicago at the time.

I caught a vision during those days of what God could do to change an entire community. It began in Monroe, Louisiana, when a youth meeting in a church turned into a genuine revival that affected the entire city. The meetings began in a local church with about twenty-five people in attendance, and they grew until the church couldn't contain those coming. We moved to the local college campus, and it was unable to contain all of those in attendance. Finally, we moved into the civic center with thousands of young people present. Scores of young people turned to Christ. Racial tensions in the local schools were relieved. Drug dealers were converted. The evening TV news carried reports of what God was doing in the city. God intervened in the affairs of that community.

It was then that I knew it was possible to see a genuine spiritual awakening and moral renewal in America. I led a team of young people to march across the southern part of the United States and issue a call for revival. I met Arthur Blessitt in Washington, D.C., and held a rally calling for revival. During that same time period, there was an unusual move of God's Spirit in Christian colleges across the nation. It began at Asbury College and Seminary. A chapel service that was scheduled to last for thirty minutes ended up lasting for seven days and nights without stop when God intervened in the affairs of the campus. The word of what God had done quickly spread across the land. Other schools also began to experience revival. I spoke at Asbury a few weeks after the initial outbreak. It was incredible to watch what God was doing. After I spoke and before I could return to my seat, there were nearly one hundred students at the altar praying and crying out to God for forgiveness.

It seemed as though there was a wave of young people turning to Christ. All over the country, from California to D.C.; from Asbury (a Methodist institution) to Southwestern Baptist Theological Seminary; from the streets of Chicago to the Bible Belt, God was changing the lives of scores of young people. No single human personality seemed to direct what was transpiring. Only the Holy Spirit seemed to be orchestrating the events taking place. However, one question has continued to trouble me. I have had to ask myself, "Why didn't the Jesus Movement become that which turned the moral and spiritual tide in those critical days of American history?"

Weaknesses of the Movements

If there's to be a national revival, then we must return to the root cause of our falling away. America turned away from the Bible as its basic foundation in the '60s, and only a movement centered in strong Bible teaching and discipleship would be able to turn the tide of relativism in the nation. God used the Jesus Movement to bring many to Christ. However, the fundamental weakness of the movement was the lack of strong Bible-centered preaching and teaching. Music and experience, in many instances, took precedent over biblical exposition. Music and wonderful experiences with God have always been a part of revival movements. But they are not at the core of the movement. The core of the movement is a turning back to the fallen standard of the Word of God.

Second, there wasn't a strong call for repentance in many circles. There was too much "get high on Jesus" theology and not enough preaching the message of Christ: "I tell you, no! But unless you repent, you too will all perish" (Luke 13:3). We must turn from self-centeredness to God-centeredness if there's to be a national revival. This lack of strong preaching on repentance is evidenced in the fact that many of the leaders eventually fell into sin. There will never be a national revival unless the sin issue is dealt with thoroughly by those who are leaders. Every great spiritual awakening has struck at the heart of the sin issue in the nation. The Jesus Movement fell short in doing that. I don't say that as a critic, but as one who was considered a leader in the movement.

Finally, churches weren't prepared for the harvest. In the words of Jesus, we need a "wineskin" able to hold "the new wine." The wineskin is discipleship, and those who come to Christ are the new wine. The further a nation drifts from the Bible, the more deeply committed the church will have to be to the process of making disciples. Discipleship is the practical method through which we are brought back to building our lives on God's Word. Many churches had no idea what to do with the scores of young people who were expressing their desire to know Christ.

Even though the Jesus Movement of the '60s didn't produce a national revival, there was definitely a stirring in the land. That gives me great hope that God is not through with America. He has moved in mighty spiritual awakenings in times past and desires to move mightily today. There's one final reason that I believe revival is possible today. There's presently a quiet moving of God's Spirit in several areas of spiritual life within the nation. Just as the boomers have come of age, so have the "Jesus People." Many of those who came to Christ in the late '60s and early '70s have grown and matured. They have experienced "him who is able to do immeasurably more than all we ask or imagine, according to his power that is at work within us" (Ephesians 3:20).

Today's Stirrings

But there have also been spiritual movements in the land during the last few years. Some appear to have the marks of God, and others are questionable. If there's going to be a genuine revival in the land that produces a change in the moral climate of the nation, we will first return to God's Word as the standard for our lives. A number of national spiritual movements have been rooted in experience and emotions rather than the Scriptures. That can be dangerous and ultimately produce a superficial renewal that does not strike at the root problem facing this generation. Donald Gray Barnhouse, who pastored Philadelphia's historic Tenth Presbyterian Church, once said, "When a Christian begins to look for emotional experiences instead of looking for the quiet application of the Word to the heart by the Holy Spirit, he is on a wrong track, that can lead to nothing but deception, and can only delay the reality of blessing."[5] Unfortunately, most of what is being reported as revival in the nation is having little effect on the moral behavior of ordinary Americans. I've heard reports of revivals where the main attraction is "spiritual laughing, roaring, slaying, jumping and rolling." However, when genuine revival comes, the evidence is not how high we jump, but rather how straight we walk. The chief characteristic of revival in the land will be a return to the Word of God.

However, some things transpiring in the nation do have the marks of the beginning of a national awakening. An unprecedented wave of prayer is sweeping the land. Tom Elliff, president of the Southern Baptist Convention, said in our interview that his denomination has documented more than 130 national prayer movements that have emerged recently in America. Also, Bill Bright is calling for 2 million Christians to pray and fast for revival. Already thousands of Christian leaders have begun to meet together throughout the nation to pray and fast. A men's movement, The Promise Keepers, has emerged across the nation. America's largest stadiums are filling with men making commitments to God and their families. There's a new generation of political leaders such as Governor Mike Huckabee emerging. They are men and women who are refusing to compromise God's Word for the passing fancy of fame.

I'm convinced that it's possible that we could see a national revival. But someone will have to stand up, step up, and be willing to pay the price to be God's instrument to bring change to this nation. It's not likely that revival will come easily. A price tag comes with surrendering to the will of God. As you will see in the following chapter, when Governor Huckabee decided to become involved in changing his community, it cost him much. There will be no resurrection power without first going to the Cross. That means suffering. There will be no revival in the land until someone is willing to meet God's conditions. That may not feel too good.

13
MIKE HUCKABEE ON
LEADERSHIP WITH INTEGRITY

The Honorable Mike Huckabee, governor of Arkansas, was elected lieutenant governor of Arkansas after then Governor Bill Clinton was elected president of the United States. President Clinton's successor, Governor Jim Guy Tucker, was later convicted of crimes investigated by the Independent Counsel appointed by the attorney general of the U.S. Tucker then resigned and Mike Huckabee became the governor of Arkansas.

"We've got crime problems, pregnancy problems, drug addiction problems. . . . The problem is not going to be fixed by more money. Every one of these things that are costing us huge amounts of money are essentially moral or character problems. It's a character issue."

MIKE HUCKABEE ON
LEADERSHIP WITH INTEGRITY

SAMMY TIPPIT: Governor Huckabee, you haven't always been in politics. You were a pastor before becoming lieutenant governor and then later governor. Could you tell us a little about your relationship with the Lord and where you began in this journey that you're on?

GOV. HUCKABEE: I became a Christian at the age of ten during a Vacation Bible School, and I went to a small Baptist church in Hope, Arkansas, my hometown. I really was not so much from a church-oriented family, but from a very moral family. Right and wrong were clearly distinguished in our lives. But at the age of ten, I went to Bible school, mainly because my friends were going. It wasn't a real spiritual motivation that took me there, but that day the pastor talked about what it meant to know Jesus. I remember him speaking about it in a way that I knew that it had never happened to me. He led us in prayer. I was a very bashful kid, extremely shy. People find that hard to believe now, but it really was the case. When he asked people to raise their hands if they wanted to receive Christ, I said to myself, *No, I'm not going to do that because he'll probably call on me and embarrass me.* So, I just stood there and thought, *He can't keep me from praying.* I did pray, and I can still remember very vividly that it was just as if there was a cleansing that took place within my heart.

I have always been able to know that was the beginning point. That rebirth was really the start of my spiritual life. It was five years later, at the age of fifteen, through Campus Crusade's "Ten Basic Steps of Christian Maturity" that I began to really grow in the Lord.

I'm of the Expo '72 generation. [Expo was a movement of young people that gathered in Dallas in 1972 to be challenged to evangelize the world for Christ.] But there were some people in Hope that had this Bible study on Wednesday nights in their home.

These were the first adults that I had known in my life that really believed the Bible. I mean, they really believed it to the point that it was not just Sunday morning stuff for them. I was just flabbergasted. It wasn't that they were so educated. He was a bulldozer operator. But here was a guy that was comfortably talking about his relationship with Jesus, witnessing, and things that I'd never really been exposed to. I grew up in a little church that taught you that you needed to get saved, go to church, and then you go to heaven—in that order.

The attitude was that now you're saved, that's great. Now you've bought your fire insurance, then you should go to church—that's your discipline. You've got to do that. It doesn't matter whether you get anything out of it, it's just you've got to do that. Then when you die, you go to heaven. So, that was the totality of the Christian life to me. But that Bible study at age fifteen was a turning point. I felt that the Lord wanted my life to be more than just sitting on the shelf. I really never intended to go into the pastorate. I was in communications and worked for the James Robison organization during the 1970s. I ended up backing into the pastorate when a church needed someone for supply preaching. I went there, and they asked me to come down and preach a week of meetings. I did, and then they asked me to be interim pastor. I did that, and then they asked me to stay. I was there for six years. After that, I went to Texarkana and was pastor another six years. It was a wonderful experience.

But it was during that time I saw so much of what was going on in our culture that the church was not addressing. The church had become an isolated club. It was no longer that penetrating arm of God in a community. It was a refuge and retreat point—not the point of launching an offensive. It was a defensive fortress, and people came there to escape, not to be equipped. I tell people I really preached myself into politics because I continued to talk about the needs of the community.

ST: At what point in time did you feel that you were really speaking to yourself? When did you feel that you needed to be making more of a difference in the public life?

HUCKABEE: Throughout my pastorate, from the very beginning. I was very community-oriented and active in the Chamber of Commerce, United Way, and all sorts of community functions. I felt that it was critical for the church to involve itself in the community. It couldn't be salt and light if the salt was in the shaker and the light was in the well-lit rooms. If we were to penetrate society, then we needed to go where things were putrefying and decaying. That's what salt was to do—to preserve. It couldn't preserve if it was only around that which was already preserved and carefully chilled.

I had this wonderful love of politics dating back to my teen years. I figured that was something that would never happen. Once I got into the pastorate, I shelved the idea that I would ever be in politics. But I became convinced that a lot of our institutions—government, schools, and even churches—had completely unhitched from their moorings and were adrift. Government was no longer based upon the principle of moral absolutes. The church was no longer based on the principle of servanthood and outreach. Schools were no longer trying to build young citizens. A whole series of things began to take place, one of which was about a two-hour meeting I had with Dr. Joycelyn Elders. It was at the request of then Governor Bill Clinton.

ST: Why did you have that meeting?

HUCKABEE: In 1989 I was elected president of the Arkansas Baptist Convention. It was during a rather tumultuous time in Southern Baptist life. Bill Clinton was governor and also a member of a Southern Baptist church. He was very sensitive to what the state's largest denomination was doing and thinking. So, we had a rapport. Joycelyn Elders was director of the State Department of Health. At that time, she was really giving fits to evangelicals who were protesting condoms in the schools and abortion programs. I think there was a program that was promoting homosexual rights. She would make some pretty wild statements in public about "ministers needing to quit moralizing from the pulpit," and "Christians need to get over their love affair with the fetus."

It created a real uproar for then Governor Clinton. He called me and said, "What do you think this is doing?" I told him, "I think you're in real trouble with this. People don't really feel that a state employee, who is paid for by all of us, should be out there attacking a significant segment of the population of decent people." That conversation led him to ask if I would be willing to sit down with Joycelyn Elders and express the concerns of the evangelical community. I said that I would. I came away from that meeting with her with this deep conviction. Here was a person that really believed what she was saying and very committed to it. She was in a position to make things happen in government that would affect the way my children were educated. Her decisions would affect the way they lived and everybody around me lived. That was one of those watershed moments. I remember talking with my wife and saying, "If people like that are going to set public policy, then we can't sit on the sidelines forever."

That began a long process of asking people to pray with me about my involvement in political life. In 1991, I decided to run for the United States Senate against an eighteen-year incumbent, a two-time former governor. It was hard to do that in 1992 with Bill Clinton on the ballot. I was running against an extremely well financed, well established incumbent Democrat Senator. I didn't win the race, but neither did I lose the fire for what I was doing. Bill Clinton's election to the presidency opened a vacancy in the lieutenant governor's office. That gave me an opportunity to run. No one thought I could win because I was going against the political machinery of Arkansas. Here I was, an upstart Republican, versus Bill Clinton's former legal counsel in this race for lieutenant governor. It was the only thing on the ballot and the first election in Arkansas since [Bill Clinton had] gone to the White House. It really stunned not only the state, but a lot of people in the country when I won.

ST: When you became lieutenant governor of Arkansas, I know there must have been a tremendous transition for you personally. But it would have been a tremendous transition for the entire political machinery around here as well. You're a Republican, and Arkansas is primarily Democratic. What was the transition like? Were there difficulties that you faced?

HUCKABEE: I was only the fourth Republican elected to state office in 150 years. So they didn't know what to do with me. What they did do was nail the door shut to my office. Now, this was not an apocryphal story. Literally, the door to the lieutenant governor's office was nailed shut, and it remained nailed for fifty-nine days.

ST: Why?

Huckabee: Basically to harass me.

ST: Could they do that legally?

HUCKABEE: They could because the Democrats controlled all the other offices, and there really was not a lot I could do. When you're the only minority party person down here, what power do you have? What authority do you have? Nothing! And the only real power came because the people of Arkansas were outraged. Even Democrats said, "We didn't vote for the guy, but he did get elected. That's just wrong!"

So many turns in my whole political career, Sammy, have been like Joseph who was thrown in the well and then sold [into] slavery by his brothers. He said, "You intended to harm me, but God intended it for good" (Genesis 50:20). That really has been the case. All the computer equipment had been taken out of the office. All the printers were gone. They took out all the office furniture. This desk, for example, is still a borrowed desk. It's sort of a badge of honor with me now. I had no paper. I had to have my letterhead printed by private contributions because I couldn't get the state to cooperate even for something as simple as that. It was just extraordinary.

ST: You're on this great mountaintop of winning a prominent statewide election and all of a sudden you're slamdunked! How did you handle that?

HUCKABEE: Well, I knew very clearly that I was going to be tested, not only spiritually, but politically also. I knew that part of their strategy was "if we can get this guy mad enough, he'll blow up and explode. When he does, then we'll just say, well look, he's just a whiner." So, I told my small staff, "The meaner they get, the nicer we become. The more belligerent they act, the more cooperative we are. The more difficult they are, the more accommodating we will be." I felt like we needed to live out Proverbs 15:1, "A gentle answer turns away wrath, but a harsh word stirs up anger."

You never can win playing on that kind of playing field because you're outmanned. You're outnumbered. The dumbest thing you could do is try to play the game with the person who is challenging you. You must change the rules of the game. You change the rules of engagement. So, they got meaner, and meaner, and meaner. And we would try to be nicer, and nicer, and nicer. That position before the public eye caused such an incredible outpouring of support for me that finally the nails had to come out of the door. To this day—it's been almost four years—I'll go to some remote place in Arkansas [and] the first thing somebody might say is, "They didn't treat you right when you first went down there. Did you ever get those nails out of your door? I bet they didn't nail your door shut when you became governor!". . . . It is sort of a legend now in Arkansas politics.

ST: Let's talk about some of the transition concerning issues you faced. You came into a situation where the values and the moral beliefs were perhaps different from yours. You're facing people who have different standards. When you became lieutenant governor, did you find it difficult dealing with some of those issues?

HUCKABEE: Not really. It's been a surprise to people who ask, "Has it been an adjustment getting into politics from the ministry?" I tell them, "Sometimes the politics of government are not as brutal as the politics of church." That's the most brutal politics I've ever been through in my life. . . .

The other part is that as a pastor, Sammy, you will never please everybody. Every day you're going to make somebody unhappy. You have to make decisions and take positions on things that won't quite be understood by the people who ought to be your friends and support you. But they'll turn on you. Part of what you learn as a pastor is that you can't even tell others why you've made some decisions. To do so would violate the trust of someone who has entrusted you with confidential matters. You have to just live with some information that you can never disclose. You can never disclose all the details because it would hurt the person who has given you their trust.

Politics is no different. I have to make decisions whether or not to carry out an execution. I have carried out four, and it's a gut-wrenching thing. I have to decide on paroles, different requests, all sorts of legislation. So I can't always justify in public what I've done because I might violate confidential information that I have. That's part of the transition.

My wife has said it, I think, very eloquently: "They're so much alike" (her role as first lady [and that of] a pastor's wife), "but the real difference is that in the church, the people put you on a pedestal, and they really want you to be there. They want to keep you there and believe the best about you. But in politics, they put you on the pedestal, and they spend every waking moment trying to tear you off of it." But you're still out there in the spotlight, and people look at you differently than they look at the other people around them.

ST: You came into the governor's office differently from most governors in the United States. Jim Guy Tucker resigned as governor, having been convicted and sentenced to prison over Whitewater-related activities. A number of prominent political people here in Arkansas have been convicted of crimes. Web Hubbell, assistant to the attorney general of the United States, and the McDougals, who were business partners with President Clinton, are from Arkansas. Now you're the leading politician in the state. Do you find cynicism or skepticism when you talk about moral values as a political leader in the context of the Arkansas situation?

HUCKABEE: I have two very strong, almost polarizing reactions. One is strong support from people who say, "It's so nice to have somebody who really has convictions. We're praying for you." Those are great reactions. Then, I have the reactions from the very, very cynical people; the ones who just believe that everybody ever elected to public office is pure scum. They believe that all of us are playing games. They think that some have been caught and the rest haven't. But in their minds, we're all alike. There's simply nothing you can do to convince that person. Some are in the press. They believe that you're just a complete sham. You just can't keep your focus on their criticisms. It's hard to do, but that's very important for survival.

ST: How do you think that leaders can create a climate of trust and confidence within the general population? I think that since the Nixon years, there's been basically a lack of trust in the general population, not just of political authorities, but religious authorities as well. Is there anything that can be done as leaders to reestablish moral credibility?

HUCKABEE: I think the timing you picked, the Nixon era, was sort of the shattering of whatever innocence might have been left in American public life. And it's gotten just incredibly worse since that time. I believe that we must start at the level of every individual. For example, I think it's very important that there is consistency with a person's public life and his private life. By private, [I mean] not only in [a person's] home, but even within his own inner circle of friends and office personnel. I think there's got to be a consistency between when you're out there and the lights are on you, and when the doors are closed and you're alone with your staff. . . . If you're not genuine, then, to me, everything else is immaterial.

I think it's important to understand the role you play as a public official. For example, being governor of Arkansas gives me a level of prominence that has nothing to do with Mike Huckabee. It's because of the governor's office. When I'm out of this job, it'll be a different story. Other people have had it before me, and other people will have it after me. There's all these people who right now are saying, "Oh, Governor, we want to talk to you. Oh, you're so important. We just need to see you." That's all just temporary. I've got to keep in perspective that these people don't love me. It's not that they're enamored with me. They weren't before I was governor, and they won't be after I'm gone. You have to keep that from ever becoming something that you think about. A lot of that is just a spiritual walk day by day.

ST: Right, but pride and arrogance can easily come with leadership. You can easily fall into that trap.

HUCKABEE: I think you have to avoid two things: You have to avoid the most superfluous things people say about you, and you have to avoid the most horrible things people say about you. Some people honestly think you're the worst thing that ever breathed. I get those letters and calls every day. Then you get the other people that think you're the greatest thing since toasted sliced bread. You have to be sure and not believe that either. You must realize that you're a human being, and you're the same person you were before you had the position of leadership. You make mistakes. You say stupid things. You get proud, and you have to be dealt with on that. You get discouraged, and you have to be dealt with on that. The walk you had with God is the same walk you had before. It's just a little more visible than it used to be.

But I think also that we've got to move from this talk of "the family" to my family; not "marriage" but my marriage. I can't get out there and talk about how we need to have strong family values if I don't try to personally have strong family values. I can't talk about the institution of marriage if I'm not interested in my marriage being as good as it can be. It's absurd for me to talk about the children of America if I'm indifferent about my children. The morality of America needs to be my morality. Am I faithful to my wife? I said that in the "State of the State" address to our legislature. I told them, "Guys, let's quit talking about the nebulous sort of values and ask ourselves, 'Am I the person that I need to be as a role model?'"

ST: Our message is a real outgrowth of our own personal character. There's been a dramatic rise in divorce, single-parent families, drug abuse, all of these social problems since the '60s. Much data shows quite significant percentages of rise in these areas. What can be done to turn the tide of moral values, and turn the country back to biblical values? What would you say to the people of Arkansas who have chosen you to be their leader?

HUCKABEE: What I have already said to them, and will continue to say to them, is that we have to change the paradigm. For too long we've believed that money is the issue that changes what we do in government. Everything in government is built around the budget and money. We have this attitude that if we spend enough money in the right places, and we change certain things, then character will follow. People will be better, and we'll eliminate poverty, disease, and crime. Well, I go back to Matthew 6:33 (KJV), "Seek ye first the kingdom of God, and his righteousness; and all these things shall be added." I'm not trying to say we can ever, from a government's perspective, infuse the kingdom of God into society. I would not be in favor of any kind of imposed faith.

But let's deal with the broad universal need of character. We've got crime problems, pregnancy problems, drug addiction problems, and all these things. So we need to attack these problems. Well, the problem is not going to be fixed by more money. Every one of these things that are costing us huge amounts of money are essentially moral or character problems. It's a character issue. Why do we have so many people in prison? We can't build prisons fast enough in Arkansas. It costs us $13,000 a year in Arkansas to house an inmate. It's one of the cheapest costs in the country, but that's more money than it would cost to put a kid in any one of our universities, give [him] spending money, plus pay his every expense, including books. Why are we spending that money? Because people lack character. They end up in prison because they're drug addicted and they're thieving and murdering. . . . We spend $40,000 per year per juvenile in our juvenile justice system for rehabilitation and for treatment. Forty thousand a year! That's a huge amount of money. The reason we do that is because their families are broken down. These kids are really, really lost. They're lost spiritually, emotionally, and even in their families.

And we just keep thinking that we must put more money in education. But education isn't the key. I remember my conversation with Joycelyn Elders. Her whole thing was "We have to educate, educate, educate." I think something's wrong with that approach. We have more sex education than we've ever had, and teen pregnancy rates continue to climb. We have better education. We have computers and all this technology we've never had before. Yet we have kids who are attacking teachers and each other. We have drug dogs in the hallway, armed guards patrolling, and metal detectors to get into some of the schools here in Little Rock. If it's more money and more education, then what's wrong? The problem is that it's a breakdown of character and respect. . . .

The "more money and education principle" is based on the idea that man is essentially good. He's going to do the right thing if he knows better. Therefore, if we educate him, tell him what's good, and give him enough economic stability, then he'll do right. That's a totally false basis. We have to understand that man is basically selfish. He'll do whatever he can get away with. If he thinks he can get by with killing somebody to get what he wants, he'll do it. We know that some people will kill for a pair of shoes. We have to understand that the only thing able to change that kind of pattern is when the person's character is changed. He must come to the place where he doesn't want to kill. That will take place when he's not selfish. His self-centeredness must give way to a sense of community.

Now, obviously the church would call that rebirth or God

changing our hearts. But even for a secular society, we can still understand it in terms of character. Let the churches do the specifics, but the government can say that some things are right and others are wrong. It's wrong to steal. It's wrong to lie. It's wrong to cheat. Those kinds of things need to be imparted.

ST: What are you doing to try to build character within the young people of single-parent homes? They're facing some difficult things. Many of them don't have a father to be that strong hand. How do you build character within them?

HUCKABEE: As it relates to public policy, there are several things. One, we're introducing a "Character First" curriculum in the schools. We're not mandating it because we don't like the concept of forcing schools. But we are offering to public schools, 311 school districts, character education materials. The course teaches about nature and life. Meanwhile, the student is really learning character qualities such as responsibility and honesty. The second thing we're doing is that we're trying to change some of our tax laws. Currently, we penalize married couples for filing as married couples. So, we no longer want to penalize the young mother should she get married. Currently we really reward single parenthood, and we penalize marriage. Well, that's crazy. We're never going to see marriage increase that way.

ST: Let me ask you this: What do you think it will take for a spiritual awakening and moral renewal within America?

HUCKABEE: I don't think that it will ever be that the government does something to bring that about. One of the things I feel very strongly about, as a Christian believer in politics, is that too many Christians look to see what the government is going to do for the awakening. Well, it's not going to happen. All government really can do is basically try to get its hands on the throttles and decelerate the problems, not accelerate. My motive for getting into government is not to see what government can do to fix the problems. I want to try to awaken people to realize that government can't fix these things. These have to be moved back into the private sector of the church, that is—the spiritual world. The awakening will happen when God's people realize that the true power to change the world is in their hearts. It's in the prayer closets, not in the legislative halls. . . .

A lot of evangelical Christians have gotten involved in politics, not out of a heart for God and America. They're tired of paying fifty cents on the dollar for taxes. It's economic. It's out of their own selfishness. They want more money for themselves. So, they get involved in politics because they're angry at the tax situation. These are the same people who are mad because government is taking so much of their money to do things with welfare, helping these "deadbeats" out here, as they call them.

The truth is, if they had given a dime out of every dollar that they'd earned to take care of the widows, the poor, the orphans, the hungry, the sick, and the imprisoned, we would never have had these government programs. These programs have totally failed because they were based on the faulty premise that people are imprisoned and teens have gotten pregnant because they didn't know any better. Christians have forgotten that this is a character breakdown. The church is sitting out here with the answer and won't share it. The government's over here without an answer, and it's trying to solve it. It's no wonder—it's just a miracle that the social breakdown didn't take place sooner.

Whatever level we're decreasing taxes and government intrusion into these social problems, then the church is going to have to accept a greater challenge. Every church ought to say, "We will adopt a prisoner and help that person's family. We'll take a welfare mother and teach her how to buy groceries on a hundred-dollar budget. We'll help her to see how far she can stretch a budget and to teach her how to buy clothes." Many of these women don't know how to do some of these things. We assume that everybody grew up upper-middle-class or even middle-class and [knows] how to spend money wisely. Not everyone knows how to earn and save money. Sometimes you have a person who thinks if you rent a TV for fifteen dollars a week for the next fourteen years, that's a great bargain! You have to explain that this isn't a very wise thing, and that they can't afford it. It's many of those little things where the church can make a big difference. Government can never fix those things. And if churches don't help, then we're never going to get a handle on some of our problems.

ST: So you're saying there must be a revival within the church that thrusts the church out into the community to be that salt and light that you talked about at the beginning of this interview.

HUCKABEE: I think that many churches have become clubs. When I was starting out as a pastor, I envisioned that the role of the pastor was like a captain of a warship. He was to be equipping, training, and leading his army into battle against the forces of darkness. I later came to find out that the people's expectation of the pastor was not that he was the captain of a warship. They thought that he would be the captain of a love boat, making sure that everybody had a great time. As long as he kept the people entertained—their trips for the youth were better than other churches' trips; their senior adult program had more activities and catfish suppers than any other church; and their young adult fellowships went to really neat places—then it was a great church.

When I'd call on people who'd visited our church, very rarely would they say, "Pastor, I'm thinking about coming to your church. Where is it that I could serve, and in what capacity do you think God can use me to make a difference in this community?" The response was more like, "Tell me about your youth program. What can you do for our children? What kind of activities do you have for people our age?" In other words, it was such a consumer-oriented mentality that was driving the decisions about who goes to church and what they expected out of it. I became increasingly disgusted that we had totally abandoned the New Testament model of the church. We had become an organization where people were coming to stoke their own selfishness. Many Christians want worship services that are as entertaining as any movie they've seen. There's nothing wrong with worship that is exciting. But if the entertainment value of the sermon and songs is the criteria by which we judge the effectiveness of the church, then we're missing the purpose of the church. It's not the pleasure quotient of the Wednesday night suppers or having a family life center with great weight lifting equipment that we need. It's not having a wonderful softball team or well-respected friends that makes a church great.

I have to ask myself, "What real changes are taking place in the world as a result of my being related to Jesus and my being a part of this church?" The sad truth is that often the answer is "Nothing!" Too much of the time our Christianity is a total in-reach. All we're doing is huddling away from the world, patting ourselves on the back thinking that we're better than those folks out there. We're happy that we're not like those scummy people on the outside:

those adulterers and homosexuals, the drug addicts and dealers, and all those nasty people. We pat ourselves on the breast like the Pharisee in the temple, and we've totally missed what God has for the church. I'm appalled with the Americanization of the Christian faith.

ST: What final message would you have for the Christian community?

HUCKABEE: Christianity is a process, not just an event. We have to begin to recognize that America, the world, and the church are never going to rise any higher than our own personal walk with God. I can pray for God to change America, but it's ridiculous if I'm not praying for God to change me. It's absurd for me to say, "Oh, God, bless our leaders," but I'm not asking God to use me. There are a lot of people in the pews who are always praying for someone else to stand up, step up, and do the right thing. We need to be praying that I will do the right thing. It must be me, personally, on my face before God. Revival is first and foremost personal before it can ever become corporate. I believe that corporate revival is nothing more than a mass of individual revivals taking place in the lives of a large group of people.

EPILOGUE

---★---

Governor Huckabee is right—revival begins with you and me. It must be personal before it can become national. The problems affecting the nation are the same problems that we personally face day in and day out. If revival is to come to the nation, we must cease pointing fingers at everyone else and allow God to search our hearts and show us our need for revival. We need to see where the spirit of self-centeredness has gripped our own lives.

Just as the pastor in Romania said to his congregation, "The repenters must repent," Christians in America must repent. We must turn from self to Christ. We must not be conformed to the culture, but transformed into the image of Christ. It's time for each of us to take a long, hard look at our walk with God and make any changes necessary.

I pray that this book will be more than just another book on your shelf. My prayer is that it will challenge you to pray as you've never prayed; to obey God in a fresh way; and to be light during a time of increasing darkness. That is the hope for our nation and our world. Take some time to seek God's face today. That's the starting place. Once you've met Him in a fresh manner, He'll do the rest.

NOTES

---★---

CHAPTER 1

1. George Washington, cited in *Moral Ideas for America*—Appendix A, ed. Larry P. Arnn and Douglas A. Jeffrey (Claremont, Calif.: The Claremont Institute for the Study of Statesmanship and Political Philosophy, 1993), 100.
2. Michael Medved, *Hollywood vs. Religion* (Dallas: Chatham Hill Foundation, 1994).
3. Ibid.
4. Ibid.
5. Rick Marin and Sue Miller, "Ellen Steps Out," *Newsweek*, 14 April 1997, 67.
6. Ibid.
7. Larry Flynt with Kenneth Ross, *An Unseemly Man* (Los Angeles: Dove, 1996), xi.
8. Ibid., 6.
9. Michael Levin, "Flynt Doesn't Deserve Heroic Film Treatment," *Los Angeles Times*, 6 January 1997, Calendar, 3.
10. Flynt, *An Unseemly Man*, 258.
11. David B. Larson, M.D., and Susan Larson, *The Forgotten Factor in Physical and Mental Health: What Does the Research Show* (copyright David and Susan Larson, 1994), 1.
12. Ibid., 66, 67.
13. Ibid., 75.
14. Ibid., 69.
15. Ibid., 70, 71.
16. Ibid., 72.
17. Ibid., 95.
18. Ibid., 111, 112, 116, 117.
19. Ibid., 120, 121.
20. Matt Labash, "The Truth vs. Larry Flynt," *The Weekly Standard*, 17 February 1997, 19.
21. Scott Alexander and Larry Karaszewski, *The People vs. Larry Flynt, The Shooting Script* (New York: Newmarket, 1996), 199.
22. Labash, "The Truth vs. Larry Flynt," 23.
23. Alexis de Tocqueville, *Democracy in America*, trans. George Lawrence, and ed. J. P. Meyer (Garden City, N.Y.: Doubleday, 1969), 293.
24. Ibid.
25. Francis Canavan, "The First Amendment and Pornography," in *Moral Ideas for America* (Claremont, Calif.: The Claremont Institute, 1993), 8, 10.
26. *Chaplinsky v. New Hampshire*, 315 US 568, 571–572 (1942), cited in Canavan, "The First Amendment and Pornography," 5.
27. American Psychological Association, cited in William Bennett, *The Index of Leading Cultural Indicators* (New York: Simon and Schuster, 1994), 104.

CHAPTER 2

1. Abraham Lincoln, cited in *Moral Ideas for America*, Appendix A, 104-5.
2. Source for 1970-1994 data: National Data Book and Guide to Sources (U.S. Department of Commerce; U.S. Census Bureau; Ronald H. Brown, editor; Washington D.C., September 1995), 55. Source for 1960 data: U.S. Bureau of the Census, 1960 Census of Population, PC(2)-4B, "Persons by Family Characteristics," Table 11.
3. Ibid.
4. James Lincoln Collier, *The Rise of Selfishness in America* (New York: Oxford Univ. Press, 1991), 221.
5. Ibid.
6. Ibid., 227, 228.
7. Robert Bork, *Slouching Towards Gomorrah* (New York: Regal, 1996), 50, 51.
8. Engel et al. V. Vitale et al., No. 468. Argued April 3, 1962—Denied June 25, 1962, cited in David Barton, *America: To Pray or Not to Pray* (Specialty Research Associates, P.O. Box 397, Aledo, Tex. 76008), 152, 154.
9. Arnn and Jeffrey, *Moral Ideas for America*, 104.
10. Collier, *The Rise of Selfishness in America*, 230.
11. Robert H. Knight, *Dr. Kinsey and the Children of Table 34* (Washington D.C.: Family Research Council, n.d.), 1.
12. "Dr. Kinsey and the Children of Table 34," *In Focus* (Washington D.C.: Family Research Council, n.d.).
13. Knight, *Dr. Kinsey and the Children of Table 34*, 9.
14. Bork, *Slouching Towards Gomorrah*, 22.
15. Centers for Disease Control, AIDS Death Rate Annual, deaths by half year and age group, through 1995, United States, Table 13.
16. Robert Swenson, "Plagues, History, and AIDS," *American Scholar*, Spring 1988, 191, 192.
17. Bork, *Slouching Towards Gomorrah*, 51.
18. Vital Statistics of the U.S.—1970, Volume III (U. S. Department of Health, Education and Welfare, Health Resources Administration, National Center for Health Statistics, Rockville, Md., 1974), "Estimated Number of Marriages and Divorce from 1920-1970," Table 2-1.
19. Statistical Abstract of the U.S., 109th Edition, "Marriage and Divorces—Number and Rate, by State; 1980 to 1987" (National Data Book and Guide to Sources, U.S. Department of Commerce, U.S. Bureau of the Census, January 1989, Washington D.C.), 88.
20. David B. Larson M.D., James Swyers, and Susan Larson, *The Costly Consequences of Divorce: Assessing the Clinical, Economic, and Public Health Impact of Marital Disruption in the United States*, (Rockville, Md.: National Institute for Healthcare Research, n.d.), 26.
21. William J. Bennett, *The Index of Leading Cultural Indicators* (New York: Simon and Schuster, 1994), 46.
22. Charles Krauthammer, "Defining Deviancy Up," *The New Republic*, 22 November 1993, 20.
23. Ibid., 48.
24. Patrick Fagan, "The Real Root Causes of Violent Crime: The Breakdown of Marriage, Family, and Community" (Washington D.C.: The Backgrounder, The Heritage Foundation, March 17, 1995), No. 1026, p. 36.
25. Eric Schlosser, "The Business of Pornography," *U.S. News & World Report*, 10 February 1997, 44.
26. Ibid., 43-44.
27. Jane D. Brown and Jeanne Steele, "Sex and the Mass Media" (paper presented at

the American Enterprise Institute, 29 September 29, 1995).

28. Ibid.

29. Ibid.

30. Bennett, *The Index of Leading Cultural Indicators,* 104.

31. Ibid., 103.

32. Robert Maginnis, "Juvenile Violence Increasing," *Perspectives* (Family Research Council), 7 February 1996.

33. Ibid.

34. U.S. Bureau of the Census, Forcible Rape—Number and Rate: 1970-1993, Table no. 315, p. 203.

35. Cited in Walter Berns, "Popular Culture and Popular Government" (paper presented at the American Enterprise Institute, 10 March 1992), 5.

CHAPTER 3

1. Dan Quayle, *Standing Firm* (New York: HarperCollins-Zondervan, 1994), 319.

2. U.S. Bureau of the Census, Current Population Reports, Series P20-484, "Marital Status and Living Arrangements: March 1994," Source for 1960 data: U.S. Bureau of the Census, 1960 Census of Population, PC(2)-4B, "Persons by Family Characteristics," Tables 1 and 19.

3. Barbara Dafoe Whitehead, *The Divorce Culture* (New York: Knopf, 1997), 3.

4. Ibid.

5. Centers for Disease Control and Prevention, Monthly Vital Statistics Report, Volume 43, No. 13, supplement, October 25, 1995.

6. U.S. Bureau of the Census, Current Population Reports, Series P20-484, "Marital Status and Living Arrangements: March 1994" and 1960 Census of the Population, PC(2)-4B, "Persons by Family Characteristics," Tables 1 and 19.

7. Ibid., 18.

8. Collier, *The Rise of Selfishness,* 246.

9. David Blankenhorn, *Fatherless America* (New York: HarperCollins, 1995), 60.

10. Ibid., 61.

11. Ibid., 99.

12. Ibid.

13. "Divorce: One Way to Sacrifice Kids," letter to columnist Roddy Stinson, *San Antonio Express News,* Sunday, 2 March 1997, 3A.

14. Larson, Swyers, Larson, *The Costly Consequences of Divorce,* 50.

15. Ibid., 47.

16. Ibid.

17. As cited in Whitehead, *The Divorce Culture,* 149.

18. Centers for Disease Control, Monthly Vital Statistics Report, Vol. 44, No. 11(S), 24 June 1996, 8.

19. Blankenhorn, *Fatherless America,* 69.

20. Cheryl Wetzstein, "The Fatherhood Deficit," *The World & I,* November 1995—article can be found on the Internet at: http://www.worldandi.com/archive/cinov.htm

21. Collier, *The Rise of Selfishness in America,* 246.

CHAPTER 4

1. President Lyndon Johnson, as cited in William J. Bennett, *Index of Leading Cultural Indicators* (New York: Simon and Schuster, 1994), 45.

2. U.S. Bureau of the Census, Statistical Abstract of the U.S., 109th Edition (U.S. Department of Commerce, Washington D.C., January 1989), 85. The 1994 Statistics came from the Centers for Disease Control Monthly Vital Statistics Report, Volume 43, Number 13, supplement, October 1995.

3. Dick Morris, *Behind the Oval Office* (New York: Random House, 1997), 212, 213.
4. Ibid., 209.
5. "Idolizing of Morris Shows Modern Culture's Bankruptcy," *Albuquerque Journal,* 24 September 1996, A6.
6. Whitehead, *The Divorce Culture,* 6.
7. Ibid., 7, 8.
8. Patrick Fagan, "Social Breakdown in America," Issues 96, The Heritage Foundation (Can be found on the Internet at: http://www.heritage.org:80/heritage/issues96/chpt6.html).
9. Cal Thomas, *The Things That Matter Most* (New York: HarperCollins/Zondervan, 1994), 96.
10. "The Business of Pornography," *U.S. News & World Report,* 10 February 1997, 44.
11. Ibid., 49.
12. Bennett, *The Index of Leading Cultural Indicators,* 103.
13. Ibid.
14. "How Viewers Grow Addicted to Television," *New York Times,* 16 October 1990, C1.
15. As cited by Robert H. Bork, "Popular Culture and American Values" (paper presented at the American Enterprise Institute, 10 March 1992), 5, 6.
16. Andrew Fletcher of Saltoun, *Conversation Concerning a Right Regulation of Governments for the Common Good of Mankind,* 1704; cited in John Bartlett, *Bartlett's Familiar Quotations,* ed. Justin Kaplan, 16th ed. (Boston: Little, Brown and Company, 1992), 285.
17. Bork, "Popular Culture and American Values," 2.
18. Corie Brown, "Hollywood Lesbians: It's a 'Girl World,'" *Newsweek,* 14 April 1997, 68.
19. Ibid.
20. Marin and Miller, "Ellen Steps Out," 66.

CHAPTER 5
1. Arnn and Jeffrey, *Moral Ideas for America,* 110, 111.
2. Federal Bureau of Investigation, as cited in Bennett, *The Index of Leading Cultural Indicators,* 22.
3. Collier, *The Rise of Selfishness in America,* 264.
4. Bennett, *The Index of Leading Cultural Indicators,* 22, 23.
5. Births to Unmarried Mothers: United States, 1980–92, Vital and Health Statistics Series 21, No. 53, Released 6 June 1995 by the National Center for Health Statistics.
6. Patrick Fagan, "Rising Illegitimacy: America's Social Catastrophe," F.Y.I. (Published by the Heritage Foundation, Washington D.C., 29 June 1994).
7. Daniel Patrick Moynihan, "Defining Deviancy Down," *The American Scholar,* Winter 1993, 24.
8. "Preventing Crime, Saving Children: Mentoring, Monitoring and Ministering," The Second Report of the Council on Crime in America, Co-Chairs: William J. Bennett and Griffin Bell (Center for Civic Innovation at the Manhattan Institute, New York, February 1997), 3.
9. Ibid.
10. Bob Greene, "Our Greatest Threat? Ourselves, It Turns Out," *USA Today,* 11 February 1997, 11A.
11. Robert Maginnis, "Violence in the Schoolhouse: A 10-Year Update," *Insight* (Washington D.C.: Family Research Council, May 1994), 1.
12. Ibid.
13. Ibid., 2.

14. Youth Suicide Surveillance, Center for Disease Control, Selected Suicide Statistics for Persons 15-24 Years of Age, by Age Group, Race, and Sex, U.S., Selected Years 1950-1980, Issued November 1986, 9.
15. Suicide in the United States, National Center for Injury Prevention and Control, Center for Disease Control, Atlanta, Georgia, 1.
16. Attempted Suicide Among High School Students—United States, Centers for Disease Control, from Morbidity and Mortality Weekly Report, September 20, 1991, Vol. 40, No. 37, 633-35.
17. Patrick Fagan, "Why Religion Matters: The Impact of Religious Practice on Social Stability," Cultural Policy Studies Project, The Heritage Foundation, 25 January 1996.
18. Katie Hafner, Jennifer Tanaka, and Brad Stone, "Blaming the Web," *Newsweek,* 7 April 1997, 46.
19. Ibid.
20. Ibid.
21. "ABC News Aids Gay Military Drive," *Accuracy in Media AIM Report,* ed. Reed Irvine, January-A 1993, 2.
22. Ibid.
23. Ibid.
24. AIDS Death Rate Annual, Table 13, AIDS cases through December 1995, United States, Centers for Disease Control, Atlanta, Georgia.
25. Robert Knight and Ken Ervin, "Homosexual Group Aims to Silence Opponents," *Insight* (Washington D.C.: Family Research Council, 3 April 1996), 2.
26. Ibid.
27. "Homosexual Realities—The Seamy Truth," *Accuracy in Media, AIM Report,* ed. Reed Irvine, February-B 1993, 2.
28. Ibid., 3.
29. Ibid.
30. Ibid.
31. Bennett, *The Index of Leading Cultural Indicators,* 69.
32. Ibid.
33. "How Effective Are Condoms in Preventing Pregnancy and STD's in Adolescents?" a study by J. Thomas Fitch, M.D., September 1996, 15.
34. Ibid., 6.
35. Ibid., 15, 16.
36. "A.D. 1995 Restatement of the Oath of Hippocrates, Circa 400 B.C." (Brighton, Ma.: Value of Life Committee, 1995).
37. Cited in Leon L. Bram, ed., *Funk & Wagnalls New Encyclopedia,* 1996, vol 13, 120.
38. Nigel M. de S. Cameron, "You Are Not Your Own," *Physician,* January/February 1997, 19.
39. "Physician Assisted Death," *Family Policy,* a publication of the Family Research Council, n.d., 7.
40. Ibid., 6.

CHAPTER 6

1. L. E. Maxwell, *Born Crucified* (Chicago: Moody, 1973), 55.
2. Ibid., 60.
3. Ibid., 63.

CHAPTER 8

1. Charles R. Swindoll, *Strike the Original Match* (Portland, Oreg.: Multnomah, 1980), 40.

CHAPTER 10

1. Charles G. Finney, *How to Experience Revival* (Springdale, Pa.: Whitaker House, 1984), 9.
2. W. E. Vine, *Vine's Expository Dictionary of New Testament Words*, unabridged edition (McLean, Va.: Mac Donald, n.d.), 961, 962.

CHAPTER 12

1. Jonathan Edwards, "The Great Awakening," in *The Works of Jonathan Edwards,* ed. C. C. Goen (New Haven and London: Yale Univ. Press, 1972), 118, 120.
2. Arnold A. Dallimore, *George Whitefield,* vol. I (Westchester, Ill.: Cornerstone, 1979), 422.
3. Ibid., 412.
4. Ibid., 296.
5. Donald Gray Barnhouse, *How to Live a Holy Life* (Old Tappan, N.J.: Revell, 1975), 18.

Petits contes sympathiques

A reader for advanced beginning
French students

June K. Phillips

National Textbook Company
a division of NTC/CONTEMPORARY PUBLISHING GROUP
Lincolnwood, Illinois USA

The publisher would like to thank Florence A. Brodkey for her contributions to this edition.

Cover design: Lisa Buckley
Interior design: Lucy Lesiak
Interior illustrations: Andrew Grossman, the Toos Studio

ISBN: 0-658-00528-6

Published by National Textbook Company,
a division of NTC/Contemporary Publishing Group, Inc.,
4255 West Touhy Avenue,
Lincolnwood (Chicago), Illinois 60712-1975 U.S.A.

00 01 02 03 04 05 06 07 08 09 CG 0 9 8 7 6 5 4 3 2 1

‌ Contents ‌

✍ Introduction ✍

Petits contes sympathiques is an introductory reader for advanced beginning students of French. The twenty-seven humorous short stories use simple, yet authentic and natural language to deal with a variety of comical situations. Although the situations are often satirical and a bit farfetched, the topics themselves—such as learning languages, eating out, going to the doctor, studying, and traveling—are ones that are traditionally featured in basal texts. By providing imaginative situations sprinkled with humor, these stories will help students strengthen their own communication skills and thus bolster their self-confidence when they speak French. Because they are short stories, all can be read well within one class period.

Each story starts with a **prereading** activity that encourages students to use their prior knowledge and critical thinking skills to make their own special connection to the story. Lively classroom discussions can result from these **Avant de lire** activities. Each reading is followed by comprehension exercises that check students' understanding. Students answer objective questions based on what they have just read, and might also have to complete multiple-choice questions or determine if statements are true or false, correcting the false information. The **Avez-vous compris?** section ends with **Et vous?,** so everyone has a chance to express his or her opinion. Following this, there are exercises that focus on the vocabulary, verbs, and structures used in the stories. For example, students might identify cognates, synonyms, or antonyms in the **Vocabulaire** section; supply the correct verb form in the **Verbes** section; or choose the right preposition, possessive adjective, or form of *venir de* or *aller* with the infinitive in the **Structure** section. High-frequency vocabulary and expressions are used throughout to facilitate comprehension, and the more difficult terms have been glossed on the page, defined in English, and then included, along with other words, in the French-English vocabulary at the back of the book. A whimsical illustration accompanies each story and adds to the humor and meaning of the text.

Students might enjoy role-playing these stories for the rest of the class or for a smaller group. If they do, not only will the "actors" refine their interpretive reading skills, but their audience will strengthen its listening skills. Having students listen to the stories on the audiocassette that is also available will polish listening skills too. Each story has been recorded and is read by native speakers.

Petits contes sympathiques is the perfect complement to any basal text for advanced beginners and is the ideal addition to your French class. Students will enjoy reading these engaging stories as they move toward mastery of the structures needed for self-expression in French. Teachers will appreciate the book's flexible organization that lets them select stories in any order to reinforce topics or structures being studied or reviewed in class.

1.

Une langue étrangère

AVANT DE LIRE: *Pourquoi étudiez-vous le français? Etes-vous content(e) de cela? Connaissez-vous d'autres langues? Lesquelles?*

Bijou a deux ans. C'est le chien le plus intelligent du village. Le jour de la rentrée des classes, il quitte la maison à huit heures du matin. C'est un chien ambitieux: il veut arriver

5 à l'école de bonne heure. Sa mère lui demande:

   —Bijou, à quelle heure rentres-tu de l'école aujourd'hui?

   —Aujourd'hui, je rentre vers° deux heures et demie, répond Bijou.

vers around

1

10 Durant la journée, la mère de Bijou regarde la
pendule° de temps en temps. Elle se demande°
comment se passe la première journée de son
fils. Elle suit de très près ses progrès.

A trois heures précises, Bijou arrive devant la
15 maison. Il frappe à la porte avec sa queue. Sa mère
ouvre la porte et l'accueille° en lui disant:

—Bonjour, chéri!

—Miaou, miaou! répond Bijou, imitant un chat.

—Que dis-tu, Bijou? demande sa mère avec
20 surprise. Cela ressemble à du chat. Ne sais-tu
pas aboyer° et hurler° comme tout le monde?

—Bien sûr° que si. Je veux juste te montrer
ce que j'ai appris° à l'école. Cette année, nous
commençons l'étude d'une langue étrangère.
25 Pendant la première leçon, nous avons appris
comment dire bonjour. Tu vois comme
j'apprends vite.

pendule clock
se demande wonders

accueille welcomes,
   greets

aboyer to bark
hurler to howl
Bien sûr Of course
j'ai appris I learned

◖ AVEZ-VOUS COMPRIS? ◗

A. Indicate whether these statements are true or false. Write *V* for
vrai and *F* for *faux*. If the statement is false, correct it to make
it true.

   1. (   ) Bijou va à l'école aujourd'hui.
   2. (   ) Il rentre vers 5 heures.
   3. (   ) Il ouvre la porte et entre dans la maison.
   4. (   ) Bijou ne sait pas aboyer.
   5. (   ) Bijou parle couramment une langue étrangère.

B. Répondez à ces questions par une phrase complète en français.

   1. Comment s'appelle le chien?
   2. Quel âge a-t-il?
   3. Est-ce que Bijou est ambitieux?
   4. A quelle heure est-ce que Bijou quitte la maison?
   5. Où va-t-il?
   6. Quand rentre-t-il?
   7. A quoi sa mère s'intéresse-t-elle?
   8. Qui dit "Miaou, Miaou"?
   9. Qui est-ce que Bijou imite?
   10. Qu'est-ce que Bijou étudie à l'école?

C. Et vous?

   1. Comment vous appelez-vous et quel âge avez-vous?

   2. A quelle heure quittez-vous votre domicile le matin et quand rentrez-vous le soir?

   3. Depuis combien de temps étudiez-vous le français?

   4. Quels sont les premiers mots que vous avez appris?

   5. Connaissez-vous d'autres langues étrangères?

◖ VOCABULAIRE ◗

A. Cognates are words that have a similar root or element in both French and English. For example, *salade* is a cognate of *salad*. Many English words that end in *-ous* end in *-eux (-euse)* in French. Give the French equivalents of the following words.

1.	furious	**5.**	fabulous	**9.**	generous
2.	glorious	**6.**	nervous	**10.**	precious
3.	famous	**7.**	delicious	**11.**	ambitious
4.	curious	**8.**	mysterious	**12.**	serious

B. Antonyms are words that have opposite meanings. Match these antonyms.

A	**B**
1. de bonne heure	**a.** au revoir
2. demander	**b.** continuer
3. quitter	**c.** l'enfant *(m., f.)*
4. bonjour	**d.** en retard
5. la mère	**e.** chuchoter
6. hurler	**f.** répondre

◖ VERBES ◗

A. Complete the sentences with the appropriate form of the verb given in the model.

   1. Tu *imites* le professeur.

Nous _____ les autres.

J'_____ ma sœur.

Vous _____ vos parents.

Les enfants _____ leurs camarades.

Elle _____ son frère.

3

2. Pierre *réussit* à l'école.

Elles _____ leur examen.

Nous _____ toujours.

Tu _____ à lui parler.

Maman _____ tous ses gâteaux.

Vous ne _____ pas vos examens.

3. Elle *répond* au garçon.

Elles _____ aux lettres.

Marie et moi, nous _____ au professeur.

Je _____ à l'invitation.

Tu _____ à la question.

Vous ne _____ jamais en classe.

B. Complete the sentences with the correct form of the present tense of the verbs indicated.

1. Guillaume _____ un chat. *(imiter)*
2. Nous _____ à deux heures. *(rentrer)*
3. _____ -tu le français? *(apprendre)*
4. Ils _____ toujours leurs devoirs. *(finir)*
5. Nous _____ à la porte. *(frapper)*
6. Vous _____ de bonne heure. *(arriver)*
7. Je _____ une langue étrangère. *(choisir)*
8. Ma mère _____ avec surprise. *(répondre)*
9. Le chien _____ toute la journée. *(hurler)*
10. Ils _____ le miaulement du chat. *(entendre)*

ᥫ STRUCTURE ᥫ

A. Complete the sentence with the appropriate form of *de* or *à*.

MODÈLE: Bijou va _____ l'école.
Bijou va *à* l'école.

1. Pierre est l'élève le plus intelligent _____ village.
2. Ils frappent _____ la porte.
3. Elle rentre _____ la maison.
4. Il est dix heures _____ matin.
5. Le garçon s'intéresse _____ mes études.

B. Form sentences using the words in the given order. Add any necessary words and make any necessary changes.

MODÈLE: Bijou/rentrer/maison/deux/heures
Bijou rentre à la maison à deux heures.

1. Louise/Marie/imiter/garçons
2. Nous/frapper/porte
3. Tu/arriver/école/bonne heure
4. Vous/apporter/livres/rouge
5. Jean/moi/passer/devant/école

2.
Au restaurant

AVANT DE LIRE: *Aimeriez-vous être propriétaire d'un restaurant? Que feriez-vous pour faire de la publicité?*

Je m'appelle Jean Delacroix. Je passe devant un grand restaurant de la rue de la Paix. Je remarque° un monsieur assis° à la terrasse. Il savoure° une grosse portion de bifteck pommes
5 frites. J'aime bien le bifteck pommes frites. J'entre dans le restaurant et je m'assieds. Le garçon me donne la carte et me demande:

remarque notice
assis seated
savoure relishes

–Que désirez-vous, monsieur? De la viande?
10 Du poisson? Tous nos plats° sont excellents.

    –Apportez-moi de l'eau minérale,° s'il vous
plaît. J'ai soif.° Et apportez-moi un bon bifteck
pommes frites parce que j'ai très faim.°

    Au bout de quelques minutes, le garçon
15 place une assiette devant moi. Un petit bifteck
accompagné de pommes frites est placé sur une
petite assiette. Mon appétit est énorme, mais
la portion est toute petite. Je la regarde avec
tristesse.

20   –Pourquoi cette portion est-elle si petite?
Le monsieur à la terrasse a une grosse portion.
Est-ce qu'il paie plus que moi? Je ne suis pas
étranger, monsieur. Je suis de Rouen. Je crois
que vous essayez° de me tromper.°

25   –Je vous assure que non, répond le garçon.
Je ne trompe personne.

    –Je veux parler au propriétaire.

    –En ce moment vous ne pouvez pas lui
parler. Il est occupé. C'est lui qui mange le
gros bifteck et les pommes frites à la terrasse.

plats dishes

eau minérale mineral
    water
J'ai soif I am thirsty
j'ai faim I am hungry

essayez try
tromper to cheat

✎ AVEZ-VOUS COMPRIS? ✎

A. Complete the sentences to summarize the story.

A	B
1. Jean passe	**a.** le garçon veut tromper le client.
2. Jean remarque un homme	**b.** un bifteck et des pommes frites.
3. Jean veut	**c.** la grosse portion.
4. La portion n'est pas	**d.** devant un restaurant.
5. Jean pense que	**e.** avec le propriétaire.
6. Il veut parler	**f.** très grosse.
7. Le propriétaire a	**g.** assis à la terrasse.

B. Répondez à ces questions par une phrase complète en français.

1. Est-ce que Jean est américain ou français?
2. Où le monsieur est-il assis?
3. Qu'est-ce que Jean aime bien?
4. Pourquoi Jean veut-il de l'eau minérale?
5. A-t-il un grand appétit?
6. Pourquoi regarde-t-il son assiette avec tristesse?
7. Que croit Jean?
8. Pourquoi Jean ne peut-il pas parler au propriétaire?

C. Et vous?

1. Quelle est votre nationalité?
2. Aimez-vous la cuisine française, chinoise, italienne ou américaine?
3. Avez-vous bon appétit?
4. Quand mangez-vous?
5. Aimez-vous manger au restaurant?
6. Préférez-vous manger chez vous ou au restaurant?
7. Avez-vous déjà eu l'impression que l'on essaie de vous tromper? Expliquez.

⟪ VOCABULAIRE ⟫

A. Cognates: French words that end in *-ion* are generally the same as the English equivalent and are feminine. Say the French word for each of the following English words.

1. portion	6. operation
2. nation	7. composition
3. conversation	8. admiration
4. action	9. election
5. direction	10. invitation

B. Adverbs can often be formed by adding *-ment* to the feminine form of the adjective. Write the feminine form and the adverb for each of these French adjectives.

MODÈLE: naturel *naturelle* *naturellement*

1. final	5. personnel
2. général	6. sûr
3. réel	7. agréable
4. cruel	8. grand

C. Antonyms: Match the words with opposite meanings in the two columns.

A	B
1. entrer	**a.** minuscule
2. prendre	**b.** debout
3. avant	**c.** sortir
4. remarquer	**d.** ignorer
5. devant	**e.** derrière
6. énorme	**f.** donner
7. excellent	**g.** après
8. assis	**h.** mauvais

◖ VERBES ◗

A. Complete the sentences with the present tense of *être, avoir,* or *vouloir.*

1. Hélène _____ près de la porte.
2. Les clients _____ de grosses portions de viande.
3. Vous _____ très faim.
4. Ils _____ soif.
5. Vous _____ grand pour votre âge.
6. Nous _____ du poisson pour déjeuner.
7. Quel âge _____ -tu?
8. Je _____ sortir.

B. Complete the sentences with the correct form of the verb in parentheses.

1. Tu _____ toujours malade.	*(être)*
2. J' _____ trois sœurs.	*(avoir)*
3. Que _____ -vous boire?	*(vouloir)*
4. Les livres _____ près des cahiers.	*(être)*
5. Marie et moi, nous _____ soif.	*(avoir)*
6. Tu _____ de l'eau?	*(vouloir)*
7. _____ -tu des frites avec le bifteck?	*(vouloir)*
8. Ils _____ raison.	*(avoir)*
9. Les chats _____ du lait.	*(vouloir)*
10. De quelle nationalité _____ -il?	*(être)*

9

◖ STRUCTURE ◗

Form complete sentences using the words in the order given. Add any necessary words, such as *de, à, les, le, la, que,* etc.

MODÈLE: Je/voir/chien/devant/maison
Je vois le chien devant la maison.

1. Je/voir/monsieur/près de/table
2. Nicole/vouloir/eau minérale/parce que/avoir soif
3. Nous/passer/devant/grand/restaurant
4. Tu/avoir/faim de loup
5. Vous/manger/bifteck/et/pommes frites
6. Mes parents/s'asseoir/terrasse/restaurant

3.
Une question d'opinion

AVANT DE LIRE: *Quelle raison donnez-vous à votre professeur quand vous n'avez pas fait vos devoirs?*

Paul est un garçon très intelligent et poser des
questions est son passe-temps favori. Un dimanche
après-midi, Paul s'approche de° sa mère et dit:
    –Maman, qu'est-ce qui est mieux, une grande
5 voiture ou une petite?
    –Eh bien, Paul, c'est une question d'opinion.
Une petite voiture est facile à garer;° une grande
voiture est plus confortable pour voyager et aller
en vacances.

s'approche de comes
up to

garer to park

10   Paul la remercie° et retourne° jouer. Bientôt, il revient.

    —Maman, est-ce mieux de voyager° en train ou en avion?

    —Eh bien, Paul, c'est une question d'opinion,
15 répond à nouveau° la maman. Dans le train, tu peux regarder le paysage,° aller d'un wagon à l'autre, manger au wagon-restaurant,° et même° dormir dans un wagon-lit pendant que tu voyages. Mais lorsque tu voyages en avion, tu peux aller
20 d'une ville à une autre ou même d'un pays à un autre en très peu de temps parce que les avions voyagent à très grande vitesse.°

    —Maman, tu sais beaucoup de choses, dit Paul et il retourne jouer.

25   Avant de s'endormir, Paul a encore une question.°

    —Maman, vaut-il mieux° jouer au basket ou jouer aux échecs?°

    —Eh bien, Paul, c'est une question d'opinion.
30 Certains° jouent au basket parce qu'ils aiment courir,° sauter° et jeter le ballon. D'autres° préfèrent être assis devant un échiquier° et penser à leur prochain coup.°

    —Maman, tu es brillante, dit Paul en fermant
35 les yeux pour dormir.

    Le lendemain, au début du cours, le professeur, Sylvie, demande aux élèves leurs cahiers° avec leurs devoirs d'histoire. Paul lui dit que son cahier est à la maison.

40   —Tous les élèves doivent apporter leurs cahiers! répond Sylvie.

    —Eh bien, madame, c'est une question d'opinion, répond le garçon.

    —Paul, que veux-tu dire° quand tu dis "C'est
45 une question d'opinion?"

    —Eh bien, madame, dit Paul, l'élève qui fait ses devoirs devrait apporter son cahier. Mais si l'élève n'a pas fait ses devoirs, il vaut mieux qu'il laisse le cahier chez lui.

remercie thanks
retourne goes back

voyager to travel

à nouveau again
paysage landscape
wagon-restaurant dining car
même even

vitesse speed

encore une question one more question
vaut-il mieux is it better
échecs chess

Certains Some
courir to run
sauter to jump
D'autres Others
un échiquier chess board
coup move

cahiers notebooks

que veux-tu dire? what do you mean?

12

◁◁ AVEZ-VOUS COMPRIS? ◁◁

A. Indicate whether these statements are true or false. Write *V* for *vrai* and *F* for *faux*. If the statement is false, correct it to make it true.

1. ( ) Paul est un garçon très intelligent.
2. ( ) Le garçon ne remercie pas sa mère.
3. ( ) Quand on voyage en avion, on peut dormir dans le wagon-lit.
4. ( ) Les avions volent à grande vitesse.
5. ( ) Les joueurs d'échecs préfèrent courir.
6. ( ) Les basketteurs préfèrent sauter.
7. ( ) Le professeur dit que les élèves ne devraient pas emmener leurs cahiers à l'école.
8. ( ) Tout le monde aime être assis devant un échiquier.

B. Répondez à ces questions par une phrase complète en français.

1. Quel est l'un des passe-temps favori du garçon?
2. Quels sont les avantages d'une petite voiture?
3. D'après sa maman, quand Paul peut-il jouir du paysage?
4. Où les passagers dorment-ils lorsqu'ils voyagent en train?
5. Quel genre de choses un basketteur fait-il lorsqu'il joue?
6. Que fait Paul après que sa maman ait répondu à sa dernière question?
7. Qui est Sylvie? Que demande-t-elle?
8. Pourquoi Paul dit-il que c'est une question d'opinion?

C. Et vous?

1. Quel est l'une de vos distractions favorites?
2. Quel genre de voiture préférez-vous? Pourquoi?
3. Quel moyen de transport utilisez-vous lorsque vous partez en vacances?
4. Préférez-vous jouer au basket ou aux échecs? Pourquoi?
5. Avez-vous peur de voyager en avion? Pourquoi?
6. Où et avec qui partez-vous en vacances?
7. En quelle saison partez-vous en vacances?
8. Quel est votre endroit favori pour partir en vacances? Pourquoi?

◖◗ VOCABULAIRE ◖◗

A. Cognates: English words ending in *-or* or *-er* often have French cognates ending in *-eur (-euse)*. These words often refer to a person's occupation. Give the French translation for each of the following English words.

1. actor
2. dancer
3. doctor
4. director
5. professor

6. administrator
7. ambassador
8. regulator
9. porter
10. boxer

B. Antonyms: Match the words with opposite meanings in the two columns.

A	B
1. garçon	**a.** ouvrir
2. intelligent	**b.** réponse
3. finir	**c.** s'éloigner
4. s'approcher	**d.** difficile
5. facile	**e.** lenteur
6. vitesse	**f.** stupide
7. question	**g.** fille
8. fermer	**h.** commencer

◖◗ VERBES ◖◗

A. Complete these sentences with the appropriate form of the verb given in the model.

1. Nous *allons* à l'école tous les jours.
   Vous _____ chez vos grands-parents tous les dimanches.
   Ils _____ souvent au restaurant.
   Tu _____ étudier avec un camarade.
   Elle _____ au cinéma avec des amis.
   Je _____ chez le boulanger acheter du pain.

2. Tu *peux* venir chez moi aujourd'hui.
   Je ne _____ pas garer ma voiture dans ce petit espace.
   Vous _____ parler français.
   Ils _____ trouver les réponses dans le dictionnaire.
   Nous _____ le faire.
   Elle _____ danser.

14

3. Elle *vient* de partir.

Vous _____ au stade.

Nous _____ d'acheter une nouvelle maison.

Ils _____ en classe avec leurs devoirs.

Tu _____ d'arriver.

Je _____ du cinéma.

B. Complete each sentence with the correct form of the verb in parentheses.

    1. Les jeunes gens _____ au stade.   *(aller)*

    2. Alexandre _____ de jouer au football.   *(venir)*

    3. Les élèves _____ apporter leurs devoirs.   *(devoir)*

    4. Que _____ -tu dire?   *(vouloir)*

    5. _____ -tu avec les autres étudiants?   *(venir)*

    6. Il _____ mieux voyager en train.   *(valoir)*

    7. Je ne _____ pas envoyer la lettre.   *(aller)*

    8. _____ -ils s'amuser?   *(pouvoir)*

    9. Je _____ voir le match.   *(venir)*

  10. L'enfant _____ poser des questions.   *(pouvoir)*

☙ STRUCTURE ❧

Complete the sentences with the appropriate word from those given below. Make any necessary changes.

    1. Il _____ mieux faire ses devoirs avant d'aller en classe.

    2. Le professeur _____ aux questions.

    3. L'enfant trouve sa mère _____.

    4. Je ne sais pas ce que cela _____.

    5. En avion, on _____ voyager très vite.

    6. _____ de s'endormir, l'enfant lit avec sa maman.

    7. Il s'assied _____ la table.

    8. L'échiquier est _____ la table.

sur	avant	valoir	pouvoir
brillant	répondre	vouloir dire	devant

4.

La surprise

AVANT DE LIRE: *Aimez-vous les surprises ou préférez-vous toujours savoir ce qui se passe?*

La famille Durand-Dupont est enfin installée dans sa nouvelle maison. Les jeunes sont contents parce qu'ils ont beaucoup de place° pour jouer avec leurs nouveaux amis. Pourtant,° le père
5 semble un peu inquiet.° Après avoir acheté les nouveaux meubles,° il ne reste plus beaucoup d'argent° à la banque.

—Nous devons être prudents° avec nos dépenses, dit Robert à sa femme Josette.
10 —Ne t'inquiète pas, elle répond.

Quelques jours passent. Madame Durand-Dupont

beaucoup de place
lots of space
Pourtant Still
inquiet worried
meubles furniture
**il ne reste plus
beaucoup d'argent**
there's not much
money left
prudents careful

pense que bien qu'ils soient° un peu à court
d'argent,° elle devrait° organiser une fête pour
célébrer l'anniversaire de son mari. Robert le
15 mérite,° non seulement parce qu'il est un bon
mari et un bon père, mais aussi parce qu'il travaille
dur.° Comme elle est sûre que son mari ne veut
pas gaspiller° de l'argent pour une fête, Josette
demande à ses enfants de garder le secret pour
20 ne pas gâcher° la surprise.

Le jour de l'anniversaire de Robert, Josette
dit à son mari:

—Robert, quel dommage° que nous ne
puissions pas° célébrer ton anniversaire avec
25 une fête dans notre nouvelle maison!

—C'est mieux ainsi, Josette. Nous sommes à
court d'argent. La nouvelle maison est un
superbe cadeau, répond Robert.

Le soir, les invités° arrivent pour la
30 surprise-partie. Les enfants attendent° à la
fenêtre pour annoncer l'arrivée de leur père.
Au bout d'un moment, ils crient:°

—Maman, il arrive. Papa arrive.

Quand il voit la voiture de son père, le
35 petit Michel—qui n'a que trois ans—court à sa
rencontre et hurle:

—Papa! Papa! Aucun invité n'est caché dans
la maison pour ta fête!

bien qu'ils soient
   although they are
à court d'argent short
   of money
devrait should
mérite deserves
il travaille dur he
   works hard
gaspiller to waste

gâcher to spoil

quel dommage what
   a pity
ne puissions pas that
   we are not able to

invités guests

attendent wait

crient shout

ᏟᏟ AVEZ-VOUS COMPRIS? ᏬᏬ

A. Indicate whether these statements are true or false. Write *V* for
vrai and *F* for *faux*. If the statement is false, correct it to make
it true.

1. (   ) Les enfants de l'histoire sont contents dans leur
   nouvelle maison.

2. (   ) Les enfants ont de nouveaux amis.

3. (   ) Robert et Josette ont beaucoup d'argent à la banque
   après l'achat de leur maison.

4. (   ) Josette veut célébrer l'anniversaire de son mari.

5. (   ) Robert veut dépenser de l'argent pour une fête
   d'anniversaire.

6. ( ) Tous les enfants de la famille gardent le secret.
7. ( ) Les invités arrivent le soir.
8. ( ) Michel a trois ans.

B. Répondez à ces questions par une phrase complète en français.

1. Quel est le nom de famille du père de famille?
2. Pourquoi les enfants sont-ils heureux?
3. Maintenant qu'ils sont dans leur nouvelle maison, que veut faire le père?
4. Pour qui et pourquoi Josette veut-elle organiser une fête?
5. Que demande Josette aux enfants?
6. Où les invités arrivent-ils?
7. Pourquoi les invités viennent-ils?
8. Que font les enfants à la fenêtre?

C. Et vous?

1. Comment pensez-vous que Robert réagit aux paroles de Michel?
2. Comment et avec qui aimez-vous célébrer votre anniversaire?
3. Aimez-vous les surprise-parties? Pourquoi?
4. Si vous n'avez pas beaucoup d'argent, organiserez-vous une fête surprise pour votre ami(e)? Pourquoi?
5. Si vous organisez une soirée, combien d'amis invitez-vous? Quelles activités organisez-vous pour la soirée?
6. Pour y vivre avec votre famille, préférez-vous une vieille maison ou une neuve? Pourquoi?
7. Décrivez la maison que vous souhaitez acquérir un jour.
8. Pourquoi cette histoire est-elle drôle?

৩৩ VOCABULAIRE ৩৩

A. Word groups: French nouns ending in *-eur* often refer to a person's actions. These nouns are generally related to *-er* verbs. Give the verbs that are related to the following nouns and write a sentence using each of them.

MODÈLE: danseur *danser*

1. travailleur
2. visiteur
3. joueur
4. chanteur
5. donneur
6. nageur
7. acheteur
8. traiteur

B. Match the synonyms in the two columns.

A	B
1. beaucoup	**a.** interroger
2. inquiet	**b.** c'est regrettable
3. demander	**c.** présent
4. c'est dommage	**d.** guetter
5. cadeau	**e.** angoissé
6. voir	**f.** dissimuler
7. cacher	**g.** énormément
8. attendre	**h.** remarquer

C. Match the antonyms in the two columns.

A	B
1. beaucoup	**a.** ancien
2. prudent	**b.** trouver
3. la dépense	**c.** partir
4. demander	**d.** l'économie
5. s'inquiéter	**e.** peu
6. arriver	**f.** se calmer
7. nouveau	**g.** aventureux
8. cacher	**h.** répondre

⟪ VERBES ⟫

A. Complete each sentence with the appropriate form of the *-er* verb in parentheses.

1. L'enfant _____ dans le jardin. *(jouer)*
2. La dame _____ une fête pour son mari. *(organiser)*
3. Les invités _____ dans la soirée. *(arriver)*
4. Nous lui _____ l'arrivée de la lettre. *(annoncer)*
5. Vous _____ votre amie pour déjeuner. *(rencontrer)*
6. Tu _____ la réponse à ta question. *(demander)*
7. Pourquoi les enfants _____ -ils si fort? *(crier)*
8. Je _____ le secret. *(garder)*

B. Complete each sentence with the appropriate form of the verb in parentheses.

1. Les enfants _____ leur père.   *(attendre)*
2. Je ne vous _____ pas.   *(entendre)*
3. Le peintre _____ la toile.   *(tendre)*
4. Est-ce que vous _____ le paysage?   *(voir)*
5. Pour l'anniversaire de Sophie,
   il _____ une fête.   *(prévoir)*
6. Nous _____ pour lui faire une surprise. *(se cacher)*

❦ STRUCTURE ❧

Rewrite each sentence in the negative.

1. Un invité est caché dans la maison.
2. Il aime gaspiller de l'argent.
3. Ils sont contents dans leur nouvelle maison.
4. Mes parents organisent toujours une fête pour mon anniversaire.
5. Tous les enfants gardent le secret.
6. Mon frère fait ses devoirs tout seul.

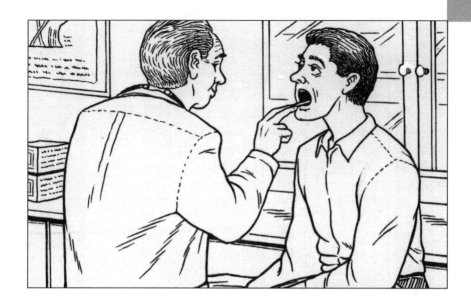

5.
Le charlatan

AVANT DE LIRE: *Comment est votre docteur?*
Est-ce que votre docteur ressemble à celui
de l'histoire? Pourquoi?

Le docteur Bernard a très peu de patients.
Un jour, son infirmière° lui annonce:

—Docteur Bernard, il y a un malade dans la
salle d'attente.°

5 —Donnez-lui le numéro dix et faites-le° entrer
dans une demi-heure, dit le médecin. De cette
façon,° il pensera que j'ai beaucoup de travail.

Enfin, le malade entre dans le cabinet du
docteur Bernard.

10 —Qu'est-ce qui ne va pas, monsieur?
demande le docteur.

infirmière nurse

salle d'attente
  waiting room
faites-le have him

De cette façon That way

Qu'est-ce qui ne va
  pas? What is wrong?

J'ai toujours mal à la tête° et je ne peux pas supporter° la lumière du soleil.° Je ne sens pas bien du tout.

15   –Tirez la langue,° s'il vous plaît.
(Le monsieur ouvre la bouche et tire la langue.)
Le médecin l'examine et dit:
–Vous n'avez pas besoin de médicaments.
Je crois que vous vous reposez trop. Je vous

20 conseille° de faire de longues promenades tous les jours, au lieu de° dormir l'après-midi.
    –Je ne peux pas, docteur. Je ne peux pas supporter la lumière du soleil.
    –Alors, promenez-vous le soir.

25   –Mais je marche déjà beaucoup.
    –Très bien, mais il faut encore marcher.
    –Mais, docteur, mon travail . . .
    –Si votre occupation ne vous permet pas de marcher autant,° changez de travail.

30   –Mais, docteur . . .
    –Si vous en savez plus que moi, pourquoi venez-vous me voir? A propos, que faites-vous? Etes-vous ingénieur, avocat,° vendeur, ouvrier,° marchand?

35   –Non, monsieur. Je suis gardien° au Louvre et je fais le tour du musée trois fois par nuit.
    –Tirez la langue encore un fois, s'il vous plaît.

mal à la tête headache
supporter to bear
lumière du soleil sunlight
Tirez la langue Stick out your tongue

conseille advise
au lieu de instead

autant so much

avocat lawyer
ouvrier laborer

gardien watchman

৬৫ AVEZ-VOUS COMPRIS? ৯৯

A. Choose the proper word to complete each sentence.

   1. Un charlatan est un médecin qui _____ les malades.
     a. attend
     b. trompe
     c. aide
     d. regarde

   2. Le malade attend _____ avant de voir le docteur.
     a. trente minutes
     b. une heure
     c. dix minutes
     d. toute la journée

3. Le monsieur a _____.
   a. chaud
   b. mal à la tête
   c. froid
   d. peur
4. Il n'aime pas _____.
   a. son travail
   b. la lumière du soleil
   c. les promenades
   d. les médicaments
5. Le médecin examine _____ du malade.
   a. la bouche
   b. la langue
   c. la main
   d. les poumons
6. Selon le médecin, le monsieur se repose trop _____.
   a. la nuit
   b. l'après-midi
   c. le matin
   d. le soir
7. Cet homme marche beaucoup la nuit parce qu'il est

   _____.
   a. artiste
   b. vendeur
   c. gardien
   d. marchand
8. Le charlatan est _____.
   a. sincère
   b. correct
   c. malhonnête
   d. malade

B. Répondez à ces questions par une phrase complète en français.
   1. Combien de patients le docteur Bernard a-t-il?
   2. Quel numéro l'infirmière donne-t-elle au malade?
   3. Pourquoi l'infirmière lui donne-t-elle le numéro dix?
   4. Est-ce que le patient va bien?
   5. Quel conseil lui donne le médecin?
   6. Le malade aime-t-il le soleil?
   7. Quelle est l'occupation du patient?
   8. Que demande le charlatan à la fin?

C. Et vous?

1. Est-ce que votre médecin a une grosse clientèle?
2. Prenez-vous un numéro chez le médecin? à la boulangerie?
3. Etes-vous en bonne santé?
4. Que faites-vous pour vous maintenir en forme?
5. Aimez-vous faire des promenades ou préférez-vous vous reposer?
6. Qu'est-ce que vous ne supportez pas?
7. Avez-vous confiance en votre médecin?

◖ VOCABULAIRE ◗

A. Find a word in the story that is related to the word given. Tell its meaning.

MODÈLE: le médicament   *le médecin* (medicine, doctor)

1. une infirmerie
2. la maladie
3. le dortoir
4. le conseil
5. le repos
6. une entrée
7. vendre
8. attendre
9. se promener
10. travailler

B. Match the synonyms from the two columns.

A	B
1. se reposer	a. marcher
2. trente minutes	b. le docteur
3. se promener	c. l'occupation
4. le travail	d. dormir
5. le médecin	e. une demi-heure

C. Match the antonyms from the two columns

A	B
1. peu de	a. la lune
2. le matin	b. ignorer
3. malade	c. bien portant
4. enfin	d. le soir
5. le soleil	e. beaucoup de
6. savoir	f. d'abord

❦ VERBES ❧

A. Supply the correct form of the reflexive verbs in parentheses.

1. Il _____ très bien. *(se sentir)*
2. Je _____ tous les après-midi. *(se reposer)*
3. Nous _____ à dix heures le soir. *(se coucher)*
4. Tu _____ toujours à sept
   heures du matin. *(se lever)*
5. Mes amis _____ tous les après-midi
   dans le parc. *(se promener)*
6. Est-ce que vous _____ bien? *(s'amuser)*
7. La petite fille _____ toute seule. *(s'habiller)*
8. Vous _____ dans la salle d'attente. *(s'asseoir)*

B. Complete the sentences with the appropriate form of the verb
indicated.

1. Il _____ tout savoir. *(croire)*
2. Vous _____ tout. *(ne pas savoir)*
3. Est-ce que tu _____ tes devoirs avant
   d'aller au cours? *(faire)*
4. Je _____ que le docteur a raison. *(croire)*
5. Nous _____ de la gymnastique tous
   les jours. *(faire)*
6. Vous _____ une promenade dans
   le jardin. *(faire)*
7. Il _____ qu'il se trompe. *(savoir)*
8. Mon père et ma mère _____ en
   ce docteur. *(croire)*

❧ STRUCTURE ❧

Transform the sentences into commands.

MODÈLE: Vous lui dites bonjour.
Dites-lui *bonjour*.

1. Vous le faites entrer.

   _____

2. Vous tirez la sonnette.

   _____

3. Tu lui donnes le livre.

   _____

4. Vous lui donnez un médicament.

   _____

5. Tu fais tes devoirs.

   _____

6. Tu y vas.

   _____

6.
Un garçon terrible

AVANT DE LIRE: *Est-ce que vous connaissez des gens qui sont difficiles à vivre?° Pensez-vous qu'il soit facile de traiter° avec ce genre de personne?*

difficiles à vivre difficult to put up with
traiter to deal with

Le chien commence à hurler parce que Jacques tire° la queue° du pauvre animal.

—Jacques, crie sa mère, ne tourmente pas le chien! Ne lui tire pas la queue.

5   —Le chien fait beaucoup de bruit,° mais je ne lui tire pas la queue, répond le méchant garçon. Je la tiens bon, mais c'est lui qui tire.

tire pulls
la queue tail

bruit noise

27

La famille de Jacques habite le village de
Saint-Pierre à la Martinique. Le village est agité
10 parce que le volcan,° la montagne Pelée, fume   **volcan** volcano
beaucoup. Les parents du garçon ont peur du
volcan parce qu'il peut détruire° le village. Ils   **détruire** to destroy
décident d'envoyer l'enfant chez ses grands-
parents qui habitent Paris. Ils vont à l'aréoport.
15   Pendant le voyage, Jacques se tient° mal   **se tient** behaves
comme toujours. Les passagers ne peuvent ni se
reposer ni dormir. Le garçon court d'un bout à
l'autre° de l'avion et il crie comme un fou.°   **d'un bout à l'autre** from
L'hôtesse de l'air est très jeune et polie mais   one end to the other
20 elle est irritée° par ce garçon désagréable. Enfin, **un fou** crazy person
elle lui dit: **irritée** angry
        —Sois sage et reste assis!
    Mais l'enfant continue à courir et à faire du
bruit.
25   Arrivés à Paris, l'hôtesse de l'air et tous les
passagers sont soulagés car ils ne vont plus voir
Jacques.
        Les grands-parents sont très contents de
voir leur petit-fils. Après deux jours, les parents
30 de Jacques reçoivent un télégramme des
grands-parents: "Nous vous renvoyons Jacques;
envoyez-nous la montagne Pelée."

≪◎ AVEZ-VOUS COMPRIS? ◎≫

A. Complete each sentence with the appropriate expression.

1. Le chien hurle parce que
    a. Jacques va chez ses grands-parents.
    b. le garçon lui tire la queue.
    c. la mère fait du bruit.
    d. le petit crie.
2. Les parents de Jacques habitent
    a. la montagne Pelée.
    b. une grande ville.
    c. la Martinique.
    d. la France.

3. Les passagers sont fâchés parce que Jacques
   a. se tient bien.
   b. dit que tout le monde est fou.
   c. reste assis.
   d. fait beaucoup de bruit.
4. L'hôtesse de l'air trouve que Jacques est
   a. sage.
   b. méchant.
   c. fâché.
   d. poli.
5. Les grands-parents envoient un télégramme parce qu'ils
   a. préfèrent le volcan à leur petit-fils.
   b. sont contents de voir Jacques.
   c. veulent remercier le ciel pour leur petit-fils.
   d. se fâchent contre l'hôtesse de l'air.

B. Répondez à ces questions par une phrase complète en français.
   1. Comment s'appelle le garçon?
   2. Où habite la famille de cet enfant?
   3. Jacques est-il gentil avec le chien?
   4. Les grands-parents habitent-ils dans la même ville que leurs enfants?
   5. Où va Jacques?
   6. Comment Jacques voyage-t-il?
   7. Comment se comporte-t-il durant le voyage?
   8. Que dit l'hôtesse de l'air ?
   9. Les grands-parents sont-ils contents de voir leur petit-fils?
   10. Quel est le texte du télégramme?

C. Et vous?
   1. Avez-vous un animal? Lequel?
   2. Aimez-vous voyager avec des enfants?
   3. Comment tolérez-vous des enfants mal élevés?
   4. Que savez-vous de la Martinique?

⟨⟨ VOCABULAIRE ⟩⟩

Match the antonyms from the two columns.

A	B
1. commencer	**a.** jamais
2. tourmenter	**b.** s'arrêter
3. tenir	**c.** se réveiller
4. détruire	**d.** recevoir
5. envoyer	**e.** finir
6. toujours	**f.** construire
7. fâché	**g.** content
8. dormir	**h.** calmer
9. continuer	**i.** lâcher

⟨⟨ VERBES ⟩⟩

A. Complete the sentences with the correct form of the verb indicated.

1. Les enfants _____ beaucoup de bruit. *(faire)*

2. Je ne _____ pas venir aujourd'hui. *(pouvoir)*

3. Tu ne _____ pas partir avec un si mauvais temps. *(pouvoir)*

4. Nous _____ de la gymnastique pour nous maintenir en forme. *(faire)*

5. Vous _____ de la peinture en plein air. *(faire)*

6. Elle _____ voir le paysage de la fenêtre. *(pouvoir)*

B. Complete the following sentence with the appropriate form of the *passé composé* of the verbs indicated in parentheses.

1. Le volcan _____ en 1932. *(erupter)*

2. Les parents _____ leur fils chez ses grands-parents. *(envoyer)*

3. L'enfant _____ la queue du chien. *(tirer)*

4. La mère _____. *(crier)*

5. Le chien _____ à hurler. *(commencer)*

6. Le volcan _____ beaucoup. *(fumer)*

✎ STRUCTURE ✎

A. Replace the pronoun in parentheses by a stress pronoun to complete the sentence.

MODÈLE: C'est (il) qui tire.
   C'est *lui* qui tire.

1. C'est (je) _____ qui fais la vaisselle.
2. C'est (tu) _____ qui parles toujours.
3. C'est (nous) _____ qui partons.
4. C'est (elles) _____ qui arrivent.
5. C'est (ils) _____ qui partent.
6. C'est (elle) _____ qui est la plus jolie.
7. C'est (il) _____ qui est le plus gentil.
8. C'est (vous) _____ qui faites le plus de bruit.

B. Complete the sentences with the appropriate possessive adjective.

1. Les grands-parents sont contents de voir _____ petit-fils.
2. Je te donne _____ livre.
3. Il fait _____ devoirs tous les jours.
4. Nous apprenons _____ leçons avant les examens.
5. J'aime la robe que vous portez. J'aime _____ robe.
6. Tu aimes _____ père et _____ mère.

7.
La parole est d'argent, mais le silence est d'or

AVANT DE LIRE: *Pensez-vous qu'il soit important de faire une première bonne impression? Pourquoi?*

Alexandre Robin visite un petit village du Pays basque dans le sud de la France pour la fête du quinze août. L'après-midi, les hommes jouent à la pelote basque.° Le soir, ils dansent le

5   fandango. C'est une danse énergique qui montre que les hommes sont toujours amis après leur

pelote basque
  ball game similar to
  softball

32

partie.° Ils portent une blouse et un pantalon
blancs, le béret basque, des espadrilles° et une
large ceinture de couleur.

10   Alexandre remarque une belle jeune fille qui
regarde les danseurs. Il s'approche d'elle et lui dit:
    —Mademoiselle, permettez-moi de me présenter.°
Je m'appelle Alexandre Robin; je suis étudiant à
l'université de Bordeaux. Voulez-vous danser
15 avec moi?

    Parce qu'il est très beau et qu'il parle bien, elle
accepte son invitation. Pendant la danse Alexandre
essaie de faire bonne impression sur elle. Il exagère
en parlant de ses études (inventées), de sa riche
20 famille (seulement en enfants), de ses compétences
athlétiques (il joue aux cartes), et de ses belles
amies (qui existent dans son imagination).

    La jeune fille, qui est très intelligente, sait tout
de suite qu'il ne dit pas la vérité.° Elle décide de
25 ne pas lui dire qu'elle le trouve menteur.°

    A la fin de la fête, Alexandre lui demande:
    —Puis-je vous accompagner chez vous?
    —Non, merci, ce n'est pas nécessaire, mon
chauffeur m'attend.
30   —Puis-je vous téléphoner?
    —Mais oui, monsieur.
    —Quel est votre numéro de téléphone?
    —Il se trouve dans l'annuaire° comme tous les
numéros.
35   —Comment vous appelez-vous, mademoiselle?
    —Vous trouverez mon nom aussi dans
l'annuaire avec le numéro de téléphone.
    Et sur ces mots, elle s'en va.°

partie game
espadrilles canvas shoes

me présenter to
    introduce myself

vérité truth
menteur liar

annuaire phone book

elle s'en va she
    goes away

◖ AVEZ-VOUS COMPRIS? ◗

A. Choose the one completion that is NOT true for the story.

   1. Pour célébrer la fête du quinze août
      a. on danse.
      b. on joue à la pelote.
      c. on porte un costume typique.
      d. on invente des histoires.

33

2. Alexandre est
   a. beau.
   b. poli.
   c. honnête.
   d. étudiant.
3. En dansant, Alexandre parle
   a. des sports.
   b. de la fête.
   c. des jeunes filles.
   d. de ses parents.
4. Après la fête, la jeune fille
   a. rentre seule.
   b. ne donne pas son numéro de téléphone.
   c. ne veut pas revoir Alexandre.
   d. donne son nom à Alexandre.

B. Répondez à ces questions par une phrase complète en français.
   1. Comment s'appelle le jeune homme?
   2. Que visite-t-il?
   3. Que remarque-t-il?
   4. Comment se présente-t-il?
   5. Avec qui danse-t-il?
   6. La jeune fille croit-elle ce qu'Alexandre dit?
   7. Accepte-t-elle qu'il la raccompagne?
   8. Lui donne-t-elle son numéro de téléphone?

C. Et vous?
   1. Croyez-vous ce que vous raconte quelqu'un que vous rencontrez pour la première fois?
   2. Donnez-vous toujours votre numéro de téléphone lorsqu'on vous le demande?
   3. Que répondez-vous si vous ne voulez pas donner votre numéro de téléphone?
   4. Que pensez-vous de la réponse de la jeune fille?

❧ VOCABULAIRE ☙

A. Match the antonyms from the two columns.

A		B	
1.	sud	**a.**	pauvre
2.	énergique	**b.**	jamais
3.	montrer	**c.**	refuser
4.	toujours	**d.**	interdire
5.	permettre	**e.**	laid
6.	beau	**f.**	cacher
7.	accepter	**g.**	léthargique
8.	riche	**h.**	se taire
9.	parler	**i.**	nord

B. Telephone numbers: In French you say phone numbers by groups of two numbers. Say the following French phone numbers aloud.

1. 46 60 17 90   **4.** 56 32 49 72
2. 38 72 30 54   **5.** 67 29 54 43
3. 46 28 01 10   **6.** 23 12 78 03

❧ VERBES ☙

A. Reflexive verbs: Complete the sentences with the appropriate form of the verb in parentheses.

1. Comment _____? *(s'appeler; tu)*

2. Où _____ le numéro de téléphone? *(se trouver)*

3. A quelle heure _____ -t-il le matin? *(se lever)*

4. Les enfants _____ les dents avant de se coucher. *(se laver)*

5. Je ne _____ pas à ce qu'il vienne. *(s'attendre)*

6. Alexandre _____. *(se vanter)*

7. Nous _____ bien à la fête. *(s'amuser)*

8. Vous ne _____ pas bien. *(se sentir)*

35

B. Rewrite the sentences in the negative.

MODÈLE: Il dit la vérité.
Il ne dit pas la vérité.

1. Elle lui donne son numéro de téléphone.
2. Je peux vous accompagner.
3. Nous vous permettons de partir.
4. Ils sont venus.
5. Vous parlez français.
6. Tu crois ce qu'il dit.

◖◗ STRUCTURE ◖◗

Complete the sentences with the correct form of the adjective given in parentheses.

1. La jeune fille est _____.   *(intelligent)*
2. Tu portes une _____ robe.   *(beau)*
3. Il parle de ses _____ amies.   *(beau)*
4. Elle croit que les enfants sont _____.   *(menteur)*
5. C'est un garçon _____.   *(énergique)*
6. Ils portent une veste et des
   pantalons _____.   *(vert)*
7. Les filles portent une _____ ceinture et
   les garçons un _____ ceinturon.   *(large)/ (large)*

36

8.
Le professeur distrait°

distrait absent-minded

AVANT DE LIRE: *Prêtez-vous beaucoup
d'attention à votre façon de vous habiller?*

Vincent est quelqu'un° de très bien. Il
est agréable,° amical,° et c'est un professeur
formidable. Ses élèves l'admirent parce qu'il est
équitable,° a un bon sens de l'humour et connaît
parfaitement le sujet qu'il enseigne. Néanmoins,°
il y a quelque chose à son sujet que ses élèves
ne comprennent pas. Il y a toujours un élément
de ses vêtements qui n'est pas assorti° avec le
reste. Par exemple, il porte une chemise jaune
avec des pantalons bleus et une veste rouge.

quelqu'un somebody
agréable pleasant
amical friendly
équitable fair
Néanmoins Nevertheless

assorti matched

5

10

D'autres fois, ses vêtements rappellent° une fête, telle que° Noël, parce qu'il porte une chemise rouge avec une cravate verte. Il semble que ce professeur ne se soucie° pas de sa mise.°

15   Un jour après les cours, Nicole s'approche du° professeur et lui demande la permission de lui poser une question. D'abord,° elle craint que le professeur se mette en colère,° mais Vincent lui affirme° que non.

20   —Que voulez-vous savoir? dit Vincent.

    Alors Nicole lui demande combien de paires de chaussures il possède.°

    —Euh . . . je ne sais pas, répond le professeur.

    —Avez-vous donné vos chaussures au

25 cordonnier° la semaine dernière? continue Nicole.

    —Je ne pense pas, répond encore le professeur.

    —Avez-vous un problème avec vos pieds? demande Nicole.

    —Pas que je sache.°

30   —Alors, monsieur . . . Pourquoi portez-vous une chaussure de cuir à un pied et une chaussure de tennis à l'autre depuis jeudi dernier?

    Vincent regarde ses pieds, réfléchit un instant, et sans sourciller° répond:

35   —Elles sont toutes les deux noires, et de plus° elles sont de première qualité.

rappellent reminds
telle que such as

se soucie cares
mise appearance
s'approche goes up to

D'abord At first
se mette en colère would get angry
affirme assures

possède owns

cordonnier shoemaker

Pas que je sache. Not that I know.

sans sourciller undisturbed
de plus furthermore

◖◖ AVEZ-VOUS COMPRIS? ◗◗

A. Répondez à ces questions par une phrase complète en français.

    1. Pourquoi les étudiants admirent-ils Vincent?

    2 Quel problème Vincent a-t-il avec ses vêtements?

    3. Qui s'approche de Vincent?

    4. Quelle est l'attitude de Vincent vis-à-vis de l'étudiante?

    5. Vincent sait-il combien de paires de chaussures il possède?

    6. Quel genre de chaussures Vincent porte-t-il?

    7. Pourquoi est-ce que cela ne dérange pas Vincent de porter deux chaussures différentes?

    8. Qu'est-ce qui vous fait penser que le professeur est distrait?

B. Complete each numbered statement with the proper expression from the second list.

A	B
1. Vincent est	**a.** Vincent porte une chemise rouge avec une cravate verte.
2. L'étudiant dit	
3. Le professeur porte	**b.** sont de première qualité.
4. Nicole s'approche de Vincent	**c.** pour lui poser des questions sur ses chaussures.
5. Le professeur n'a qu'une	**d.** avec sa façon de s'habiller.
6. L'étudiant veut savoir	**e.** que Vincent connaît son sujet.
7. Vincent a un problème	**f.** Vincent regarde ses chaussures.
8. Les étudiants ne comprennent pas pourquoi	**g.** une chemise jaune avec des pantalons bleus.
	h. professeur.
9. Les chaussures du professeur	**i.** chaussure de cuir.
10. Sans sourciller,	**j.** si le professeur a un problème avec ses pieds.

C. Et vous?

1. Est-ce que vous pensez que vous êtes quelqu'un de sympathique?
2. Comment vous habillez-vous pour aller en classe?
3. Quel genre de chaussures préférez-vous? Pourquoi?
4. Pourquoi pensez-vous que certains étudiants sont nerveux lorsqu'ils parlent à leur professeur?
5. Quelle couleur préférez-vous pour vos vêtements? Pourquoi?
6. Est-ce que la façon dont s'habillent vos professeurs vous importe? Pourquoi?
7. Qu'est-ce qui est plus important pour vous, la qualité ou le prix des vêtements? Pourquoi?
8. Comment réagissez-vous lorsque vous parlez à une personne distraite?

ꙮ VOCABULAIRE ꙮ

A. Adjectives: Adding *dé-* to an adjective can create a word that has an opposite meaning. For example, *classé/déclassé*. Form the opposites of the following words. Verify their meanings and write a sentence with each of them.

1. agréable
2. muni
3. pourvu
4. fait
5. bouché
6. bridé

B. Match the antonyms in the two columns.

A	B
1. admirer	a. nier
2. amical	b. dernier
3. équitable	c. arrêter
4. assortir	d. injuste
5. comprendre	e. mépriser
6. affirmer	f. hostile
7. continuer	g. ignorer
8. premier	h. contraster

ꙮ VERBES ꙮ

A. Complete the sentences with the appropriate form of *connaître* or *savoir*.

1. Il _____ plusieurs langues.
2. Ils _____ tout faire.
3. Vous croyez tout _____.
4. Tu ne _____ pas ce dont tu parles.
5. Est-ce que nous _____ vos amis?
6. Je _____ les parents de ce jeune homme.
7. Est-ce que vous _____ à quelle heure part le train?
8. Ils ne _____ pas cette ville.

40

B. Complete the sentences with the appropriate form of *répondre, comprendre,* or *craindre.*

1. Est-ce que vous _____ toujours aux lettres?
2. Je ne _____ pas ce qu'il dit.
3. Les élèves _____ le professeur.
4. Tu _____ à la question de ton père.
5. Ils ne _____ pas la question.
6. Nous _____ de sortir lorsqu'il y a un orage.

❦ STRUCTURE ❧

Complete the sentences with the appropriate relative pronouns.

1. Je ne connais pas la personne _____ entre.
2. Le sujet _____ il enseigne est très intéressant.
3. Le pantalon _____ il porte n'est pas assorti à sa chemise.
4. Savez-vous _____ vous allez?
5. Vous ne savez pas ce _____ vous parlez.

9.
Bon appétit!

AVANT DE LIRE: *Pensez-vous qu'il soit important de comprendre la langue du pays que vous visitez? Pourquoi?*

Monsieur Jones se rend° en France pour la première fois.° Il va y séjourner° un mois. Il passe la première semaine de ses vacances dans un hôtel à Paris tout près du jardin° des Tuileries.

5 Ce lundi, il se lève de bonne heure pour flâner° dans les petites rues et sur les grands boulevards de cette belle ville. Il visite les musées, les grands magasins, les boutiques,° les théâtres, les cafés, les églises et tous les autres bâtiments.° L'après-midi,

10 il trouve une chaise dans le jardin et il s'amuse en regardant les enfants qui jouent avec leurs bateaux dans le bassin.° Vers huit heures, il va

se rend goes to

fois time
séjourner to stay in one place
jardin garden
flâner to stroll

boutiques small shops
bâtiments buildings

bassin pool of water

42

dîner au restaurant de l'hôtel. Il se met à table° avec un monsieur distingué. Le monsieur se lève et

15 dit à Monsieur Jones:

–Bon appétit!

Monsieur Jones, qui ne parle pas le français, répond:

–Sam Jones!

Tous les deux dînent en silence parce que le

20 Français ne parle pas anglais.

Le lendemain, Monsieur Jones s'assied à la même table.

–Bon appétit, dit le Français.

Et Monsieur Jones répond:

25 –Sam Jones!

Après le repas, l'Américain rencontre° un ami qui parle bien le français et lui raconte° cette histoire. Son ami explique que "Bon appétit" n'est pas le nom du monsieur. C'est une formule de

30 politesse qui veut dire° "je vous souhaite° un repas délicieux." Monsieur Jones est ravi° de l'apprendre.

Le troisième jour, Sam Jones se met à table à huit heures moins le quart. En voyant le monsieur distingué, Monsieur Jones se lève tout de suite° et

35 dit amicalement:°

–Bon appétit!

En entendant ces mots, le monsieur répond avec un grand sourire:

–Sam Jones!

Il se met à table He sits down to eat

rencontre meets
raconte tells

veut dire means
souhaite wishes
ravi delighted

tout de suite immediately
amicalement in a friendly way

◖◉ AVEZ-VOUS COMPRIS? ◉◗

A. Indicate whether these statements are true or false. Write *V* for *vrai* and *F* for *faux*. If the statement is false, correct it to make it true.

1. ( ) Monsieur Jones visite la France une fois par mois.

2. ( ) Il aime flâner dans les rues de Paris.

3. ( ) Il se repose dans le jardin avant de dîner.

4. ( ) Le monsieur à sa table dit que les repas à l'hôtel sont excellents.

5. ( ) Monsieur Jones pense que le Français s'appelle Monsieur Bonappétit.

6. ( ) Un ami de Monsieur Jones lui dit que "Bon appétit" est une formule de politesse.

7. ( ) Monsieur Jones hésite à employer cette nouvelle expression.

8. ( ) Le monsieur français ne sait pas ce que "Sam Jones" veut dire.

B. Répondez à ces questions par une phrase complète en français.

1. D'où vient Monsieur Jones? de France ou des Etats-Unis?
2. Quelle ville visite-t-il d'abord?
3. Où habite-t-il à Paris?
4. Où dîne-t-il?
5. Qui est assis à sa table?
6. Que dit le Français à Monsieur Jones?
7. Qui parle deux langues?
8. Que répond le monsieur quand Monsieur Jones lui dit "Bon appétit"?

C. Et vous?

1. Quel pays habitez-vous?
2. Quelle ville habitez-vous?
3. Aimez-vous passer vos vacances dans un hôtel ou chez des amis?
4. Avec qui déjeunez-vous à l'école?
5. Combien de personnes sont assises à table avec vous?
6. Que disent vos amis avant de manger?
7. Quelles langues parlez-vous?
8. Quelles autres formules de politesse connaissez-vous en français?

◖ VOCABULAIRE ◗

A. Word groups: The letters *im-* or *in-* at the beginning of a French word indicate the root word takes on a negative meaning and are similar to *un-* or *im-* in English. Find the root word in the following words and give the meaning of both forms.

MODÈLE: impoli   *poli* (impolite, polite)

1. impossible
2. immoral
3. immortel
4. impatient
5. inactif

6. improbable
7. imprudent
8. injuste
9. indiscrète
10. incroyable

B. Find synonyms from the story for these words or phrases.

1. quatre semaines
2. tôt
3. marcher
4. le jour suivant
5. un conte
6. manger

C. Find antonyms from the story for these words or phrases.

1. les jours de travail
2. la dernière
3. se coucher
4. le bruit
5. triste
6. se presser

ᕦ VERBES ᕤ

A. Change the tense of the verbs to the immediate future.

MODÈLE: Je mange au restaurant.
  Je vais manger au restaurant.

1. Il passe une semaine de vacances à Paris.
2. Nous visitons les musées de la ville.
3. Ils dînent au restaurant.
4. Vous partez en vacances.
5. Quand commencez-vous ce travail?
6. Tu joues du piano cet après-midi.

B. Complete each sentence with *en* and the present participle of the verb in parentheses.

MODÈLE: Il lit son journal _____.   *(déjeuner)*
  Il lit son journal *en déjeunant.*

1. _____, j'ai décidé d'aller faire une
   promenade.   *(se lever)*
2. _____ à l'école, j'ai rencontré un ami. *(aller)*
3. Il marchait _____.   *(chanter)*
4. _____ la photo, il a reconnu ses amis.   *(regarder)*
5. Nous marchions tout _____.   *(parler)*
6. _____ je me suis fait mal au pied.   *(danser)*

45

◖❧ STRUCTURE ❧◗

A. A quelle heure? Answer these questions using the times indicated in parentheses.

    1. A quelle heure dînez-vous? _____ (6:30 P.M.)

    2. A quelle heure dîne-t-on en France? _____ (7:30 P.M.)

    3. A quelle heure allez-vous en classe? _____ (9:00 A.M.)

    4. A quelle heure regardez-vous les nouvelles? _____
       (6:00 P.M.)

    5. A quelle heure vous couchez-vous? _____ (10:00 P.M.)

    6. Je rentre à la maison à _____ (5:55 P.M.).

    7. Je prends l'autobus à _____ (17:20).

    8. Ma pause déjeuner *(lunch break)* est à _____
       (12:10 P.M.).

    9. Mon cours de français est à _____ (9:30) tous les matins.

   10. Je fixe mon rendez-vous *(appointment)* à _____
       (1:20 P.M.).

   11. Je vais au cinéma à _____ (5:45 P.M.).

B. Complete the sentences with the appropriate preposition given below. You will use two of the prepositions twice.

    1. Mon père va _____ Italie.

    2. L'hôtel est _____ de l'église.

    3. Elle s'amuse à marcher _____ les rues.

    4. Ils dînent _____ silence.

    5. Quelquefois, nous répondons _____ comprendre.

    6. Il me l'explique _____ souriant.

    7. Je vais passer mes vacances _____ un petit hôtel.

    8. Qui vient _____ nous?

    9. _____ sa promenade, il boit un café.

après	avec	dans	en	près	sans

10.
Je ne comprends pas

AVANT DE LIRE: *Que faites-vous lorsque vous ne comprenez pas ce que quelqu'un vous dit?*

Un Américain très riche est fatigué de travailler. Il vient de vendre° son entreprise. Un de ses amis l'invite à lui rendre visite° en France. L'Américain va à l'aéroport, achète un billet° d'avion et arrive
5 à Lyon après un vol de neuf heures. Il admire la cathédrale et les autres vieux bâtiments de la ville.

Le lendemain, il voit des gens qui sortent d'une église. Qu'est-ce qui se passe?° C'est un mariage. Evidemment, il veut savoir qui vient de se marier.
10 En anglais, il demande le nom du nouveau marié à un passant. Le Français ne comprend pas. Il hausse les épaules° et répond:

–Monsieur, je ne comprends pas.

vient de vendre has just sold
rendre visite pay a visit
billet ticket

Qu'est-ce qui se passe? What's happening?

hausse les épaules shrugs his shoulders

47

L'Américain pense que le marié s'appelle
15 Jene Comprenpas.

      Vers midi, il rencontre un autre groupe de gens
dans la rue. Un homme est tombé° par terre, le   **tombé** fallen
visage° couvert de sang,° victime d'un accident.   **visage** face
      –Qui est cet homme? demande-t-il en anglais.   **sang** blood
20   Et on lui donne la même réponse:
      –Monsieur, je ne comprends pas.
      L'Américain est attristé° et pense: **attristé** saddened
      –Le pauvre! Il est marié depuis si peu de
temps et maintenant il meurt.
25   L'après-midi, il remarque un cortège funèbre.°   **cortège funèbre**
Il s'approche d'une dame qui pleure amèrement°   funeral procession
et pose la même question. La dame répond sans   **amèrement** bitterly
cesser de pleurer.
      –Mon . . . sieur . . . , je . . . ne . . . com . . .
30 prends . . . pas.
      L'Américain étonné s'écrie:
      –Je ne peux pas croire cela! Le pauvre
Monsieur Jene Comprenpas, marié, victime d'un
accident et enterré, tout cela en un seul jour.

ꙮ AVEZ-VOUS COMPRIS? ꙮ

A. Complete the numbered sentences to summarize the story.

A	B
1. Un homme d'affaires américain	**a.** s'est marié et est mort le même jour.
2. Il voyage à Lyon	**b.** la victime d'un accident.
3. Le lendemain il voit	**c.** vient de se marier.
4. Quand il demande comment s'appelle le marié	**d.** on répète le nom: –Je ne comprends pas.
5. Il croit que M. Jene Comprenpas	**e.** un mariage devant une église.
6. A midi, il voit	**f.** que c'est le jeune marié.
7. Il est triste à la pensée	**g.** quitte son travail et va en France.
8. Quand il demande le nom du mort	**h.** on répond: –Je ne comprends pas.
9. Il croit que M. Jene Comprenpas	**i.** en avion.

B. Répondez à ces questions par une phrase complète en français.

1. Pourquoi l'Américain vend-il son entreprise?
2. Comment va-t-il en France?
3. Où voit-il le mariage?
4. Pourquoi lui répond-on toujours "Je ne comprends pas"?
5. Que veut dire "Je ne comprends pas" selon l'Américain?
6. Pourquoi devient-il triste en voyant un accident?
7. Que fait la dame dans le cortège funèbre?
8. Selon l'Américain, qu'est-ce qui se passe en un seul jour?

C. Et vous?

1. Comment préférez-vous voyager? En avion ou en train?
2. Comment allez-vous à Miami? En voiture, en autobus, en avion ou en train?
3. Combien de temps faut-il pour le voyage?
4. Y a-t-il beaucoup d'accidents dans les rues de votre ville?
5. Pleurez-vous quand vous avez de mauvaises notes?
6. Qu'est-ce qui vous fait pleurer?

◖❦ VOCABULAIRE ❧◗

A. Find a verb in the story that is related to each noun given below. Give the infinitive of the verb and tell what both words mean.

1. le travail
2. l'invitation
3. l'achat
4. le mort
5. le marié
6. les cris

B. Match the synonyms from the two columns.

A	B
1. l'église	**a.** le sol
2. la terre	**b.** s'arrêter
3. le visage	**c.** avoir sommeil
4. cesser	**d.** la cathédrale
5. être fatigué	**e.** la figure

C. Find an adjective that has the same root as each noun given below and tell the meanings of both words.

1. la beauté
2. la richesse
3. la pauvreté
4. la tristesse
5. la grandeur
6. la vieillesse
7. la bêtise
8. le contentement

✣ VERBES ✣

A. Change each verb into the immediate past by using *venir de* + infinitive.

1. Je vends ma voiture.
2. Nous voyons le cortège.
3. Vous mangez votre repas.
4. Il part.
5. Ils vont au restaurant.
6. Tu fermes la porte.

B. Change each verb into the immediate past or the future by using *venir de* + infinitive or *aller* + infinitive.

1. Je dîne chez moi.
2. Nous arrivons à Paris.
3. Ils tombent dans le jardin.
4. Tu parles avec le professeur.
5. Jean voit l'accident.
6. Regardez-vous l'émission de télévision?
7. Les étudiants terminent leur classe.
8. La dame s'approche de l'agent.

✣ STRUCTURE ✣

A. Match each adjective in column A with the appropriate place name in column B.

A	B
1. parisien	a. Etats-Unis
2. espagnol	b. New York
3. américain	c. Afrique
4. québécois	d. Colombie
5. new-yorkais	e. Amérique du Sud
6. africain	f. Espagne
7. sud-américain	g. Québec
8. colombien	h. Paris

B. Comment s'appellent les habitants . . .

    1. du Canada _____

    2. d'Italie _____

    3. d'Allemagne _____

    4. de Belgique _____

    5. de Martinique _____

C. Complete each sentence with the correct word to express nationality.

    1. Le _____ rencontre des amis.
       (Français/français/Française)

    2. C'est une voiture _____.
       (Américain/américain/américaine)

    3. Qui parle _____ ici?
       (Anglais/Anglaise/anglais)

    4. L' _____? Je ne le comprends pas.
       (Italienne/Italien/italien)

    5. L' _____ est une cousine de Marc.
       (Espagnol/Espagnole/espagnol)

11.

Comment les enfants apprennent-ils?

Avant de lire: *Préférez-vous étudier seul ou avec quelqu'un? Pourquoi?*

Martine est en train d'étudier parce que demain elle va passer un examen.° Son père lit le journal, assis dans son fauteuil.°

–Papa, dit-elle timidement.° Puis-je te poser
5 quelques questions? Je veux réussir° mon examen de géographie.

–Bien sûr. Que veux-tu savoir? dit le père en posant son journal.

–Kinshasa est la capitale de quel pays?
10 –Le Congo, répond le père.

–Non, papa. Dis-moi le nouveau nom du pays.

passer un examen to take an exam
fauteuil armchair
timidement shyly
réussir to pass

–Je ne me rappelle pas cela. Je regrette.

–Papa, qu'est-ce que c'est qu'un opaki?° _{opaki}

–Ça, je sais. Je l'ai sur le bout de la langue°

15 mais je viens de l'oublier.°

–Papa, qu'est-ce que c'est que le Katanga?°

–Le katanga? Je crois que c'est un animal
mais je ne sais pas où il habite.

–Martine se tait,° fatiguée de poser des

20 questions sans obtenir de réponses correctes. Son
père commence à croire qu'elle a quelque chose.°

–Qu'y a-t-il, ma chérie?

–Rien, papa.

–Plus de questions? Tu as fini tes devoirs?

25 –J'ai beaucoup de questions mais je ne veux
pas t'ennuyer. Je ne devrais pas t'ennuyer avec
mes problèmes quand tu lis le journal et tu veux
te reposer.

Le père laisse tomber° son journal et dit:

30 –Ne sois pas bébête!° N'aie pas peur de me
poser des questions! Aie confiance en moi! Si tu
ne poses pas ces questions à ton papa, à qui les
poseras-tu et comment vas-tu apprendre?

opaki animal found in
Zaire related to the
giraffe
**sur le bout de la
langue** on the tip
of the tongue
oublier to forget
Katanga region rich in
minerals
se tait keeps quiet

elle a quelque chose
something is the
matter with her

laisse tomber drops

bébête silly

◖ AVEZ-VOUS COMPRIS? ◗

A. Complete the sentences to form a summary of the story.

1. Martine prépare une leçon de _____. (biologie /
   français / géographie)
2. Elle a un examen _____. (demain / aujourd'hui / la
   semaine prochaine)
3. Son père est en train de _____. (lire / travailler / parler)
4. Kinshasa est _____. (une nation / un fleuve / une ville)
5. Son père pense que le Katanga est _____. (un animal /
   une capitale / un habitant)
6. Il donne des réponses _____ à ses questions. (vagues /
   correctes / intelligentes)
7. La fillette _____ poser des questions. (a peur / cesse
   de / continue de)
8. Le père ne peut pas _____ sa fille. (aider / ennuyer /
   avoir confiance)

B. Répondez à ces questions par une phrase complète en français.

1. Quand est l'examen de géographie?
2. Que fait le père de Martine?
3. Pourquoi pose-t-elle des questions à son père?
4. Le Congo est-il le nouveau ou l'ancien nom d'un pays africain?
5. Le père de la fillette connaît-il bien la géographie?
6. Qu'est-ce qu'il a sur le bout de la langue?
7. Pourquoi est-ce que Martine ne pose plus de questions?
8. Finit-elle ses devoirs?
9. Quelle excuse donne-t-elle à son père?
10. A-t-elle confiance en son père?

C. Et vous?

1. Comment vous sentez-vous avant un examen?
2. Quand échouez-vous à vos examens?
3. Quelqu'un vous aide-t-il à faire vos devoirs?
4. Aimez-vous vous asseoir dans un fauteuil pour lire le journal?
5. Que savez-vous sur le Congo?

⪯⪰ VOCABULAIRE ⪯⪰

A. Word groups: Give the meanings of the less familiar words by comparing them to the basic word. Pay attention to whether each word is a noun, a verb, or an adjective.

1. étudier: un étudiant, une étudiante, une étude
2. le pays: le paysage, un paysan, une paysanne
3. le jour: la journée, le journal, le journaliste
4. habiter: un habitant, une habitation, l'habitat
5. ennuyer: les ennuis, ennuyeux
6. timide: la timidité, timidement
7. confiance: se confier, confiant
8. regretter: le regret, regrettable

B. Match the antonyms from the two columns.

A	B
1. réussir	**a.** intelligent
2. demain	**b.** commencer
3. se rappeler	**c.** échouer
4. quelque chose	**d.** hier
5. bête	**e.** rien
6. finir	**f.** oublier
7. nouveau	**g.** poser des questions
8. répondre	**h.** ancien

❧ VERBES ☙

A. Turn the sentences into commands.

MODÈLE: Nous avons confiance.
Ayons confiance!

1. Vous lisez le journal.
2. Vous êtes brillant.
3. Tu as raison.
4. Nous sommes à l'heure.
5. Tu es présent.
6. Tu chantes toute la journée.
7. Nous avons de la chance.
8. Vous avez confiance.
9. Tu es sage.
10. Vous n'avez pas peur.
11. Tu n'es pas méchant.
12. Nous ne sommes pas bêtes.

B. Change the tense of the verbs to the future.

MODÈLE: Tu poses des questions.
Tu poseras des questions.

1. Il étudie pour son examen.
2. Nous sommes à la maison.
3. Vous parlez de ce sujet.
4. Je regarde la télévision.
5. Il a de l'argent.
6. Mes parents mangent au restaurant.
7. Tu penses à ton examen.
8. Elle s'habille avec goût.

◖ STRUCTURE ◗

Rewrite the sentences in the negative.

1. Je sais où il habite.
2. Nous connaissons tout le monde.
3. Ils sont toujours en retard.
4. Mon père sait tout.
5. J'ai encore soif.
6. Pourquoi pose-t-il tant de questions?
7. Qui réussit à l'examen?
8. Elle apprend beaucoup dans cette classe.

12.

La perfection n'est pas de ce monde

AVANT DE LIRE: *Avez-vous déjà trouvé beaucoup d'argent là où vous vous y attendiez° le moins?*

vous vous y attendiez you expected it

La journée avait mal commencé pour Denis. Il était pressé. Son réveil° n'avait pas sonné° et il s'était levé en retard. Il avait rendez-vous° chez le dentiste dans une heure et pour aggraver° la
5 situation, sa voiture avait un pneu crevé.° Il n'avait pas d'autre solution que de prendre un taxi.

réveil alarm clock
n'avait pas sonné did not go off
rendez-vous appointment
aggraver to make matters worse
pneu crevé flat tire

Dans le taxi, il se rend compte° qu'il n'a qu'un billet de cinq cents francs sur lui.

10   —Comment vais-je payer le taxi? se demande-t-il. Un chauffeur de taxi ne peut pas faire la monnaie° de cinq cents francs, pense-t-il.

Toutefois,° essayant d'être optimiste, il se dit que les taxis ont quelquefois beaucoup de courses° tôt le matin. Tout de même, cinq cents francs est une grosse coupure° se dit encore Denis.

Aussi demande-t-il au chauffeur de l'arrêter devant une banque. Denis entre dans la banque, se dirige vers° un guichet° et demande à l'employée de bien vouloir lui faire la monnaie° de cinq cents francs. La caissière accepte. Avant de sortir, Denis compte l'argent.

—Mademoiselle, dit-il, il y a une erreur.°

—Je ne fais pas d'erreur, monsieur, répond la caissière.

—Pourtant, mademoiselle . . .

—Monsieur, je vous ai déjà dit que nous ne faisons pas d'erreurs ici.

Denis essaie encore une fois de lui montrer le billet de deux cents francs et lui dit:

—Regardez, mademoiselle, ce que vous me donnez . . .

Enervée, l'employée lui répond:

—Monsieur, pour la troisième et dernière fois, je vous répète qu'ici, dans cette banque, nous ne faisons pas d'erreurs. C'est ce que nous gagnons° à rendre service° à des gens comme vous!

Confronté° à la mauvaise humeur de l'employée, Denis s'exclame:

—Mademoiselle, je n'ai jamais rencontré quelqu'un qui ne fait jamais d'erreurs et est aussi parfaite que vous. Cela mérite une récompense.° Tenez, prenez le billet de deux cents francs que vous m'avez donné en trop.

15

20

25

30

35

40

se rend compte realizes

n'a pas la monnaie
does not have change

Toutefois Nevertheless
courses runs

grosse coupure
huge bill

se dirige vers goes to
guichet window
faire la monnaie
to change

erreur mistake

gagnons earn
rendre service to help

récompense reward

◖ AVEZ-VOUS COMPRIS? ◗

A. Complete each sentence with one of the words or phrases in parentheses.

1. La journée de Denis commence (bien / passablement / mal).
2. Le réveil (sonne trop tôt / a sonné dix minutes trop tard / n'a pas sonné).
3. La voiture de Denis (marche très bien / n'a pas d'essence / a un pneu crevé).
4. Pour régler le taxi, Denis pense que (il a oublié l'argent chez lui / il a perdu son porte-monnaie / le billet qu'il a est trop important).
5. Denis dit au chauffeur de taxi (de s'arrêter devant une banque / de changer le billet qu'il a / qu'il n'a pas d'argent).
6. L'employée accepte (de changer le billet / de faire des fautes / de sortir de la banque).
7. L'insistance de Denis montre qu'il est (honnête / malhonnête / ridicule).
8. L'attitude de la caissière est (très responsable / irresponsable / responsable).
9. L'employée dans l'histoire est (sympathique / gentille / de mauvaise humeur).
10. Quand Denis quitte la banque, il a (autant / moins / plus) d'argent que lorsqu'il est entré.

B. Répondez à ces questions par une phrase complète en français.

1. Quel moyen de transport Denis utilise-t-il quand sa voiture ne marche pas?
2. Avec qui Denis a-t-il un rendez-vous?
3. Combien d'argent Denis a-t-il pour payer le taxi?
4. Qu'est-ce qui préoccupe Denis pendant qu'il est dans le taxi?
5. Qu'est-ce que Denis pense que les chauffeurs de taxi font le matin?
6. Où va Denis pour résoudre son problème?
7. Que fait Denis quand il reçoit de l'argent?
8. Que fait Denis avant de quitter la banque?

C. Et vous?

    1. Allez-vous souvent chez le dentiste?

    2. Etes-vous anxieux avant d'aller chez le dentiste?

    3. Préférez-vous prendre un taxi ou l'autobus? Pourquoi?

    4. Que faites-vous si votre journée commence avec des problèmes de transport?

    5. Que faites-vous lorsque vous allez à la banque?

    6. Voudriez-vous travailler comme employé(e) de banque? Pourquoi?

    7. Si vous étiez le/la caissier(-ère) et aviez un(e) client(e) comme Denis, que feriez-vous?

    8. Que faites-vous si le/la caissier(-ère) fait une erreur et ne veut pas entendre votre explication?

☙ VOCABULAIRE ❧

Match the antonyms from the two columns.

A	B
1. en retard	**a.** donner
2. optimiste	**b.** perdre
3. tôt	**c.** punition
4. accepter	**d.** entrer
5. sortir	**e.** tard
6. gagner	**f.** refuser
7. récompense	**g.** pessimiste
8. prendre	**h.** en avance

☙ VERBES ❧

A. Change the tense of the verbs to the *passé composé*.

    1. Je trouve de l'argent dans la rue.

    2. Il se lève tard.

    3. Je paye le taxi.

    4. Tu demandes au chauffeur de t'arrêter devant la banque.

    5. Nous nous dirigeons vers le guichet.

    6. La caissière n'accepte pas l'argent.

    7. La journée commence mal.

    8. Vous faites une erreur.

    9. Ils me donnent trop d'argent.

    10. Elle rencontre son amie au café.

B. Change the tense of the verbs in the sentences in exercise A to the *imparfait*.

◁ STRUCTURE ▷

Complete the sentences with the appropriate preposition from the list.

1. Nous nous dirigeons _____ le taxi.
2. Il entre _____ le restaurant.
3. Vous pensez _____ vos enfants.
4. Les enfants sont _____ la fenêtre.
5. Le chien marche _____ son maître.
6. La chaise est _____ la table.
7. Il a rendez-vous _____ le dentiste.
8. Tu voyages _____ ton fils pour t'aider.

dans	à	derrière	chez
vers	à côté de	avec	devant

13.
A la pharmacie

AVANT DE LIRE: *Vous et votre famille fréquentez°-vous toujours la même pharmacie? Connaissez-vous le pharmacien personnellement?*

fréquentez patronize

Monsieur Girard travaille dans une pharmacie. Il habite le village de Jeumont près de la frontière° franco-belge. C'est un homme assez important. Tous les gens du village demandent son conseil quand
5   ils ont des ennuis.° Pour les habitants de Jeumont, Monsieur Girard est plus qu'un pharmacien; il est aussi médecin, avocat et ami.

Le petit Georges, un gosse° de huit ans, entre dans la pharmacie en courant et demande un

frontière border

ennuis worries, problems

gosse kid

10 médicament pour le mal d'estomac. Le pharmacien,
sans examiner le garçon, lui donne un verre de
liquide jaune.

    –Bois-le tout de suite, Georges. Vide-le.°   **Vide-le** Empty it

    –Mais, Monsieur Girard . . . , dit le garçon en
15 essayant d'expliquer quelque chose.

    –Je n'ai pas le temps de discuter. Bois-le. Si
tu as quelque chose à dire, parle-moi plus tard.
J'attends.

    Le garçon commence à boire d'un air°   **air** look
20 malheureux. Il regarde tristement Monsieur
Girard qui crie:

    –Enfin, bois-le!

    Quand il n'y a plus de médicament dans le
verre, Monsieur Girard dit à Georges:

25   –Très bien, mon petit. Maintenant, je t'écoute.
Tu peux me parler. Qu'as-tu à dire?

    –Monsieur Girard, dit le garçon. Vous vous
êtes trompé.° Ce n'est pas moi qui ai mal à   **Vous vous êtes trompé.**
l'estomac. C'est mon petit frère qui est malade.   You made a mistake.

◖ AVEZ-VOUS COMPRIS? ◗

A. Complete each sentence with the appropriate expression.

    1. Dans une pharmacie, on vend
        a. des verres.
        b. des médicaments.
        c. des boissons.
        d. des pharmaciens.

    2. Georges
        a. a mal à l'estomac.
        b. demande quelque chose à boire.
        c. aime le liquide jaune.
        d. cherche un remède pour le mal d'estomac.

    3. Monsieur Girard
        a. examine l'estomac de Georges.
        b. discute le médicament avec Georges.
        c. boit quelque chose pour un mal d'estomac.
        d. donne quelque chose pour l'estomac à Georges.

4. Le pharmacien insiste pour que Georges vide le verre parce que (qu')
   a. il a besoin du verre.
   b. il sait que le petit a soif.
   c. le garçon hésite à le boire.
   d. il a quelque chose à lui dire.
5. George a l'air triste parce qu'il
   a. cherche le médicament pour son frère.
   b. a très mal à l'estomac.
   c. veut boire plus de liquide.
   d. veut tromper le pharmacien.

B. Répondez à ces questions par une phrase complète en français.
   1. Comment s'appelle le pharmacien?
   2. Est-il seulement un pharmacien?
   3. Qui lui demande conseil?
   4. Quel âge a Georges?
   5. Est-ce que le pharmacien examine Georges?
   6. Georges est-il content de boire le liquide jaune?
   7. Pourquoi a-t-il l'air malheureux?
   8. Est-ce que Georges est maintenant guéri?

C. Et vous?
   1. Aimez-vous prendre des médicaments?
   2. Consultez-vous un médecin ou un pharmacien lorsque vous ne vous sentez pas bien?
   3. Prenez-vous des médicaments sans diagnostic?
   4. Que pensez-vous de l'attitude du pharmacien dans l'histoire?

❧ VOCABULAIRE ❧

Match the antonyms from the two columns.

	A		B
1.	important	a.	bien portant
2.	sans	b.	plus tard
3.	vider	c.	avoir raison
4.	donner	d.	se taire
5.	tout de suite	e.	prendre
6.	se tromper	f.	insignifiant
7.	malade	g.	remplir
8.	parler	h.	avec

◖ VERBES ◗

Complete each sentence with the imperative form of the verb indicated in parentheses.

1. _____ tout le verre.   *(boire; tu)*
2. _____ la bouteille.   *(vider; vous)*
3. _____ ce chemin.   *(prendre; nous)*
4. _____ au jardin.   *(travailler; nous)*
5. _____ le avant de lui donner
   un médicament.   *(examiner; vous)*
6. _____ à lire tout de suite.   *(commencer; tu)*

◖ STRUCTURE ◗

Complete each sentence by replacing the words in parentheses with a pronoun.

1. Le pharmacien _____ donne le
   médicament.   *(à l'enfant)*
2. Je _____ lis.   *(le livre)*
3. Nous _____ buvons.   *(tout le liquide)*
4. Monsieur Girard _____ travaille. *(dans une pharmacie)*
5. Vide- _____ .   *(le verre)*
6. C'est _____ qui est malade.   *(mon frère)*

14.
A quelque chose malheur est bon! (Première partie)

AVANT DE LIRE: *Préférez-vous le silence ou du brouhaha?*°

brouhaha hustle and bustle

Monsieur Dumontier est propriétaire d'un magasin où l'on vend des instruments de musique. Ses journées sont pénibles° parce qu'il trouve insupportable cette musique moderne qu'il doit
5 écouter. Le soir, quand il rentre chez lui, il désire le silence. Mais c'est impossible: sa fille téléphone à ses amis; son fils joue du tambour,° des cymbales et de la guitare électrique. Madame Dumontier

pénibles tedious

tambour drum

66

joue du piano; le chien aboie pour accompagner
10 les autres musiciens.

Enfin, Dieu merci, c'est l'heure de se coucher.
Monsieur Dumontier, épuisé,° s'endort° immédi-
atement. A deux heures du matin, sa femme le
réveille.°
15 —François, lève-toi! Il y a des voleurs° dans la
maison.

—Ah, non, Thérèse. Comment le sais-tu?
demande-t-il?

—Ne perds pas de temps° à me poser des
20 questions! Je te dis qu'il y a des voleurs dans la
maison. Ils peuvent nous tuer° pendant que° tu
m'ennuies avec tes questions ridicules. Tu as peur
de protéger ta famille, peut-être?

—Mais comment sais-tu qu'il y a des voleurs ici?
25 —Je peux les entendre, répond-elle, furieuse.
—Ne sois pas bête, Thérèse. Les voleurs ne
font pas de bruit.

*Quelques minutes plus tard, Madame
Dumontier réveille de nouveau° son mari.*
30 —François, lève-toi! Je suis sûre qu'il y a des
voleurs dans la maison.

—Je t'ai déjà dit que les voleurs ne font pas
de bruit.

—C'est pourquoi je suis sûre maintenant qu'ils
35 sont dans la maison: je n'entends rien.

épuisé exhausted
s'endort falls asleep

réveille wakes
voleurs thieves, robbers

Ne perds pas de temps
Don't waste time

tuer to kill
pendant que while

de nouveau again

◖ AVEZ-VOUS COMPRIS? ◗

A. Choose the phrase that corectly completes the sentence.

1. Monsieur Dumontier aime bien
   a. écouter les instruments de musique
   b. se reposer dans un endroit tranquille.
   c. la musique moderne.
   d. les journées pénibles au magasin.
2. Il n'y a pas de silence chez lui parce que
   a. son fils joue du piano.
   b. sa fille aboie.
   c. tout le monde fait beaucoup de bruit.
   d. sa femme parle continuellement.

3. Pendant la nuit, Monsieur Dumontier
   a. se réveille.
   b. est réveillé par sa femme.
   c. entend des voleurs.
   d. écoute encore la musique.

4. Madame Dumontier a peur
   a. des voleurs.
   b. de son mari.
   c. des bêtes féroces.
   d. de sa famille.

5. A la fin, elle croit qu'il y a des voleurs parce que (qu')
   a. ils veulent la tuer.
   b. son mari a peur.
   c. ils font du bruit.
   d. ils ne font pas de bruit.

B. Répondez à ces questions par une phrase complète en français.

1. Quelle est la profession de Monsieur Dumontier?
2. Quelle musique n'aime-t-il pas?
3. Ecoute-t-il de la musique chez lui?
4. Monsieur Dumontier a-t-il du mal à s'endormir?
5. Quel est le prénom de Madame Dumontier?
6. De quoi a-t-elle peur?
7. Pourquoi pense-t-elle qu'il y a des voleurs dans la maison?
8. Est-ce que les voleurs sont bruyants?

C. Et vous?

1. Avez-vous peur des voleurs la nuit?
2. Comment réagissez-vous lorsque vous entendez du bruit au milieu de la nuit?
3. Vous réveillez-vous au milieu de la nuit?
4. Qu'est-ce qui vous fait peur?
5. Racontez une grande frayeur que vous avez eue.

✤ VOCABULAIRE ✤

Match the synonyms from the two columns.

A	B
1. vendre	**a.** gagner
2. pénible	**b.** se lever
3. moderne	**c.** le silence
4. se coucher	**d.** acheter
5. se réveiller	**e.** s'endormir
6. perdre	**f.** ancien
7. protéger	**g.** agréable
8. le bruit	**h.** menacer

✤ VERBES ✤

A. Complete each sentence with the correct form of the verb in parentheses.

1. Tous les soirs, je _____ vers dix heures. *(s'endormir)*
2. Tous les matins, nous _____ à six heures. *(se réveiller)*
3. Il _____ toujours de la même façon. *(s'habiller)*
4. Vous _____ de chemin. *(se tromper)*
5. Ils _____ devant le magasin de musique. *(s'arrêter)*
6. Elle _____ lorsqu'elle écoute de la musique. *(s'ennuyer)*

B. Complete each sentence with the *passé composé* of the verb in parentheses.

1. Nous _____ la vérité. *(dire)*
2. Vous _____ trop tard. *(se coucher)*
3. Ils _____ hier. *(partir)*
4. Tu _____ trop vite. *(parler)*
5. Elle _____ les voleurs. *(entendre)*
6. Je _____ du piano cet après-midi. *(jouer)*
7. Il _____ du temps et _____ son travail. *(perdre/ne pas finir)*
8. Le père _____ sa famille avec courage. *(protéger)*

❦ STRUCTURE ❧

A. Complete each sentence by replacing the words in parentheses with a pronoun.

1. L'enfant _____ pose des
   questions.   *(au professeur)*
2. La femme _____ réveille.   *(son mari)*
3. Il _____ trouve insupportable.   *(la musique)*
4. Le garçon _____ joue.   *(du tambour)*
5. Nous _____ entendons.   *(les voleurs)*
6. Tu _____ désires.   *(le silence)*

B. Complete each sentence with the appropriate form of the adjective in parentheses.

1. Les enfants sont _____.   *(épuisé)*
2. La dame est _____ qu'elle a
   entendu des voleurs.   *(sûr)*
3. Les spectatrices sont _____.   *(furieux)*
4. Il s'habille avec des vêtements
   _____.   *(ridicule)*
5. Je trouve ce garçon _____.   *(insupportable)*
6. Le travail est _____.   *(pénible)*

15.
A quelque chose malheur est bon! (Deuxième partie)

AVANT DE LIRE: *Croyez-vous dans le dicton que toute mauvaise chose a ses bons côtés?*°

toute mauvaise chose
a ses bons côtés
every cloud has a
silver lining

Monsieur Dumontier ne veut ni ciritquer la
logique de sa femme, ni sortir du lit. Il veut tout
simplement dormir. Mais son épouse ne le laisse
pas dormir. Enfin, il se lève, met ses pantoufles°

5 et attrape une énorme poêle° dans la cuisine. Très
lentement, il se dirige vers le salon. Il ouvre la
porte mais reste prudent. Devant lui, il y a deux

pantoufles slippers

poêle frying pan

hommes. Ils mettent les instruments de musique
de son fils dans de grands sacs. Le chien féroce,
10 qui d'ordinaire aboie toute la journée, dort dans
un fauteuil.

Quand les voleurs aperçoivent° le propriétaire,   **aperçoivent** notice
menaçant° avec sa poêle à la main, ils s'inquiètent.   **menaçant** threatening
Ils laissent tomber les sacs et lèvent les mains.

15 —Je vous en prie, monsieur, ne nous faites pas   **ne nous faites pas de**
de mal.° Nous sommes de gentils voleurs. Nous   **mal** don't hurt us
n'entrons que dans des maisons décentes.

—Silence! crie Monsieur Dumontier. Cessez.
Ecoutez-moi bien si vous ne voulez pas aller
20 en prison. Téléphonez à vos copains très vite.
Dites-leur de venir tout de suite° avec un camion°   **tout de suite** immediately
pour enlever le piano. Et pendant que vous y   **camion** truck
êtes,° prenez aussi le téléphone et le chien.   **pendant que vous y êtes**
    while you are at it

◖ℚ AVEZ-VOUS COMPRIS? ℚ◗

A. Complete each sentence with the appropriate expression.

   1. Quand sa femme le réveille, Monsieur Dumontier veut
      a. se lever.
      b. parler avec elle.
      c. aller dans le salon.
      d. rester au lit.

   2. Il va au salon avec
      a. un livre.
      b. une poêle.
      c. son chien.
      d. sa femme.

   3. Le chien n'aboie plus parce qu'
      a. il aime les voleurs.
      b. il est dans le sac avec les instruments.
      c. il dort.
      d. il est féroce et sauvage.

   4. Les voleurs ont peur
      a. du chien.
      b. de la poêle.
      c. de leurs camarades.
      d. de Monsieur Dumontier.

5. Pour ne pas aller en prison, les voleurs doivent
   a. enlever Madame Dumontier et le chien.
   b. laisser tous les instruments dans le salon.
   c. donner un camion à Monsieur Dumontier.
   d. emporter le téléphone, les instruments de musique et le chien.

B. Répondez à ces questions par une phrase complète en français.
   1. Combien y a-t-il de voleurs?
   2. Est-ce que Monsieur Dumontier ouvre la porte avec bruit?
   3. Quel genre de voleurs sont dans la maison?
   4. Ont-ils peur de Monsieur Dumontier?
   5. Que font-ils lorsqu'ils aperçoivent Monsieur Dumontier?
   6. Que doivent-ils faire pour ne pas aller en prison?

C. Et vous?
   1. Que pensez-vous des voleurs?
   2. Que feriez-vous si vous découvriez des voleurs chez vous?
   3. Quelle sera d'après vous la réaction de Madame Dumontier?

⦿ VOCABULAIRE ⦿

A. Adverbs: A number of French adverbs are formed by adding -*ment* to the feminine form of the adjective. Write the feminine form and the adverb corresponding to each of the following adjectives.

MODÈLE: lent   *lente   lentement*

   1. simple
   2. triste
   3. calme
   4. fort
   5. chaud
   6. froid
   7. rapide
   8. vert

B. Find synonyms in the text for the following words.

1. s'il vous plaît
2. Taisez-vous!
3. appeler
4. incarcérer
5. quitter
6. se reposer
7. remarquer
8. craindre

ℳℚ VERBES ℘℘

A. Change the sentences into the negative.

1. Il veut critiquer sa femme.
2. La mère laisse dormir son fils.
3. Dites-moi la vérité.
4. Vous voulez aller en prison.
5. Il veut tout savoir.
6. Nous sommes toujours à la maison.

B. Complete the sentences by putting the verbs in parentheses in the imperative form.

1. _____ la vérité! *(dire; tu)*
2. _____ à votre frère! *(téléphoner; vous)*
3. _____ dans la maison! *(entrer; nous)*
4. _____ la queue du chien! *(ne pas tirer; tu)*
5. _____ de bêtises! *(ne pas dire; vous)*
6. _____ vos sacs! *(laisser tomber)*
7. _____ la porte! *(prendre; vous)*
8. _____ ce que le professeur dit! *(écouter; nous)*

ℳℚ STRUCTURE ℘℘

Complete each sentence with the appropriate possessive adjective.

1. C'est _____ (je) sac.
2. Nous prenons tous _____ bagages.
3. Voici _____ (vous) chambre.
4. C'est ici qu'elle passe _____ vacances.
5. Il conduit _____ voiture.
6. Tu te promènes avec _____ père.

16.
Un pompier a un problème

AVANT DE LIRE: *Pouvez-vous imaginer être un pompier bénévole?° Comment seriez-vous?*

bénévole volunteer

Pierre a toujours rêvé d'être pompier, mais dans la petite ville où il habite, il n'y a pas de caserne de pompiers.° Rien n'arrive jamais dans cette ville. Il n'y a jamais aucune sorte d'urgence.°
5 La vie y est très paisible.° Avec un gros effort, Pierre a réussi à convaincre° ses voisins qu'il serait utile de fonder une caserne de pompiers pour faire face à toutes les urgences, comme un incendie,° une attaque cardiaque° ou pour

caserne de pompiers
fire station
urgence emergency
paisible peaceful
convaincre to convince

incendie fire
attaque cardiaque
heart attack

75

10　éviter° une noyade°. Enfin, Pierre a atteint° son
but. Son ami René a même offert sa jeep comme
moyen° de transport en cas d'urgence.

Deux semaines plus tard, après déjeuner, des
cris se font entendre de la place principale de la
15　ville.

—A l'aide! A l'aide! La maison de Madame
Leroy sur la colline° est en flammes.°

Quatre volontaires sortent en courant de chez
eux° et montent dans la jeep. Pierre, qui faisait la
20　sieste,° entendant le remue-ménage° dans son
sommeil, s'est levé, et a mis ses chaussures et sa
chemise. Quand il est arrivé à la porte de sa
maison, il ne pouvait plus voir la jeep.

—Prête-moi ta moto, Jean, il demande au fils
25　du voisin.

Pierre enfourche° la moto, et le voilà parti,
pour tenter° de rattraper° la jeep qui a déjà
traversé le pont.

Après que le feu ait été éteint,° tous les voisins
30　se sont rassemblés sur la place principale pour
parler de l'incendie et féliciter° les pompiers
bénévoles. Soudain, quelqu'un a dit:

—Pierre, tu as fait un travail extraordinaire.
Tu sembles épuisé. Regarde tes vêtements.

35　—Oh, dit Pierre, la moto est tombée en panne
quand j'essayais de traverser le ravin, et j'ai dû la
porter sur mon épaule pour empêcher l'eau de
l'emporter.

éviter to avoid
noyade drowning
a atteint achieved
moyen means

A l'aide! Help!

colline hill
en flammes on fire
de chez eux from their
　　houses
faisait la sieste was
　　taking a nap
remue-ménage hubhub

enfourche gets on

tenter to try
rattraper to catch up to

ait été éteint had been
　　put out

féliciter to congratulate

☙ AVEZ-VOUS COMPRIS? ☚

A. Choose the proper word to complete each sentence.

1.　La vie dans le village de Pierre était _____.
    a. paisible
    b. agitée
    c. mouvementée

2. Pierre réussit à _____ ses voisins.
   a. rencontrer
   b. convaincre
   c. mettre en colère
3. _____ passent avant qu'une urgence se présente.
   a. Deux mois
   b. Deux semaines
   c. Trois semaines
4. Sur la colline, la maison de _____ brûlait.
   a. Pierre
   b. Madame Leroy
   c. René
5. Pendant que Pierre faisait la sieste, il a entendu

   _____.
   a. Madame Leroy
   b. le remue-ménage
   c. René
6. Quand Pierre est arrivé à la porte, il a remarqué que
   _____ n'était plus là.
   a. la jeep
   b. la maison de Madame Leroy
   c. la moto
7. Pour atteindre la colline, Pierre _____.
   a. a sauté dans la jeep
   b. a enfourché la moto
   c. a couru
8. Les bénévoles _____.
   a. ont cherché Pierre
   b. ont éteint le feu
   c. sont restés dans le ravin
9. Tous les voisins sont allés célébrer _____.
   a. chez Pierre
   b. dans un parc
   c. sur la place principale du village
10. Pendant que les voisins célébraient, Pierre était _____.
    a. bien habillé
    b. épuisé
    c. affamé

B. Répondez à ces questions par une phrase complète en français.

1. Pourquoi Pierre veut-il un groupe de volontaires?
2. Qu'est-ce qui manque dans la petite ville de Pierre?
3. De quoi Pierre a-t-il toujours rêvé?
4. Quand les volontaires dans l'histoire peuvent-ils aider?
5. Dans l'histoire combien de volontaires se précipitent-ils vers l'incendie?
6. Pourquoi les pompiers vont-ils chez Madame Leroy?
7. Que faisait Pierre quand les gens criaient "A l'aide"?
8. Qu'a demandé Pierre lorsqu'il s'est levé? De qui?
9. Qu'est-ce que les voisins ont célébré?
10. Pourquoi Pierre n'est-il pas arrivé à l'incendie?

C. Et vous?

1. Après avoir terminé vos études, voudriez-vous vivre dans une petite ville comme celle de Pierre? Pourquoi?
2. Quelle est la population de la ville où vous vivez?
3. A quoi ressemble la vie dans votre ville?
4. Aimez-vous monter sur un scooter? Pourquoi?
5. Vous êtes-vous porté volontaire dans votre école?
6. Aimeriez-vous être pompier? Pourquoi?
7. Avez-vous jamais organisé un groupe dans votre communauté? Dans quel but?
8. Pensez-vous que faire la sieste est une bonne ou mauvaise habitude?
9. Si votre maison prenait feu, que feriez-vous en premier lieu?
10. Que pensez-vous de la personnalité de Pierre? Pourquoi?

◈ VOCABULAIRE ◈

Match the synonyms from the two columns.

A	B
1. volontaire	**a.** rattraper
2. être dans les nuages	**b.** petite ville
3. bourgade	**c.** rêver
4. incendie	**d.** habiter
5. demeurer	**e.** bénévole
6. se produire	**f.** fonder
7. essayer	**g.** feu
8. branle-bas	**h.** tenter
9. rejoindre	**i.** arriver
10. bâtir	**j.** remue-ménage

◈ VERBES ◈

A. Complete each sentence with the present participle of the verb in parentheses.

1. En _____ dans la maison, il a senti le feu. *(entrer)*

2. Il est sorti en _____. *(courir)*

3. Elle fait ses devoirs en _____. *(chanter)*

4. J'y suis allé en _____. *(marcher)*

5. Nous rêvons en _____. *(dormir)*

6. En _____ mieux faire, il a fait moins bien. *(vouloir)*

7. Il est tombé en _____ de les rattraper. *(essayer)*

8. Vous vous êtes levé en _____ le bruit. *(entendre)*

79

B. Complete each sentence with the appropriate form of the verb in parentheses—*imparfait* or *passé composé*.

1. La voiture _____ quand
   il allait chez ses parents.   *(tomber en panne)*
2. Le feu _____ pendant
   qu'il _____.   *(commencer/faire la sieste)*
3. Ils _____ en courant
   pour arriver à l'heure.   *(partir)*
4. Les pompiers _____
   d'éteindre le feu.   *(essayer)*
5. Jean _____ sa jeep
   pour y aller.   *(offrir)*
6. Nous _____ quand tout
   _____ fini.   *(arriver/être)*
7. Tu _____ tôt pour aller
   à l'école.   *(se lever)*
8. Il _____ à convaincre ses
   parents de le laisser sortir.   *(réussir)*

◄⊘ STRUCTURE ⊘►

Change the following sentences into the negative.

1. Il a toujours voulu venir le voir.
2. Nous avons tout fait.
3. Je suis grande.
4. Il a tout mangé.
5. Il faut sortir vite.
6. Vous pouvez encore venir.

17.
La ponctuation

AVANT DE LIRE: *Que faites-vous si quelqu'un vous embarrasse devant un groupe de gens?*

Pierre Ledoux est un jeune homme de vingt-deux ans. Pierre est beau, intelligent et idéaliste. Sa devise° est "Ne maudissez° pas l'obscurité, allumez° plutôt° une chandelle." Pierre a fait ses
5   études à l'université de Clermont-Ferrand et il est devenu professeur. Il est allé enseigner dans un lycée de Champeix.

devise moto
maudissez curse
allumez light
plutôt rather

Le premier jour, il s'est présenté à la classe et
il a commencé la leçon:

10 —Aujourd'hui, nous allons étudier l'importance
de la ponctuation. Je vais vous expliquer les
signes et les règles de la ponctuation.

Il a commencé avec le point final (.), la
virgule (,), le point-virgule (;) et les guillemets

15 (" "), quand Laurent, le plus mauvais élève de la
classe, a posé toutes sortes de questions idiotes:

—Pourquoi faut-il mettre deux guillemets,
l'un au commencement de la phrase et l'autre à
la fin?

20 Le professeur savait que Laurent ne
s'intéressait pas vraiment à la réponse. Aussi
lui a-t-il donné une réponse humoristique.

—Nous mettons deux guillemets parce
que nous avons deux yeux, un guillemet pour

25 chaque œil. Cependant, si tu viens me voir après
la classe, j'essayerai de mieux te l'expliquer.

Laurent s'est fâché parce qu'il n'a pas pu
irriter le professeur. Cet élève désagréable a
continué à poser des questions bêtes, mais il

30 n'a pas réussi à mettre le professeur en colère.
Alors, il a dit à haute voix:°   à haute voix aloud

—Je pense que ce professeur est bête.

Toute la classe s'est étonnée, mais le
professeur a conservé son calme° et ne s'est pas   a conservé son calme

35 emporté° contre ce garçon insolent. Il a pris la   kept his calm
craie° et il a écrit au tableau la phrase suivante: emporté upset
                                                          craie chalk
—L'élève impoli dit: "Ce professeur est bête."

—Comment peut-on changer le sens de la
phrase sans changer les mots? a-t-il demandé.

40 Pendant que la classe réfléchissait, il a pris
l'éponge° et la craie pour créer une nouvelle   l'éponge sponge
phrase:

—"L'élève impoli, dit ce professeur, est bête."

❦ AVEZ-VOUS COMPRIS? ❧

A. Choose the phrase that correctly completes the sentence.

A	B
1. Le nouveau professeur est	**a.** pourquoi il y a deux guillemets.
2. Il a commencé avec une leçon	**b.** parce qu'on a deux yeux.
3. Laurent voulait savoir	**c.** parce que le professeur ne s'est pas irrité.
4. Le professeur lui a donné	**d.** sur les signes de ponctuation.
5. Il y deux guillemets	**e.** une réponse humoristique.
6. Le mauvais élève s'est fâché	**f.** le professeur était stupide.
7. L'élève impoli a dit que	**g.** a écrit ce que Laurent a dit.
8. Au lieu de le punir, le professeur	**h.** jeune, gentil et intelligent.

B. Répondez à ces questions par une phrase complète en français.

1. Où Pierre Ledoux a-t-il fait ses études?

2. Quelle est sa devise?

3. Quelle est sa profession?

4. Qu'est-ce qu'il a enseigné le premier jour?

5. Pourquoi Laurent a-t-il posé des questions ridicules?

6. Pourquoi le professeur a-t-il répondu avec humour?

7. Pourquoi a-t-il invité Laurent à venir le voir après la classe?

8. Comment est-ce que Laurent a interrompu la classe la dernière fois?

9. Qu'est-ce que le professeur a fait au lieu de punir l'élève?

10. Pierre a-t-il réagi selon sa devise?

C. Et vous?

1. Avez-vous peur de l'obscurité?

2. Posez-vous beaucoup de questions durant vos cours?

3. Votre professeur donne-t-il des réponses sérieuses ou humoristiques?

4. Votre professeur se fâche-t-il facilement?

5. Que faites-vous lorsqu'il y a une panne d'électricité?

6. Etes-vous ennuyé, étonné, paisible lorsque votre professeur vous réprimande?

7. Quel genre de punitions votre professeur donne-t-il?

VOCABULAIRE

A. Word groups: The letters *dés-* at the beginning of a French word indicate that the root word has a negative meaning like *dis-* in English. Find the root word in the following and give the meanings of both words.

1. désaccord
2. désarmé
3. déshériter
4. désavantage
5. désintéressé

6. désapprouver
7. désassembler
8. déshonorer
9. désenchanté
10. désordre

B. Find the antonyms for the following words in the text of the story.

1. bénir
2. prosaïque
3. insignifiance
4. bon
5. éteindre
6. réponse
7. début
8. respectueux

VERBES

A. Complete each sentence with the *passé composé* of the verb in parentheses.

1. Jacques _____ du football au lycée. *(faire)*
2. Nous _____ au théâtre hier soir. *(aller)*
3. Je _____ au directeur. *(se présenter)*
4. Vous _____ par la première page. *(commencer)*
5. Avant d'accepter, tu _____ beaucoup de questions. *(poser)*
6. Ses parents _____ parce qu'il avait de mauvaises notes. *(se fâcher)*
7. Est-ce que ta sœur _____ l'examen? *(réussir)*
8. Qu'est-ce que tu lui _____? *(dire)*

B. Change the sentences to the *passé composé*.

1. Il vient en retard.
2. La grand-mère monte dans sa chambre.
3. Nous allons en vacances sans nos parents.
4. Solange, est-ce que tu pars à six heures?
5. Mes sœurs restent au parc.
6. J'arrive de bonne heure à la réunion.
7. Ses parents sortent du restaurant.
8. Descendez-vous ici?

◀◉ STRUCTURE ◉▶

Provide correct punctuation marks for the following sentences.

1. aujourd'hui nous allons étudier la grammaire la prononciation et le vocabulaire
2. pourquoi nous donne t il des réponses stupides
3. vite apportez moi de l'eau bouillante
4. il m'a dit attendez moi ici
5. le professeur a regardé l'élève puis il est allé au tableau
6. on leur a demandé des haricots des oignons et un peu de viande n'est ce pas
7. en voyant ce qu'il faisait sa mère a dit tel père tel fils
8. que tu es méchant

18.

L'astronaute

AVANT DE LIRE: *Quelle profession voudriez-vous
avoir? Quelles autres professions vous
intéressent? Pourquoi?*

    C'était le douze octobre. La famille Dubois
était assise dans le salon après le dîner. Jacques
leur racontait un film sur Christophe Colomb qu'il
avait vu en classe d'histoire. Son professeur avait
5 comparé Christophe Colomb aux astronautres
américains qui reviennent vers la terre après
leurs voyages fantastiques sur la lune. Qu'ils sont
courageux pour faire un tel° voyage dans le ciel!   **un tel** such a
    A ce moment-là, Delphine, une gosse de six
10 ans, a interrompu le récit de son frère.

–Je veux devenir astronaute, moi aussi, a-t-elle déclaré. Je n'ai peur ni d'aller dans la lune, ni sur les planètes. J'irai même jusqu'au soleil.

–Mais, Delphine, tu as dit que tu voulais être

15 agent de police, ou pompier, ou soldat. Maintenant, tu veux devenir° astronaute. Sais-tu que c'est un travail difficile et dangereux?

devenir to become

–Je n'aurai pas peur, a répondu la petite. Je suis beaucoup plus courageuse que Christophe

20 Colomb.

–Mon trésor, a dit sa mère, je sais que tu es courageuse. Mais on ne peut pas aller sur le soleil parce qu'il y fait très chaud. C'est une boule de feu et le feu te brûlera.° Comment pourras-tu te

brûlera will burn

25 protéger contre les rayons du soleil?

–Je me couvrirai le corps d'une crème solaire.° Je porterai des lunettes° de soleil comme toi, maman, quand nous allons à la plage.°

crème solaire sunscreen
lunettes glasses

plage beach

–Ce n'est pas suffisamment de protection, ma

30 chérie.

–Je sais ce qu'il faut que je fasse. Je ferai mon voyage la nuit.

ꞔ AVEZ-VOUS COMPRIS? ꞕ

A. Indicate whether these statements are true or false. Write *V* for *vrai* and *F* for *faux*. If the statement is false, correct it to make it true.

1. (   ) La famille Dubois se réunit dans la cuisine après le déjeuner.

2. (   ) On discute du livre que Jacques a lu.

3. (   ) Les astronautes sont allés sur la lune.

4. (   ) Delphine décide qu'elle veut devenir astronaute.

5. (   ) Delphine veut aller sur Mars.

6. (   ) Delphine est une fille peureuse.

7. (   ) Il fait très froid sur le soleil parce que c'est une boule de neige.

8. (   ) Les astronautes ont une occupation facile et sûre.

9. (   ) Delphine se protégera en portant un maillot de bain.

10. (   ) Son idée est de voyager le matin.

B. Répondez à ces questions par une phrase complète en français.

1. Qu'est-ce que Jacques a étudié à l'école?
2. Pourquoi a-t-on parlé de Christophe Colomb ce jour-là?
3. Où Delphine veut-elle aller?
4. Quel travail est dangereux?
5. Qui est plus courageux que les astronautes?
6. Pourquoi est-ce qu'un voyage au soleil est impossible?
7. Que fera Delphine pour se protéger?
8. Est-ce que l'idée de la petite est raisonnable? Pourquoi?

C. Et vous?

1. A votre avis, qui a découvert l'Amérique?
2. Que voulez-vous devenir?
3. Est-ce un travail dangereux?
4. Comment imaginez-vous la lune?
5. Aimeriez-vous explorer la terre, les cieux ou l'océan? Pourquoi?
6. Etes-vous brave ou timide?
7. Que portez-vous lorsqu'il fait du soleil?
8. Avez-vous besoin de lunettes? Quand les portez-vous?

⟪ VOCABULAIRE ⟫

A. Cognates: Many French words ending in *-ique* are cognates of English words that end in *-ic* or *-cal*. Give the English equivalent of each of the following French words.

1. fantastique
2. athlétique
3. politique
4. énergique
5. publique
6. électrique
7. authentique
8. ironique
9. historique
10. psychologique

88

B. Complete the sentences with one of the words given below. Use each word only once.

1. Pour nager, on va à _____.
2. Le travail d'un agent de police est _____.
3. Pendant la journée, nous sommes éclairés par la lumière du _____.
4. Jupiter est une _____.
5. Beaucoup de gens portent des _____ pour lire.
6. On appelle les _____ quand il y a un incendie.
7. Le bois _____ dans la cheminée.

brûle	lunettes	planète	soleil
dangereux	plage	pompiers	

⟪ VERBES ⟫

A. Indicate the tense of the verbs in the sentences: present *(P)*, *passé composé (PC)*, or future *(F)*.

1. Jacques raconte un film. _____
2. Son professeur a comparé les astronautes à Christophe Colomb. _____
3. Delphine a interrompu le récit de son frère. _____
4. Le soleil te brûlera. _____
5. Je me couvrirai le corps de crème solaire. _____
6. Je porterai des lunettes de soleil. _____
7. Nous allons à la plage. _____
8. Il a eu une bonne idée. _____

B. Change the sentences from the immediate future to the future.

MODÈLE: Je vais parler avec le docteur.
Je parlerai avec le docteur.

1. Mon père va détester cette musique.
2. Allez-vous porter un chapeau?
3. Nous allons finir ce travail.
4. Les voyageurs vont descendre à un hôtel.
5. Je ne vais pas sortir avec ce garçon.
6. Vas-tu vendre cette vieille voiture?
7. Comment va-t-il protéger sa montre dans le bateau?
8. Je vais dormir très tard.

◖◗ STRUCTURE ◖◗

Use the comparative to combine the two sentences.

MODÈLE: François est brave. Jacques est plus brave.
Jacques est plus brave que François.

1. Je suis sage. Ma sœur est plus sage.
2. Mon père est sévère. Mon professeur est moins sévère.
3. Mon chien est timide. Mon chat est aussi timide.
4. Jean-Paul est impoli. Son frère est plus impoli.
5. La robe est chère. La jupe est moins chère.
6. Le film est amusant. Le livre est moins amusant.
7. Les Dupont sont riches. Les Rothschild sont plus riches.
8. Il fait chaud au printemps. Il fait plus chaud en été.

On ne parle pas le
français ici,
mais les prix
sont moins chers.

19.
Ici on parle français

AVANT DE LIRE: *Aimeriez-vous avoir votre
propre affaire? Quel genre? Quelle publicité
feriez-vous?*

Au Canada, on parle anglais et français.
Officiellement, c'est un pays bilingue, mais en
réalité on y pratique l'anglais plus que le français.
Les gens d'expression française veulent protéger
5 leur langue et leur culture bien qu'ils parlent
anglais. Ils préfèrent donc faire leurs achats chez
les commerçants° qui parlent français. Dans
beaucoup de magasins, on voit cette notice:°

commerçants
businesspeople
notice sign

91

"On parle français." Quelquefois, ce sont les clients
10 qui parlent français, et souvent le propriétaire ne
sait que quelques mots.

Un commerçant avait ouvert un magasin de
confection° dans un quartier francophone. La
première semaine, personne ne venait acheter
15 parce qu'il n'y avait pas de notice. Un des amis
du propriétaire,° lui-même un commerçant avisé°
lui a conseillé:

—Si tu veux améliorer° tes affaires,° tu devrais
mettre une notice dans ta vitrine.°

20 —Mais je ne sais ni dire ni écrire un seul mot
dans cette langue, a déclaré le commerçant
honnête. Je ne veux tromper personne.

—Ce n'est pas important, a dit son ami. Je vais
venir t'aider demain. Nous allons changer
25 quelques mots dans l'affiche ordinaire.

Le lendemain, dans la vitrine est apparue cette
notice inhabituelle: "On ne parle pas le français
ici, mais les prix sont moins chers."

Depuis ce jour-là, le magasin ne désemplit plus.°

confection ready-to-wear clothes

propriétaire owner
avisé wise, skillful

améliorer to improve
affaires business
vitrine store window

ne désemplit plus
is always full
(of customers)

◖◈ AVEZ-VOUS COMPRIS? ◈◗

A. Complete each sentence with the appropriate expression.

    1. Le Canada est un pays bilingue. Officiellement, on y parle
        a. quatre langues.
        b. deux langues.
        c. une langue.
    2. La majorité parle
        a. anglais.
        b. canadien.
        c. français.
    3. Ce commerçant n'a pas mis _____ dans sa vitrine.
        a. de notice
        b. de robes
        c. de vêtements

4. Le commerçant _____ le français.
   a. parle et écrit
   b. parle mais n'écrit pas
   c. ne comprend pas du tout
5. Maintenant, le commerçant a beaucoup de clients parce que les _____ sont raisonnables.
   a. prix
   b. vêtements
   c. notices

B. Répondez à ces questions par une phrase complète en français.
   1. Que parlent les Canadiens?
   2. Comment protègent-ils leur culture d'expression française?
   3. Où se trouve le magasin du commerçant?
   4. Combien de clients a-t-il?
   5. Pourquoi est-ce que les clients ne viennent pas?
   6. Pourquoi ne met-il pas de notice dans sa vitrine?
   7. En quoi sa notice est-elle différente?
   8. Qu'est-ce qui fait plaisir au commerçant?

C. Et vous?
   1. Quelles langues parlez-vous?
   2. Parle-t-on d'autres langues dans votre famille? Dans votre voisinnage?
   3. Achetez-vous des vêtements de confection ou avez-vous une couturière qui coud pour vous?
   4. Préférez-vous un magasin qui vend des articles cher ou bon marché?
   5. Pourquoi faites-vous vos achats dans un magasin particulier?
   6. Quelle notice a attiré votre attention récemment? Pourquoi?

ᑦᑭ VOCABULAIRE ᑫᑀ

A. Cognates: Often the circumflex accent (∧) in French can be converted to a similar word containing the letter *s* in English. Give the English for the following words.

1. la forêt
2. une île
3. la croûte
4. la pâte

5. la fête
6. honnête
7. la bête
8. la crête

B. Word groups: Find synonyms for the following words in the story.

1. vêtements
2. acquérir
3. sage
4. assister
5. boutique
6. commerçant

ᑦᑭ VERBES ᑫᑀ

A. Complete each sentence with the *imparfait* of the verb in parentheses.

1. Vous _____ le tennis. *(pratiquer)*
2. Dans ce pays, on _____
   seulement l'anglais. *(parler)*
3. Si tu _____ parler français,
   tu ferais de meilleures affaires. *(savoir)*
4. Nous _____ acheter dans des
   magasins où on parlait notre langue. *(préférer)*
5. La propriétaire _____ de mettre
   une nouvelle notice dans sa vitrine. *(venir)*
6. Ses parents _____ partir quand
   il s'est mis à pleuvoir. *(aller)*
7. Les prix _____ moins chers et
   le magasin ne _____ pas. *(être/désemplir)*
8. Son ami _____ qu'il fallait
   mettre une affiche dans la vitrine. *(dire)*

B. Complete each sentence with the appropriate past tense (*passé composé, imparfait,* or *plus-que-parfait*) of the verb in parentheses.

1. Mon frère et moi, nous _____ en vacances chaque année chez mes grands-parents. *(partir)*

2. Nous _____ un nouveau magasin. *(établir)*

3. Il _____ mettre une notice dans la vitrine pour attirer les clients. *(falloir)*

4. Le propriétaire _____ quand vous _____ français. *(ne pas vous comprendre/ parler)*

5. Les jeunes gens _____ jusqu'à trois heures du matin. *(danser)*

6. Le professeur _____ la phrase au tableau. *(écrire)*

7. Vous _____ et vous _____ à vos examens. *(ne pas étudier/ne pas réussir)*

8. Je _____ tard hier soir. *(arriver)*

⟪ STRUCTURE ⟫

Change the following sentences into the negative.

1. Je parle le français et l'anglais.
2. Je connais tout le monde.
3. Tout le monde vient ici.
4. Tous les vendeurs parlaient le français.
5. Tout ici est bon marché.
6. Le magasin est toujours vide.
7. Quelqu'un est venu le voir.

20.

Les devoirs

AVANT DE LIRE: *Est-il important pour les parents d'aider leurs enfants avec leurs devoirs? Pourquoi?*

–Fernand, éteins° la télévision et viens aider
Madeleine à faire ses devoirs! a crié Madame
Bertin à son mari. C'est plus important de l'aider
que de regarder un match de football ou de lire
5 le journal. Maintenant, c'est ta dernière occasion°
de l'aider.
    –Pourquoi dis-tu que c'est ma dernière
occasion de l'aider? Est-ce que Madeleine ne
va plus aller à l'école l'année prochaine?

éteins turn off

occasion opportunity

96

10   —Mais si, a répondu sa femme d'une manière
sarcastique. Mais l'année prochaine, elle sera en
troisième° et tu ne pourras plus l'aider à ce niveau.°   **en troisième** 9th grade
      Monsieur Bertin est irrité par le sarcasme de   **niveau** level
son épouse. Mais il aime sa fille et il veut l'aider.
15   Il a abandonné son journal, il a éteint la télévision
et il s'est mis à travailler avec Madeleine. Mais
pendant qu'il essayait de répondre à ses questions,
il pensait toujours au match de football qu'il venait
de voir à la télévision. Evidemment, il faisait
20   beaucoup de fautes. Le travail terminé,
Madeleine a remercié son père pour son aide.
      Le lendemain, le professeur a vérifié° les   **a vérifié** checked
devoirs. A chaque question, Madeleine levait la
main pour répondre, pensant qu'elle avait la
25   bonne réponse. Malheureusement, la plupart de
ses réponses étaient mauvaises.
      Le professeur a remarqué avec surprise:
      —Je ne peux pas comprendre comment une
seule personne peut faire tant de fautes,
30   Madeleine.
      Madeleine embarrassée, a dû alors lui confier:
      —Vous faites erreur,° Madame. Mon père m'a   **faites erreur** you are
aidée à faire mes devoirs.   mistaken

☾ AVEZ-VOUS COMPRIS? ☽

A. Choose the phrase that correctly completes the sentence.

1. Monsieur Bertin regardait
   a. un livre sur le football.
   b. un journal avec des photos d'un match de football.
   c. la télévision où il y a un match de football.
   d. un match de football au stade.
2. Madame Bertin pense que son mari
   a. est très intelligent.
   b. est assez bête.
   c. s'amuse à faire les devoirs.
   d. aidera sa fille l'année prochaine.

3. En étudiant avec Madeleine, le père pensait au
   a. journal.
   b. devoir.
   c. sarcasme de sa femme.
   d. programme de télévision.
4. Le père a répondu _____ aux questions de sa fille.
   a. très bien
   b. sans faute
   c. mal
   d. avec ironie
5. Le professeur pensait que
   a. Madeleine avait fait trop de fautes.
   b. Monsieur Bertin avait aidé sa fille.
   c. Madame Bertin était gentille.
   d. les réponses de Madeleine étaient excellentes.

B. Répondez à ces questions par une phrase complète en français.
   1. Que fait Monsieur Bertin?
   2. Qu'est-ce qui est plus important que de regarder la télévision selon Madame Bertin?
   3. En quelle classe est Madeleine?
   4. Est-ce que Monsieur Bertin est content d'aider sa fille?
   5. Est-ce que Monsieur Bertin fait attention aux questions de sa fille?
   6. Est-ce que Madeleine avait les réponses justes aux questions?
   7. Qu'est-ce que le professeur ne comprend pas?
   8. Comment Madeleine explique-t-elle toutes les fautes qu'elle a faites?

C. Et vous?
   1. Est-ce que vos parents vous aident à faire vos devoirs?
   2. Faites-vous confiance à leurs réponses?
   3. Pensez-vous que ce soit une bonne chose que les parents aident leurs enfants pour leurs devoirs?
   4. Aimez-vous étudier avec des camarades ou seul?

◁◁ VOCABULAIRE ▷▷

Match the antonyms from both columns.

	A		B
1.	allumer	**a.**	mauvais
2.	femme	**b.**	terminer
3.	première	**d.**	éteindre
4.	commencer	**d.**	important
5.	bon	**e.**	dernière
6.	insignifiant	**f.**	mari

◁◁ VERBES ▷▷

A. Complete each sentence with the *passé composé* of the verb in parentheses. Watch the agreement of the past participle.

1. Madeleine _____ aux questions
   que le professeur _____.   *(répondre/poser)*
2. Madeleine _____ ses devoirs
   seule. Son père l' _____.   *(ne pas faire/aider)*
3. Mon père _____ le match de
   football à la télévision.   *(regarder)*
4. Est-ce que tu _____ la cassette
   que je t' _____.   *(écouter/prêter)*
5. Je _____ mon amie pour le livre. *(remercier)*
6. Vous _____ de l'aider.   *(essayer)*
7. Mes parents _____ au restaurant.
   Ils l' _____.   *(aller/aimer)*

B. Change the verbs in the paragraph to the past tense.

Tous les soirs je fais **(1)** _____ mes devoirs. Quelquefois mon frère m'aide **(2)** _____. Il n'est **(3)** _____ pas toujours très attentif. Alors, il fait **(4)** _____ beaucoup de fautes. Quand le professeur m'interroge **(5)** _____, je crois **(6)** _____ que mes réponses sont **(7)** _____ justes. Mais très vite, je réalise **(8)** _____ que tout est **(9)** _____ faux. Je suis **(10)** _____ très embarrassée. Je dois **(11)** _____ alors lui avouer que quelqu'un m'aide **(12)** _____ pour mes devoirs. La prochaine fois, je ne demande **(13)** _____ aucune assistance.

⚔ STRUCTURE ⚘

Complete each sentence by replacing the noun in parentheses with a pronoun.

1. Elle _____ fait avec son copain. *(ses devoirs)*
2. Madeleine _____ levait à chaque question. *(la main)*
3. Madeleine _____ répondait. *(à toutes les questions)*
4. Madeleine _____ a regardé avant de répondre. *(son professeur)*
5. Elle _____ faisait partie. *(de la classe)*
6. Le professeur _____ a posées à toute la classe. *(les questions)*

21.
Un ami par excellence

AVENT DE LIRE: *Prétendez que cinq ans se sont écoulés° depuis que vous avez terminé vos études. Tout d'un coup,° vous rencontrez un de vos anciens professeurs. Abordez°-vous le professeur ou essayez-vous de l'éviter?°*

se sont écoulés have
 gone by
Tout d'un coup All of a
 sudden
Abordez Approach
éviter to avoid

L'autre jour, j'attendais le train dans une station de métro à New York. Tout d'un coup, j'ai aperçu Monsieur Dufour, mon ancien professeur d'anglais à Paris. Quand j'étais dans sa classe, je n'étais
5 pas très bon élève. Une fois, il m'a demandé:

—Donnez-moi le présent du verbe anglais pour
"s'en aller"!°   **s'en aller** to go away

Au lieu° de dire "je m'en vais, tu t'en vas,"
j'ai répondu: "Tout le monde s'en va."   **Au lieu** Instead of

10   Cette réponse m'a valu° un double zéro.   **m'a valu** earned me

Je me suis avancé de Monsieur Dufour.

—Quel plaisir de vous rencontrer ici, a-t-il dit
en me serrant la main.

Je n'en revenais pas.°   **Je n'en revenais pas.** I could not believe it.

15   —Monsieur, ai-je demandé, vous vous souvenez
de moi, Raymond Fournier, le plus mauvais élève
de votre classe d'anglais?

—Mais oui, a-t-il répondu. Les professeurs se
souviennent souvent des pires° étudiants.   **pires** worse

20   Nous avons bavardé un moment. Puis il m'a dit:

—Je me rends à l'université de Columbia. J'ai
l'intention d'assister° à un cours de littérature
anglaise.   **assister** to attend

Je lui ai donné les renseignements nécessaires
25   pour y arriver et il m'a remercié amicalement.

—Raymond, m'a-t-il dit en me quittant, vous
êtes l'ami par excellence.

—Vous voulez dire un de vos amis sans
excellence, ai-je répondu en souriant. Au fait,
30   pourquoi ne vous êtes-vous pas renseigné°
auprès de l'employé? Vous parlez l'anglais
couramment.   **pourquoi ne vous êtes-vous pas renseigné** why didn't you ask

—J'ai demandé à l'employé et à des passants. Il
me semble que personne ne comprend l'anglais
35   à New York, en tout cas pas MON anglais.

⸿ AVEZ-VOUS COMPRIS? ⸾

A. Choose the phrase that correctly completes the sentence.

   1. Cette conversation a lieu

     a. à Paris.

     b. en Angleterre.

     c. à New York.

     d. à l'université de Columbia.

2. Raymond a reçu deux zéros parce que (qu')
   a. tout le monde s'en est allé.
   b. le professeur ne l'aimait pas.
   c. il ne savait pas le présent du verbe "s'en aller."
   d. c'était une très bonne note.
3. Monsieur Dufour allait
   a. étudier la littérature anglaise.
   b. enseigner à l'université de Columbia.
   c. retourner tout de suite à Paris.
   d. donner des leçons d'anglais à Raymond.
4. Monsieur Dufour enseignait
   a. l'histoire ancienne.
   b. le français.
   c. l'anglais.
   d. la littérature.
5. Selon Monsieur Dufour, à New York,
   a. l'employé parle bien l'anglais.
   b. tout le monde parle anglais.
   c. les passants parlent anglais.
   d. personne ne comprend l'anglais.

B. Répondez à ces questions par une phrase complète en français.
   1. Quelle est la profession de Monsieur Dufour?
   2. Où va-t-il quand Raymond le rencontre?
   3. Raymond était-il un bon élève en anglais?
   4. Monsieur Dufour a-t-il du mal à se rappeler Raymond? Pourquoi?
   5. Quel genre d'élèves les professeurs se rappellent-ils?
   6. Pourquoi Monsieur Dufour demande-t-il à Raymond des renseignements?
   7. Pourquoi Monsieur Dufour va-t-il à l'université de Columbia?
   8. Quelle sorte d'ami est Raymond selon Monsieur Dufour?

C. Et vous?
   1. Aimez-vous rencontrer d'anciens professeurs?
   2. Comment réagissez-vous lorsque vous rencontrez quelqu'un que vous n'avez pas vu depuis longtemps?
   3. Avez-vous de mauvais souvenirs de l'un de vos cours de langue?
   4. Aimez-vous être accoster pour donner des renseignements?
   5. Racontez une rencontre inattendue dans un endroit insolite.

⟪ VOCABULAIRE ⟫

Match the antonyms from the two columns.

A	B
1. attendre	**a.** prendre
2. nouveau	**b.** s'en aller
3. mauvais	**c.** nécessaire
4. revenir	**d.** partir
5. oublier	**e.** demander
6. donner	**f.** bon
7. inutile	**g.** ancien
8. répondre	**h.** se rappeler

⟪ VERBES ⟫

A. Complete each sentence with the appropriate past-tense form of the verb in parentheses.

Après avoir fini mes études à l'université, je (partir) **(1)** _____ en voyage pour améliorer mon anglais. Par hasard, dans l'avion j' (rencontrer) **(2)** _____ Martine. C'(être) **(3)** _____ une bonne camarade lorsque nous (étudier) **(4)** _____ ensembles. Maintenant, je (trouver) **(5)** _____ bizarre de la retrouver ici quand je (ne pas s'attendre) **(6)** _____.

B. Complete each sentence with the appropriate form of the *passé composé* of the verb in parentheses.

1. Vous _____ l'allemand.	*(étudier)*
2. J' _____ à mon professeur.	*(parler)*
3. Nous _____ à l'université en métro.	*(aller)*
4. Mes parents _____ longtemps.	*(attendre)*
5. Tu _____ trop tôt.	*(partir)*
6. Mon frère _____ ce film à Paris.	*(voir)*

☙ STRUCTURE ❧

Complete each sentence with the comparative or the superlative of the adjective in parentheses.

1. Mon frère est _____ (+ bon) élève de sa classe.
2. Les professeurs se rappellent _____ (+ mauvais) élèves.
3. Jacques est _____ (+ grand) de sa classe.
4. Michelle est _____ (+ grand) que Suzanne.
5. Cette robe est _____ (- cher) que l'autre.
6. Il était _____ (+ heureux) à la campagne qu'à la ville.

22.
Un poulet pas ordinaire

AVANT DE LIRE: *Quand vous partez en voyage, quel genre de souvenirs aimez-vous ramener pour votre famille et vos amis?*

Henri, un jeune Québécois, aime beaucoup voyager. Quand il est de par le monde, il cherche des cadeaux pour sa famille. Il aime surtout trouver des soldes.° Cette année, Henri est allé à Haïti. Au
5 retour, il a passé trois heures à la douane° pendant que le douanier examinait ses achats. Pour son grand-père, il a acheté un chapeau de paille° et un asson, une courge° qui est le symbole d'autorité des prêtres vaudou.° Pour son père, il a trouvé
10 des sandales de caoutchouc,° et pour son frère de quinze ans, un tam-tam. Il voulait acheter un

soldes bargains
à la douane at customs

paille straw
courge gourd
prêtres vaudou
  voodoo priests
caoutchouc rubber

106

tambourin d'acier,° mais c'était trop lourd. Et pour les enfants? Pour les filles, des poupées de paille et pour les garçons, de petites flûtes de bambou.

acier steel

15 Il a apporté pour sa mère un joli perroquet qui parle plusieurs langues étrangères (en tout cas, selon le vendeur).

De retour chez lui, Henri a vite distribué les cadeaux. Puis il est sorti pour se faire couper les
20 cheveux. Le soir, sa maman a préparé un excellent dîner pour célébrer son retour. La famille s'est mise à table à sept heures. Le plat de résistance° était un coq au vin, le plat favori d'Henri.

plat de résistance main course

—Est-ce que l'oiseau te plaît, maman? a
25 demandé Henri. Parlant du cadeau qu'il avait donné à sa mère le matin.

Sa mère, parlant du poulet, a répondu:

—Je pense qu'il n'a pas beaucoup de goût, mon chéri.

30 —Je ne veux pas dire le poulet, maman. Je parle du perroquet que je t'ai rapporté d'Haïti.

—Le perroquet? a demandé sa mère. J'ai cru que c'était un poulet. C'est pourquoi, j'ai préparé le coq au vin.

35 —Comment? Tu as fait cuire le perroquet? Cet oiseau si intelligent qui parlait sept langues?

—S'il parlait tant de langues, pourquoi ne m'a-t-il rien dit quand je l'ai mis dans la marmite,° a interrogé la mère.

marmite pot

❧ AVEZ-VOUS COMPRIS? ❧

A. Indicate whether these statements are true or false. Write *V* for *vrai* and *F* for *faux*. If the statement is false, correct it to make it true.

1. (   ) Pendant son voyage Henri a acheté des cadeaux bon marché pour ses parents.
2. (   ) Les achats d'Henri ont été examinés dans l'avion.
3. (   ) La mère d'Henri parle plusieurs langues étrangères.
4. (   ) La mère d'Henri est allée chez le coiffeur.
5. (   ) Quand elle l'a mis dans la marmite, le perroquet n'a pas parlé.

107

B. Répondez à ces questions par une phrase complète en français.

1. Où était Henri?
2. Que fait-il pendant ses voyages?
3. Qu'a-t-il acheté pour son frère de quinze ans?
4. Est-ce que la mère d'Henri a apprécié son cadeau?
5. Combien de langues le perroquet parle-t-il?
6. Est-ce que le coq au vin a bon goût?
7. Qu'est-ce que le perroquet a dit quand la mère d'Henri l'a mis dans la marmite?

C. Et vous?

1. Aimez-vous voyager?
2. Quel genre de voyages aimez-vous faire? Seul? En groupe?
3. Passez-vous beaucoup de temps à choisir des cadeaux pour votre famille durant vos voyages?
4. Quel genre de souvenirs aimez-vous rapporter de vos voyages?

◖◖ VOCABULAIRE ◗◗

Feminine forms: Masculine words ending in *-er* often have feminine forms ending in *-ère*. Give the feminine form of each of the following words and write a short paragraph using five of them.

1. boulanger
2. fermier
3. étranger
4. potager
5. dernier
6. crémier
7. laitier
8. premier

◖◖ VERBES ◗◗

Change the verbs in the first paragraph of the *conte* to the *imparfait* or the *plus-que-parfait*.

◖ STRUCTURE ◗

A. Use a relative pronoun to combine the two sentences into one.

MODÈLE: Je vois le livre. Le livre est sur la table.
Je vois le livre qui est sur la table.

1. Mes parents achètent des cadeaux. Ils donnent les cadeaux à leurs amis.
2. Sa mère a beaucoup aimé son cadeau. Son fils lui a offert un cadeau.
3. C'est le livre. Je me sers de ce livre.
4. Vous allez au cinéma. Je vous rencontrerai au cinéma.
5. Je connais le jeune homme. Le jeune homme s'avance vers nous.
6. Je t'ai offert une poupée. Est-ce que tu aimes la poupée?

B. Complete the sentences by replacing the words in parentheses with personal pronouns.

1. Il _____ a donné à sa mère. *(un cadeau)*
2. Il _____ admire beaucoup. *(cet artiste)*
3. Le perroquet ne _____ a rien dit. *(à sa mère)*
4. J' _____ parle. *(du cadeau)*
5. Pour _____ célébrer, sa mère a préparé un bon dîner. *(son retour)*
6. Je _____ vais. *(au cinéma)*

23.
Quand je serai grand . . .

AVANT DE LIRE: *Quels seraient vos critères°*   **critères** criteria
pour choisir une profession?

Le petit Michel voudrait imiter son papa et
exercer la même profession que lui. Son père
est professeur dans l'enseignement supérieur.
Mais Michel ne sait pas quelle matière il
5 voudrait enseigner.
–Papa, qu'est-ce que je pourrais enseigner,
d'après toi? demande Michel.
–Eh bien! Voyons! Tu aimes l'histoire. Tu
pourrais être professeur d'histoire.
10 –Que fait un professeur d'histoire, papa?
–Il enseigne les évènements importants. Il parle
des grands hommes. Tiens, je vais te poser une question pour évaluer si tu serais un bon prof d'histoire:

Quelle était la couleur du cheval blanc d'Henri IV?

15 —Je crois qu'il est célèbre pour son cheval
noir, répond Michel.

—Je ne crois pas que l'histoire serait un bon
sujet pour toi.

—Peut-être les sciences alors? De quoi parle
20 un professeur de sciences?

—Des caractéristiques des éléments, de la
densité, de leurs propriétés. Tiens, voyons si
tu peux répondre à cette question de science:
Qu'est-ce qui pèse le plus lourd, un kilo de
25 plumes° ou un kilo de plomb?°

plumes feathers
plomb lead

—Oh! Ça, c'est facile, un kilo de plomb, bien sûr.
—Tu en es si sûr? Un kilo c'est un kilo. On
met beaucoup de plumes jusqu'à ce qu'il° y en

jusqu'à ce que until

ait un kilo. Mais si tu mets un kilo de plumes sur
30 un plateau de la balance° et un kilo de plomb

balance scale

de l'autre côté, c'est en équilibre°. Les sciences

en équilibre balanced

ne sont peut-être pas le bon choix non plus.

Le père de Michel avec beaucoup de patience
lui explique ce qu'enseignent les professeurs de
35 chaque discipline° à laquelle pense le petit.

discipline subject

Finalement il déclare:

—Je crois que j'ai trouvé. Tu pourrais être professeur d'astronomie, tu es toujours dans la lune.°

dans la lune in the moon

◁◖ AVEZ-VOUS COMPRIS? ◗▷

A. Indicate whether these statements are true or false. Write *V* for *vrai*
and *F* for *faux*. If the statement is false, correct it to make it true.

1. (   ) Le père et son fils discutent des devoirs du garçon.
2. (   ) Le père est ingénieur.
3. (   ) Michel veut devenir professeur.
4. (   ) Michel n'aime pas l'histoire.
5. (   ) Le père de Michel n'a aucune patience pour les
        questions de son fils.
6. (   ) Michel donne de bonnes réponses aux questions de
        son père.
7. (   ) Les plumes sont plus lourdes que le plomb.
8. (   ) Le père de Michel pense qu'il devrait être professeur
        de musique.

B. Répondez à ces questions par une phrase complète en français.

1. Comment s'appelle le petit garçon de l'histoire?
2. Que veut-il devenir lorsqu'il sera grand?
3. Pourquoi veut-il devenir professeur?
4. Quelle matière veut-il enseigner?
5. Pourquoi son père pense-t-il qu'il ne peut pas enseigner l'histoire?
6. De quelle couleur était le cheval d'Henri IV?
7. Donne-t-il une bonne réponse à la deuxième question de son père?
8. Quelle matière le père de Michel suggère-t-il? Pourquoi?

C. Et vous?

1. Quand vous étiez jeune, saviez-vous ce que vous vouliez faire professionnellement?
2. De quelle façon choisiriez-vous une carrière possible pour vous?
3. Que pensez-vous des questions du père de Michel?
4. Aimez-vous discuter de votre avenir avec vos parents?
5. Comment vous préparerez-vous à la carrière que vous choisissez?

✎ VOCABULAIRE ✎

Indicate the word that does not belong in the group.

1. profession / occupation / travail / carrière
2. matière / discipline / sujet / objet
3. évaluer / coordonner / apprécier / peser
4. déclarer / dire / penser / remarquer
5. facile / ardu / aisé / sans problème
6. enseignant / surveillant / instituteur / professeur

◆◇ VERBES ◇◆

Verb review: Complete each sentence with the appropriate forms of the verbs in parentheses.

1. S'il _____ mieux l'histoire,
   il _____ l'enseigner.   *(connaître/pouvoir)*
2. Je _____ imiter ma sœur,
   mais je _____ ses talents.   *(vouloir/ne pas avoir)*
3. Nous _____ au théâtre,
   mais il _____.   *(aller/pleuvoir)*
4. Vous _____ venir, mais
   je _____.   *(pouvoir/être absent)*
5. Mes parents _____ au restaurant,
   mais ils _____ fatigués.   *(aller/être)*
6. Que _____ -tu si
   tu _____ des voleurs?   *(faire/rencontrer)*

◆◇ STRUCTURE ◇◆

Change each sentence into the negative.

1. Il voudrait imiter son père.
2. Je sais quelle matière je vais enseigner.
3. Tu aimes les sciences. Sois professeur de sciences.
4. Il enseigne tous les évènements importants.
5. Vous parlez de quelques-uns des grands hommes.
6. Pourquoi lui posez-vous ces questions?

24.
Le concert

AVANT DE LIRE: *Quel genre de musique considérez-vous dans le coup?° Pensez-vous que la valse pourrait être dans le coup? Pourquoi?*

dans le coup hot, fashionable

Il était génial, un génie musical. Ses compositions musicales étaient supérieures à celles de Debussy ou Ravel. Il jouait du piano, et aussi de la guitare et du violon. Qui a découvert
5 ce génie? Son professeur de musique, bien sûr. Qui avait confiance en lui? Seulement son père, un riche négociant° en vin. Et quand on a un fils

négociant dealer

114

unique, un enfant prodige, il est absolument
nécessaire d'organiser un concert pour le faire
10 connaître.

Monsieur Legendre, le père de Thibault, avait
invité tous les parents de sa classe. Il avait
promis des rafraîchissements et autres friandises.°   **friandises** goodies
Il avait promis:
15 —Chacun recevra une corbeille° de fruits, des   **corbeille** basket
oranges, des pommes, des raisins et des cerises
après le concert.

—Il y aura un monde fou,° avait déclaré   **un monde fou** a lot of
Monsieur Legendre. Les portes craqueront.°   people
    craqueront will burst
20 Mais les parents ont refusé de venir. Ils
n'avaient pas envie d'écouter Thibault. Qui
pouvait aider ce père si fier du génie de son
fils? Que faire?

L'idée lumineuse lui est alors venue qu'il y a
25 beaucoup de Legendre dans l'annuaire. Oui, il
allait envoyer une invitation à tous les Legendre.
Chacun penserait que Thibault était sans doute
un distant parent. Tous viendraient sûrement
écouter ce génie musical.

30 Le soir du concert arriva. Toute une foule°   **foule** crowd
de Legendre se pressait dans la salle. Il n'y avait
plus une place de libre. Beaucoup se plaignaient°   **se plaignaient** were
parce qu'ils devaient rester debout dans le corridor.   complaining
Thibault a commencé à jouer "La valse en une
35 minute." Tout d'un coup, un homme est entré
en criant:

—Monsieur Legendre, votre maison est en feu!
Tous sont aussitôt sortis en courant de la salle.

Le lendemain, dans le journal, on pouvait lire
40 cette critique:

—Le jeune génie musical, Thibault Legendre,
a établi un nouveau record. Il a joué "La valse
en une minute" en dix secondes.

AVEZ-VOUS COMPRIS?

A. Indicate whether these statements are true or false. Write *V* for *vrai* and *F* for *faux*. If the statement is false, correct it to make it true.

   1. (   ) Thibault écrit et joue des chansons.
   2. (   ) Son père vend du vin.
   3. (   ) Le père a offert toutes sortes de choses à boire et à manger aux invités.
   4. (   ) Personne ne voulait venir écouter Thibault jouer.
   5. (   ) Le père a invité tous les Legendre de l'annuaire.
   6. (   ) Il n'y avait pas beaucoup de monde au concert.
   7. (   ) Il fallait acheter un billet pour assister à ce concert.
   8. (   ) Un homme est entré dans la salle avec de bonnes nouvelles.
   9. (   ) Chacun croyait que c'était sa propre maison qui brûlait.
   10. (   ) On a critiqué le jeune musicien d'avoir joué trop lentement.

B. Répondez à ces questions par une phrase complète en français.

   1. Qui sont Debussy et Ravel, des violonistes ou des compositeurs?
   2. Qui a dit que Thibault est génial?
   3. Quelle est l'occupation de Monsieur Legendre?
   4. Pourquoi les invités ne voulaient-ils pas venir au concert?
   5. Combien de Legendre y avait-il dans l'annuaire?
   6. Y avait-il assez de places au concert?
   7. Comment est-ce qu'un homme a interrompu le programme?
   8. Pourquoi est-ce que tout le monde sort?
   9. Quel record Thibault détient-il maintenant?

C. Et vous?

   1. Jouez-vous d'un instrument? Lequel?
   2. Quelle sorte de musique aimez-vous? Classique? Pop? Jazz?
   3. Connaissez-vous la musique de Debussy et Ravel? L'aimez-vous?
   4. Y a-t-il un enfant prodige dans votre famille?
   5. Beaucoup de personnes ont-elles le même nom que vous dans l'annuaire?
   6. Avez-vous un plan d'évacuation de votre maison en cas d'incendie?
   7. Avez-vous déjà battu un record? Lequel?

≪ VOCABULAIRE ≫

A. Faux amis: Some words that look like cognates are misleading because the French and English meanings are not the same. These words are called *faux amis*. Give the English equivalent of the following *faux amis*.

1. assister
2. crier
3. la chance
4. la journée
5. garder
6. attendre
7. pratiquer
8. le journal

B. Word groups: The ending *-ier* added to the name of a fruit refers to the tree that bears that fruit. Give the French word for the fruit produced by these trees and tell what kind of tree it is in English.

1. un cerisier
2. un pommier
3. un bananier
4. un abricotier
5. un poirier
6. un olivier
7. un prunier
8. un figuier

≪ VERBES ≫

A. Change the verbs from the future to the immediate future.

1. Chacun recevra _____ une corbeille de fruits.
2. Il y aura _____ des cadeaux pour tout le monde.
3. Ils viendront _____ en masse.
4. Tu seras _____ récompensé.
5. Je voudrai _____ cette robe.
6. Nous irons _____ au restaurant.
7. Vous pourrez _____ l'admirer.
8. Il fera _____ beau demain.

B. Change the verbs from the immediate future to the future.

1. Elle va être _____ musicienne.
2. Nous allons recevoir _____ de bonnes notes.
3. Je vais venir _____ vous voir.
4. Vous allez avoir _____ peur du volcan.
5. Vas-tu faire _____ un voyage cet été?
6. Ils vont aller _____ au concert parce que le pianiste est célèbre.
7. Je vais accepter _____ ton invitation.
8. Son père va nous donner _____ des rafraîchissements.

⪞ STRUCTURE ⪟

A. Complete the sentences with the appropriate interrogative pronoun—*qui, que,* or *quoi.*

1. _____ a trouvé mon livre?
2. _____ vient chez moi?
3. _____ organise ce concert?
4. _____ voyez-vous dans cette salle?
5. A _____ bon?
6. _____ penses-tu du programme?
7. _____ faire?
8. _____ peut aider ce père fier?

B. Ask questions using *qui, que,* or *quoi* according to the answer.

1. Ma mère me donne une pomme.
2. Je lis un article dans le journal.
3. Mon oncle travaille au théâtre.
4. On peut étudier davantage.
5. Nous mettons les fruits dans la corbeille.
6. Raoul est mon meilleur ami.

25.
Le procès
(Première partie)

AVANT DE LIRE: *Pouvez-vous discerner° quand quelqu'un vous dit des mensonges?°
Comment le savez-vous?*

discerner to detect
mensonges lies

Le premier procès:°
—Je ne suis pas coupable,° Monsieur le Juge.
Je suis innocent, a déclaré le premier accusé.
Je n'ai pas volé le poste de radio. Je vais vous
5 expliquer. Je flânais° dans la rue à trois heures

procès trial
coupable guilty

flânais was strolling

du matin quand j'ai vu la vitrine cassée.° **cassée** broken
Evidemment, je me suis arrêté. Au fond de la
vitrine, il y avait un paquet. Et dans ce paquet,
il y avait la radio. Je ne savais pas à qui elle
10 était. Je n'ai pas voulu la laisser parce qu'une
personne malhonnête aurait pu la voler. J'ai
cherché un agent mais en vain. J'ai donc décidé
de la porter au bureau de police au coin de la
rue. J'étais agité et confus. Voilà pourquoi je suis
15 allé en sens inverse.° Tout d'un coup, un agent **en sens inverse** in the
opposite direction
m'a attrapé et il m'a demandé la radio. Comme
je respecte les agents de police, je leur obéis
toujours et je la lui ai donnée. Je l'ai même
accompagné au bureau et ensuite, il m'a amené
20 ici au tribunal.

    Le deuxième procès:

    –Monsieur le Juge, ainsi a commencé l'aîné
des deux jeunes gens qui sont accusés du vol
d'un sac à main. Monsieur le Juge, mon copain
25 et moi, nous sommes innocents. La vieille dame
s'est trompée. Ce gars et moi, nous nous prome-
nions dans la rue et cette dame marchait devant
nous. Tout à coup, elle s'est retournée et elle a
commencé à nous frapper avec son sac. Nous
30 voulions nous défendre, et j'ai pris le sac. Elle a
commencé à pousser des cris. Nous ne voulions
pas réveiller tous les voisins qui dormaient et nous
nous sommes enfuis.° A ce moment-là, nous **nous nous sommes
enfuis** we fled
avons vu l'agent. Nous nous sommes approchés
35 de lui pour demander sa protection contre cette
vieille enragée. C'est pour cette raison que nous
sommes venus au tribunal. Pour vous prouver° **prouver** to show
que nous sommes des gens honorables, tous les
deux, nous voulons lui rendre l'argent qui est
40 tombé par terre pendant qu'elle nous frappait.

◖ AVEZ-VOUS COMPRIS? ◗

A. Indicate whether these statements are true or false. Write *V* for *vrai* and *F* for *faux*. If the statement is false, correct it to make it true.

1. (　) Le premier homme est accusé d'avoir volé une radio.
2. (　) Le premier crime s'est passé la nuit.
3. (　) Cet homme a cassé la vitrine d'un magasin.
4. (　) Il a réussi à trouver un agent.
5. (　) Il n'a pas résisté à l'agent.
6. (　) Dans le deuxième procès une vielle dame a trompé deux garçons.
7. (　) Les garçons marchaient derrière la dame.
8. (　) Ils ont essayé de réveiller quelqu'un pour les aider.
9. (　) Une vieille dame est certainement moins forte que les deux jeunes gens.
10. (　) Les jeunes gens ont volé l'argent à la dame.

B. Répondez à ces questions par une phrase complète en français.

1. A quelle heure le premier accusé flânait-il?
2. Qu'a-t-il vu?
3. Pourquoi a-t-il pris la radio de la vitrine?
4. Quelle erreur a-t-il faite?
5. Pourquoi a-t-il donné la radio à l'agent?
6. De quoi accuse-t-on les deux jeunes gens?
7. A qui était le sac à main?
8. Pourquoi les deux jeunes gens se sont-ils enfuis?
9. Est-ce que l'agent a cru leur histoire?
10. Selon eux, comment ont-ils obtenu l'argent?

C. Et vous?

1. Quand aimez-vous flâner dans les rues?
2. Quelles vitrines aimez-vous regarder?
3. Avez-vous jamais cassé une vitrine?
4. Avez-vous jamais été la victime d'un vol? Que vous a-t-on volé?
5. Quand vous vous promenez avec un ami, marchez-vous devant, derrière ou à côté?
6. A votre avis, les accusés sont-ils coupables ou innocents?

❧ VOCABULAIRE ☙

A. Reflexive verbs: The addition of the reflexive pronoun to a French verb slightly changes the meaning of the new verb. Give the English for the following pairs of verbs.

1. lever; se lever
2. trouver; se trouver
3. retourner; se retourner
4. réveiller; se réveiller
5. tromper; se tromper
6. appeler; s'appeler
7. rappeler; se rappeler
8. conduire; se conduire
9. fâcher; se fâcher
10. inquiéter; s'inquiéter

B. Match the words in column A with their antonyms or synonyms in column B.

A	B
1. coupable	a. flâner
2. acheter	b. mentir
3. se promener	c. toujours
4. tromper	d. aller avec
5. accompagner	e. rendre
6. jamais	f. s'en aller
7. se défendre	g. innocent
8. prendre	h. vendre
9. s'enfuir	i. attaquer
10. enragé	j. fâché

ꙮ VERBES ꙮ

A. Complete each sentence with the *passé composé* of the verb in parentheses.

1. La dame _____ de personne.   *(se tromper)*
2. Jean et Philippe _____ devant le juge.   *(se défendre)*
3. Jacques, tu _____ avec dignité.   *(se conduire)*
4. Ce matin, je _____ à six heures.   *(se lever)*
5. Quand elle a vu l'agent, elle _____.   *(s'arrêter)*
6. En entendant le bruit, nous _____.   *(se retourner)*
7. Quand la maison a pris feu, mes parents _____.   *(s'enfuir)*
8. Mon frère _____ doucement du bébé.   *(s'approcher)*

B. Change the verbs to the *passé composé.*

1. Il s'amuse à regarder des westerns à la télévision.
2. Nous ne nous inquiétons pas.
3. Je me lève de bonne heure.
4. Maman, est-ce que tu te fâches?
5. Elle s'approche de la victime.
6. Les voleurs s'enfuient.
7. Matthieu, tu ne te retournes pas?
8. Les trois jeunes filles se trompent.
9. Ma petite sœur se conduit mal.
10. A quelle heure Charlotte se couche-t-elle?

⮜ STRUCTURE ⮞

A. Complete each sentence with the correct pronoun form.

1. _____ ne suis pas coupable. *(Je/Me/Moi)*
2. Elle marchait devant _____. *(il/le/lui)*
3. Mon copain et _____, nous sommes
   innocents. *(je/me/moi)*
4. Il _____ est arrêté. *(l'/lui/s')*
5. Les assassins, personne ne _____
   voit jamais. *(les/leur/se)*
6. Elle a commencé à _____ frapper. *(je/me/moi)*
7. Je _____ ai donné l'argent. *(les/leur/se)*
8. Ils se sont approchés de _____. *(te/toi/tu)*

B. Substitute pronouns for the underlined words.

1. La dame marchait devant les garçons.
2. Mon père a lu l'article à mes frères.
3. Les agents ont posé des questions aux voisins.
4. Le malade va aller chez le médecin.
5. Le juge écoute le témoignage.
6. Qui veut annoncer les nouvelles à l'accusé?
7. Mes parents sont allés en vacances sans mes frères et moi.

26.
Le procès (Deuxième partie)

AVANT DE LIRE: *Que pensez-vous des magistrats qui acquittent les coupables et condamnent les innocents? Pensez-vous que cela arrive souvent?*

–Monsieur le Juge, je ne suis pas voleur de bijoux. Un étranger s'est approché de moi au coin de la rue et il m'a dit:

–Mon vieux, tu as l'air honnête. Prends ce
5 paquet et mets-le dans ta poche. J'ai un trou°   **trou** hole
dans ma poche et je rentre chez moi pour la
raccommoder.° Je reviendrai dans quelques   **raccommoder** to mend
minutes.

J'ai cru ce qu'il m'a dit. Il m'a donné le paquet
10 et il a disparu.

Bientôt, mes camarades sont arrivés et ils
m'ont dit:

—Ouvre le paquet! C'est peut-être une bombe.
Nous sommes entrés sous un porche.° Nous   **porche** doorway
15 étions en train d'ouvrir le paquet quand un agent
nous a surpris. Il m'a conduit devant ce tribunal.

—Je suis coupable, a déclaré le quatrième
accusé. Je suis coupable d'entrer en compétition
avec le gouvernement. Je contrefais° de l'argent;   **contrefais** counterfeit
20 de plus, je vends la fausse monnaie moins chère
que le gouvernement. Par patriotisme, je vais
renoncer à cette entreprise pour mener° une   **mener** lead
existence honorable.

Le juge écoute le témoignage° des accusés.   **témoignage** testimony
25 Puis il annonce sa décision.

—Je condamne les accusés des trois premiers
procès à six mois de prison. J'annule° le jugement   **annule** cancel
contre le dernier accusé. Libérez le dernier accusé.

—Monsieur, dit le procureur,° pourquoi   **procureur** prosecutor
30 mettez-vous en liberté cet homme qui a aussi
commis un crime? Il était coupable, n'est-ce pas?

—Vous avez raison, Monsieur le Procureur, il
est coupable. Mais si je le mets en prison, tous les
innocents se plaindront.° Eux, ils ne voudraient   **se plaindront** will
35 certainement pas cohabiter avec un criminel.   complain
Je dois donc le libérer.

⟪ AVEZ-VOUS COMPRIS? ⟫

A. Choose the phrase that corectly completes the sentence.

   1. Un voleur de bijoux
      a. fabrique des bijoux.
      b. est bijoutier.
      c. s'approprie des bijoux par force.
      d. achète et vend des bijoux.

   2. L'étranger n'a pas gardé le paquet parce que (qu')
      a. sa poche avait un trou.
      b. il y avait un trou dans le paquet.
      c. il n'avait pas de poche.
      d. il n'était pas honnête.

3. Dans le paquet mystérieux, il y avait
   a. une bombe.
   b. des voleurs.
   c. des bijoux.
   d. un trou.
4. Le dernier accusé était
   a. vendeur.
   b. faux-monnayeur.
   c. innocent.
   d. négociant.
5. Le juge a condamné
   a. tous les accusés.
   b. ceux qui n'ont pas avoué leur crime.
   c. les innocents.
   d. seulement le dernier accusé.

B. Répondez à ces questions par une phrase complète en français.
   1. Où l'accusé a-t-il rencontré l'étranger?
   2. Que lui a donné l'étranger?
   3. Pourquoi l'étranger a-t-il donné un paquet à l'accusé?
   4. De quoi les camarades de l'accusé ont-ils eu peur?
   5. Est-ce que le dernier accusé était innocent?
   6. De quoi s'accuse-t-il?
   7. Pourquoi veut-il renoncer à son activité criminelle?
   8. Est-ce que le juge est indulgent?

C. Et vous?
   1. Avez-vous déjà accepté de recevoir des paquets d'un inconnu?
   2. Comment réagissez-vous lorsqu'un étranger vous aborde?
   3. Avez-vous été appelé à faire partie d'un jury?
   4. Qu'est-ce qui vous fait peur?
   5. Quelqu'un a-t-il essayé de vous vendre quelque chose de volé?

ᘓ VOCABULAIRE ᘔ

Match the antonyms from the two columns.

A	B
1. s'approcher	**a.** confirmer
2. honnête	**b.** s'éloigner
3. mettre	**c.** apparaître
4. revenir	**d.** sortir
5. disparaître	**e.** acheter
6. entrer	**f.** fermer
7. ouvrir	**g.** partir
8. vendre	**h.** enlever
9. annuler	**i.** incarcérer
10. libérer	**j.** malhonnête

ᘓ VERBES ᘔ

A. Complete each sentence with the future form of the verb in parentheses.

1. Je _____ un voleur de bijoux. *(ne pas être)*
2. Nous _____ des animaux tout doucement. *(s'approcher)*
3. Vous _____ le paquet. *(prendre)*
4. Ils _____ dans quelques minutes. *(revenir)*
5. Tu _____ à l'heure. *(arriver)*
6. Elle _____ qu'il fait trop chaud. *(se plaindre)*

B. Verb review: Complete each sentence with the appropriate tense of the verb in parentheses.

1. Le juge _____ son verdict s'il le pouvait. *(annuler)*
2. Il m'a dit qu'il _____ plus tard. *(revenir)*
3. Hier, je _____ de lui et il m' _____. *(s'approcher/ repousser)*
4. Nous ouvrions le paquet quand l'agent _____. *(arriver)*
5. Il pourrait y avoir une bombe. _____ le paquet! *(ne pas ouvrir; vous)*
6. Pourquoi _____ en liberté ce coupable? *(mettre; vous)*
7. Je voudrais _____ tout de suite. *(partir)*
8. A leur place, je _____ habiter ici. *(ne pas vouloir)*

❦ STRUCTURE ❧

Complete the sentences with the appropriate pronoun.

1. _____ s'est approché de moi. *(Lui/Il/Elle)*
2. _____, tu ne voudrais pas venir. *(Tu/Toi/Ton)*
3. Mes parents _____ ont donné un
   joli cadeau. *(ils/leur/nous)*
4. Quand _____ est arrivée, il venait
   de partir. *(nous/elle/tu)*
5. _____ avez toujours raison. *(Tu/Vous/Ils)*
6. J'étais inquiète parce que (qu') _____
   étaient très en retard. *(elles/vous/ils)*

27.
En ligne

AVANT DE LIRE: *Que savez-vous sur les ordinateurs? Est-ce que les ordinateurs jouent un rôle important pour vous?*

Caroline, une jeune étudiante, va passer la prochaine année scolaire en Argentine. Avant son départ, son amie Nicole fait la remarque:

–Heureusement que nous vivons à l'ère° de **ère** era, age
5 la communication. Nous n'aurons pas à attendre l'arrivée des lettres par la poste, et nous n'aurons

pas des notes de téléphones exorbitantes. Nous pourrons communiquer par courrier électronique.° La famille où tu vas loger° a l'internet. De nos jours,° presque tout le monde est connecté.°

—Oh, Nicole, tu sais comment je suis avec les ordinateurs. J'ai toujours peur d'effacer° un fichier° ou de télécharger° un virus. Je ne sais pas utiliser l'internet.

—Ecoute, Caroline, après avoir démarré ton ordinateur, tu double-cliques avec ta souris d'abord sur la connexion au réseau,° puis sur ton navigateur. Après ça, clique sur l'icône de ton e-mail. Tu écris ton message, puis finalement tu cliques sur "envoyer" et tu l'envoies. C'est tout.

A Buenos Aires, Caroline, bien qu'impatiente de communiquer avec ses amis, est nerveuse à la pensée qu'un accident peut arriver avec l'ordinateur. Pour se détendre, elle allume des bougies parfumées. Elle suit les directives° pas à pas.° Tout se passe comme Nicole l'a indiqué. Mais soudain, l'écran de l'ordinateur est noir. Caroline appuie° sur une touche après une autre, mais l'écran demeure noir. Angoissée, elle appelle son amie sur son portable.° Nicole tente de la calmer en lui indiquant d'autres démarches,° mais Caroline dit:

—Il ne se passe rien.°

—Vérifie les branchements,° Nicole lui conseille.

—Je ne peux pas. Je ne vois rien.

—Comment? Tu ne vois rien? demande Nicole.

—Non, dit Caroline, je ne vois rien. Depuis un petit moment, il y a une panne d'électricité° dans toute la maison.

courrier électronique e-mail
loger to live

De nos jours Nowadays
est connecté is connected
effacer to erase
fichier file/program
télécharger to download

réseau net, network

directives instructions
pas à pas step by step
appuie press

portable cellular phone
démarches instructions
Il ne se passe rien Nothing is happening.
branchements connections

une panne d'électricité power outage

✎ AVEZ-VOUS COMPRIS? ✎

A. Choose the phrase that corectly completes the sentence.

1. Caroline est
   a. professeur.
   b. d'Argentine.
   c. l'amie de Nicole.
   d. la sœur de Nicole.
2. Caroline et Nicole pourront communiquer
   a. à distance.
   b. par internet.
   c. par courrier aérien.
   d. par panne d'électricité.
3. Caroline dit qu'elle
   a. est tout à fait à l'aise avec l'internet.
   b. manie très bien l'internet.
   c. sait très peu sur l'internet.
   d. ne sait pas utiliser l'internet.
4. Nicole explique à Caroline comment utiliser
   a. le courrier électronique.
   b. les virus.
   c. l'écran.
   d. le disque dur.
5. L'écran de l'ordinateur est devenu sombre parce que (qu')
   a. l'ordinateur est tombé en panne.
   b. Caroline a allumé une bougie parfumée.
   c. il y avait une panne d'électricité dans toute la maison.
   d. Caroline n'avait pas vérifié les branchements.

B. Répondez à ces questions par une phrase complète en français.

    1. Où part Caroline?

    2 Qui est Nicole?

    3. Comment appellent-elles l'époque où nous vivons?

    4. Quels sont les avantages du courrier électronique par rapport au courrier aérien?

    5. Pourquoi les ordinateurs rendent-ils Caroline nerveuse?

    6. Pour le faire marcher, combien de fois cliquez-vous sur l'icône du courrier?

    7. Qu'est-ce que Caroline allume pour se détendre?

    8. Pourquoi l'écran de l'ordinateur de Caroline demeure-t-il noir?

C. Et vous?

    1. Utilisez-vous beaucoup un ordinateur? Dans quel but?

    2. Etes-vous nerveux lorsque vous utilisez un ordinateur?

    3. Pourquoi les téléphones portables sont-ils populaires?

    4. Préférez-vous communiquer par internet ou par téléphone portable avec vos amis? Pourquoi?

    5. Que pensez-vous de l'idée de passer une année scolaire à l'étranger?

    6. Connaissez-vous quelqu'un qui habite à l'étranger?

    7. Quand est la dernière fois où vous avez eu une panne d'électricité chez vous? Racontez ce qui s'est passé.

    8. Quand est la dernière fois où vous êtes sorti(e) de votre pays (état)? Où êtes-vous allé(e)?

☙ VOCABULAIRE ❧

Complete the sentences with the correct forms of the words below in the order they are listed. You will find the English equivalents in the *French-English Vocabulary*.

D'abord j' **(1)** _____ mon ordinateur. Toutes les icônes **(2)** _____. Je **(3)** _____ sur le traitement de texte et je commence à **(4)** _____ pour **(5)** _____. Je **(6)** _____ sur la première ligne avec la **(7)** _____ et **(8)** _____ apparaît. Je tape mon texte. **(9)** _____ est longue. Avant de terminer, je **(10)** _____ mon document dans la **(11)** _____.

allumer	la souris
s'afficher sur l'écran	le curseur
cliquer	la saisie de données
taper	sauvegarder
créer un document	la banque de données
pointer	

☙ VERBES ❧

Complete each sentence with the imperative of the verb in parentheses.

1. _____ ton ordinateur. *(allumer; tu)*
2. _____ sur le traitement de texte. *(cliquer; vous)*
3. _____ un document. *(créer; nous)*
4. _____ toujours vos fichiers. *(sauvegarder; vous)*
5. _____ le curseur à l'endroit où tu veux écrire. *(pointer; tu)*
6. Pour voir la fin du document, _____ jusqu'au bout. *(dérouler; tu)*
7. Pour une meilleure présentation de ton devoir, _____ une jolie police de caractères. *(choisir; tu)*

❧ STRUCTURE ☙

Complete each sentence with the appropriate possessive adjective.

1. _____ famille habite Paris. *(ton/son/ma)*

2. J'aime voyager avec _____ enfants. *(mes/son/votre)*

3. Jeanne donne des directives à Nicole. Nicole suit _____ directives pas à pas. *(mes/tes/ses)*

4. Roger donne un livre à Paul. Paul est content de _____ livre. *(mon/ses/son)*

5. Si tu veux écrire un e-mail, commence par pointer _____ souris. *(sa/ma/ta)*

6. Tu écris _____ messages et tu les envoies. *(mes/ses/tes)*

◖ French-English Vocabulary ◗

A

aborder to approach
aboyer to bark
absolument absolutely
accompagner to accompany
accueillir to welcome; to greet
accusé *(m.)* defendant
achat *(m.)* purchase
acheter to buy
affaires *(f. pl.)* business
s'afficher sur l'écran to appear
  on the sceen (computer)
affirmer to assure
agent de police *(m.)* police officer
aggraver to make matters worse
agréable pleasant
aide: A l'aide! Help!
aimable likeable
aimer to love
aîné older, oldest
ainsi thus
air *(m.)* look
aller to go
  s'en aller to go away
allumer to light; to turn on
  (computer)
améliorer to improve
amener to bring
amèrement bitterly
ami *(m.)* **amie** *(f.)* friend
amical friendly
amicalement in a friendly way
an *(m.)* year
  avoir—ans to be—years old
annuaire *(m.)* phone book
annuler to cancel
apercevoir to notice
apparaître to appear
apprendre to learn
s'approcher de to come near,
  to get close
appuyer to press

après after
argent *(m.)* money
  à court d'argent short of money
arriver to happen, to arrive
asseoir: s'asseoir to sit down
assez enough
assis seated
assister to attend
assortir to match
attaque *(f.)* **cardiaque** heart
  attack
atteindre (un but) to achieve
attendre to wait
  s'attendre à to expect
attristé saddened
autant so much
avancer to go forward
avant before
avec with
avisé wise, skillful
avocat *(m.)* lawyer
avoir to have
  avoir—ans to be—years old
  avoir faim to be hungry
  avoir la monnaie to have
    change
  avoir soif to be thirsty
elle a quelque chose something
  is the matter with her
avouer to confess, to admit

B

balance *(f.)* scale
banque *(f.)* **de données** database
bassin *(m.)* pool of water
bâtiment *(m.)* building
beaucoup de lots of
bébête silly
bénévole volunteer
besoin *(m.)* need
  avoir besoin to need
bien que although

bien sûr of course
billet *(m.)* ticket
bouillant boiling
bout *(m.)*
    d'un bout à l'autre from one end
    to the other
boutique *(f.)* small shop
branchements *(m. pl.)* connections
brouhaha *(m.)* hustle and bustle
bruit *(m.)* noise
brûler to burn

C

ça that
cadeau *(m.)* present
cahier *(m.)* notebook
camion *(m.)* truck
caserne *(f.)* **de pompiers** fire station
cassé broken
cent hundred
certains some
chacun each
chandelle *(f.)* candle
charger to boot up *(computer)*
chez at the home of
client *(m.)* customer
cliquer to click
coiffeur *(m.)* hairdresser
colère *(f.)* anger
    se mettre en colère to get angry
colline *(f.)* hill
commerçant *(m.)* businessman
comprendre to understand
confection *(m.)* ready-to-wear
    clothes
confiance *(f.)* confidence, trust
connaître to know
conseil *(m.)* advice
conseiller to advise
conserver son calme to keep
    one's calm
content happy
contrefaire to counterfeit
convaincre to convince
corbeille *(f.)* basket
cordonnier *(m.)* shoemaker
corridor *(m.)* hallway
cortège *(m.)* **funèbre** funeral
    procession
coucher: se coucher to go to bed
coup *(m.)* move
    dans le coup hot, fashionable

coupable guilty
coupure *(f.)* bill
courageux(-se) brave
courir to run
courrier *(m.)* **électronique** e-mail
course *(f.)* run
craie *(f.)* chalk
craquer to burst
créer un document to create a
    document *(computer)*
crier to shout
croire to believe
curseur *(m.)* cursor

D

d'abord at first
dame *(f.)* lady
d'autres others
davantage more
debout standing
dedans inside
demain tomorrow
se demander to wonder
démarches *(f. pl.)* instructions
dérouler to scroll *(computer)*
désemplir to empty partially
détruire to destroy
deux two
devant in front of
devenir to become
devise *(f.)* moto
devoirs *(m. pl.)* homework
devrait should
difficile à vivre difficult to
    put up with
dire to say
    Que veux-tu dire? What do you
    mean?
directives *(f. pl.)* instructions
se diriger vers to go to
discerner to detect
discipline *(f.)* subject
disque dur *(m.)* hard drive
distrait absent-minded
donner to give
dormir to sleep

E

eau minérale *(f.)* mineral water
échecs *(m. pl.)* chess
échiquier *(m.)* chess board
école *(f.)* school

s'écouler to go by
écouter to listen
écrire to write
effacer to erase
emporté upset
encore again
s'endormir to fall asleep
enfant (m./f.) child
enfourcher to get on
s'enfuir to flee
ennuis (m. pl.) worries, problems
enragé furious
enseigne (f.) sign
envoyer to send
éponge (f.) sponge
épuisé exhausted
équilibre (m.) balance
  en équilibre balanced
équitable fair
ère (f.) era, age
erreur (f.) mistake
espadrilles (f. pl.) canvas shoes
essayer to try
éteindre to turn off
être branché to be connected
  (computer)
étudier to study
éviter to avoid

F

façon (f.) manner
  de cette façon that way
faim (f.) hunger
faire to make, to do
  faire erreur to be mistaken
  faire du mal to hurt
  faire la monnaie to change
  faire la sieste to take a nap
faute (f.) mistake
fauteuil (m.) armchair
féliciter to congratulate
femme (f.) woman, wife
fenêtre (f.) window
fermer to close
feu (m.) fire
fichier (m.) file, program (computer)
fin (f.) end
flâner to stroll
fois (f.) time
fou (m.) crazy person
foule (f.) crowd
frapper to knock, to beat

fréquenter to patronize, to attend
friandises (f. pl.) goodies, sweets
frontière (f.) border

G

gagner to earn, to win
gardien (m.) watchman
garer to park
gaspiller to waste
génie (m.) genius
gens (m.) people
gosse (m., f.) kid
grand big, large
guichet (m.) window

H

hausser les épaules to shrug the
  shoulders
hurler to howl, to scream

I

ici here
imiter to imitate
incendie (m.) fire
infirmière (f.) nurse
inquiet(-ète) worried
inquiéter to worry
insupportable unbearable
interroger to ask, to question
invité (m.) guest
irrité angry

J

jamais never
jardin (m.) garden
jour (m.) day
  de nos jours nowadays
journal (m.) newspaper
jusqu'à ce que until

L

laisser to leave
  laisser tomber to drop
langue (f.) tongue
  sur le bout de la langue on the
  tip of the tongue
lever to raise
lieu (m.) place
  au lieu de instead
lire to read
livre (m.) book
loger to live

lumière du soleil *(f.)* sunlight
lune *(f.)* moon
  être dans la lune to have one's
    head in the clouds
lunettes *(f. pl.)* glasses

M

magasin *(m.)* store
main *(f.)* hand
mais but
maison *(f.)* house
mal bad, not well, ill
  faire du mal to hurt
  mal *(m.)* **à la tête** headache
malade sick
manger to eat
marcher to walk
mari *(m.)* husband
marmite *(f.)* pot
maudir to curse
médicament *(m.)* medicine
meilleur better
même even
menaçant threatening
mener to lead
mensonge *(m.)* lie
menteur *(m.)* liar
mère *(f.)* mother
mériter to deserve
mettre to put
  se mettre à table to sit down to eat
meuble *(m.)* furniture
mieux better
mise *(f.)* appearance
mode *(f.)* fashion
moins less
monde *(m.)* world
  un monde fou a lot of people
monnaie *(f.)* change
monter to go up
moyen *(m.)* means

N

néanmoins nevertheless
nécessaire necessary
négociant *(m.)* dealer
ni . . . ni neither . . . nor
niveau *(m.)* grade, level
notice *(f.)* sign
nouveau, nouvelle new
  a nouveau again
  de nouveau again

noyade *(f.)* drowning
nuit *(f.)* night

O

occasion *(f.)* opportunity
oublier to forget
ouvrier *(m.)* laborer
ouvrir to open

P

paille (f.) straw
paisible peaceful
panne *(f.)* **d'électricité** power
  outage
pantoufles *(f. pl.)* slippers
parce que because
partager to share
partie *(f.)* game
pas *(m.)* step
  pas à pas step by step
Pas que je sache. Not that I know.
passer to spend
  Il ne se passe rien. Nothing is
    happening.
  passer un examen to take an
    exam
pays *(m.)* country
paysage *(m.)* landscape
pelote *(f.)* **basque** ball game similar
  to softball
pendant during
  pendant que while
pendule *(f.)* clock
pénible wearisome
penser to think
perdre to loose
  Ne perds pas de temps!
    Don't waste time!
perroquet *(m.)* parrot
pire worse
plage *(f.)* beach
plaindre to complain
  se plaindre to complain
plat *(m.)* dish
  plat *(m.)* **de résistance** main
    course
pleurer to cry
plomb *(m.)* lead
plume *(f.)* feather
plus: de plus furthermore
plutôt rather
pneu *(m.)* **crevé** flat tire

poêle *(f.)* frying pan
pointer to place the cursor
  (computer)
police *(f.)* **de caractères** font
pompier *(m.)* firefighter
porche *(m.)* doorway
portable *(m.)* cellular phone
posséder to own
poulet *(m.)* chicken
poupée *(f.)* doll
pourtant still
pouvoir to be able to
présenter to introduce
  se présenter to introduce
  oneself
prix *(m.)* price
procès *(m.)* trial
procureur *(m.)* prosecutor
promenade *(f.)* walk
propos: à propos by the way
propriétaire *(m.)* owner
prudent careful
publicité *(f.)* advertisement

Q

Quel dommage! What a pity!
quelquefois sometimes
quelqu'un somebody
Qu'est-ce qui ne va pas ?
  What is wrong?
Qu'est-ce qui se passe?
  What's happening?
question *(f.)* question
queue *(f.)* tail
quitter to leave

R

raccommoder to mend
raconter to tell
rappeler to remind
rattraper to catch up to
ravi delighted
rayon *(m.)* ray
recevoir to receive
récompense *(f.)* reward
remarquer to notice
remercier to thank
remue-ménage *(m.)* hubhub
rencontrer to meet
rendez-vous *(m.)* appointment
rendre service to help
rendre visite to pay a visit

se rendre to go to
  se rendre compte to realize
réseau *(m.)* net, network
  retourner to go back
  réussir to pass, to succeed
réveil *(m.)* alarm clock
réveiller to wake
revenir to come back
  je n'en revenais pas I could not
  believe it
robe *(f.)* dress
rue *(f.)* street

S

sac *(m.)* bag
  sac à main *(m.)* purse
saisie de données *(f.)* typing with a
  word processor
saisir to grab
salle d'attente *(f.)* waiting room
sang *(m.)* blood
sans without
santé *(f.)* health
sauter to jump
sauvegarder to save
  (computer)
savoir to know
savourer to relish
séjourner to stay in one place
serrer to shake (hands)
seulement only
soif *(f.)* thirst
soleil *(m.)* sun
sonner to go off
  (alarm clock/timer)
se soucier to care
souhaiter to wish
souris *(f.)* mouse
souvent often
supporter to bear

T

tableau *(m.)* chalk board
taire: se taire to be quiet,
  to keep quiet
tambour *(m.)* drum
taper to type
tard late
tel: un tel such a
  telle que such as
télécharger to download
témoignage *(m.)* testimony

141

se tenir to behave
tenter to try
terrasse *(f.)* porch, outside area
terre *(f.)* earth
timidement shyly
tirer to pull
tombé fallen
toujours always
tout de suite immediately
tout d'un coup all of a sudden
toutefois nevertheless
traiter to deal with
travailler to work
  il travaille dur he works hard
troisième *(f.)* 9th grade
tromper to cheat
  se tromper to make a mistake
trou *(m.)* hole
tuer to kill

U
urgence *(f.)* emergency

V
vacances *(f. pl.)* vacation
valoir to be worth
  cela m'a valu it earned me
  vaut-il mieux? is it better?
venir de to have just
vérifier to check
vérité *(f.)* truth
vers around
vider to empty
visage *(m.)* face
vitesse *(f.)* speed
vitrine *(f.)* store window
voix *(f.)* voice
  à haute voix aloud
vol *(m.)* theft
volcan *(m.)* volcano
voleur *(m.)* thief, robber
vouloir dire to mean
voyage *(m.)* trip
voyager to travel
vrai true

W
wagon-restaurant *(m.)* dining car